Contents

1: Something Is Wrong With My Brain — 11
2: A Sparkling Tornado — 31
3: Frequent Flyer Points (Without The Champagne) — 59
4: Bzz, Bzz — 81
5: 24 Hours In A Week — 99
6: A Chicken In The Oven — 121
7: Divorce, Dating And Disequilibrium — 143
8: What's One More? — 161
9: A Wedding In A Blizzard — 173
10: The Tornado Swirls Again — 183
11: 2023 - Grippy Socks — 203

This memoir is not only a story of survival but also a testament to the human spirit's capacity to grow, adapt, and thrive against all odds. With a refreshing dose of humor and unflinching honesty, Steiner opens the door to her life, offering practical tools like CBT and DBT exercises to help readers navigate their own storms. Written with a depth of insight that speaks to years of lived experience and understanding, *A Sparkling Tornado* is as therapeutic as it is inspiring.

Shelly Rush, Registered Psychotherapist

This book is an easy read. It is a non-medical story from the viewpoint of someone who is going through life coping with the ups and downs of living with Bi-polar. Open, authentic, filled with humour.

As a parent of someone living with BP, it's a daunting task filled with stress, emotions, at times a sense of helplessness and fear. But this book gives great insight and understanding of what your child is going through. It gives parents optimism that their child can lead a fulfilling life. As a parent, you can't "cure" BP, but you can help pick them up when needed, provide support, and unconditional love.

Ross Brown

This book is a must for anyone who loves a person with mental illness. Steiner approaches the topic with unflinching honesty and ongoing joy. Each chapter ends with useful resources to help individuals and families reach optimal mental health.

Kim Alexander, MD FRCSC

Sandra's writing hits that sweet spot where you are simultaneously drawn into her story by her engaging storytelling, educated about bi-polar disorder and given tools to help you navigate your own mental health issues if you are struggling. I would highly recommend this to anyone wanting to empathize with those who have bi-polar disorder or learn from her hard earned wisdom.

Lee Horton-Carter, M.A., R.P.

Psychotherapist

PROLOGUE

It took me a decade to get the courage to write this book. Each time I thought about writing, my brain would say, "Who is going to want to read about your life?" or "You are still a mess – how can you help others?" Since my diagnosis of rapid cycling bipolar disorder type 2 at age 23, I've sought out every book on bipolar I could get my hands on. These books reached out to me, made me feel understood, and gave me insight into my bipolar brain.

Eventually, though, I ran out of books to read and realized it was time to write my own story. To be proud of what I have overcome, rather than ashamed.

This book is dedicated to those newly diagnosed and confused and struggling, and for those of you who have been living with bipolar for years but are still learning new ways to cope and thrive. I write this also for friends and family members who desire to understand and support their loved ones.

I want to not only share my journey of the dark lows and exhilarating highs, but also the Cognitive Behavioural Therapy (CBT) and Dialectical Behaviour Therapy (DBT) tools that ultimately helped me live a stable and happy life. I truly believe this "toolbox of tricks" saved my life. I share these "Reflections and Resources" exercises at the end of each chapter and hope they will help you as much as they helped me.

Throughout this book, you will have the opportunity to reflect on your thoughts, symptoms and behaviours through CBT and DBT exercises. I encourage you to either use a paper notebook or a Word document to complete the exercises. For those not as "old-school" as me, I will provide online links and apps as additional resources, which are clickable links in the e-book or accessible through the QR codes in the print book. I'm not a psychologist, a therapist or a psychiatrist. My only qualification I have to share these with you is that they have been extremely helpful to me.

To keep things simple, I will refer to both hypomania and mania simply as "mania" in my story. I understand there are distinct differences, but as a non-medical professional, I am trying to keep my writing simple, flowing and enjoyable for you.

This is my story, and these are my memories, recollected as best as I can through the Swiss cheese holes left by medications, Electroconvulsive Therapy (ECT) and psychosis.

Glossary

You might be reading this because you have been diagnosed with bipolar disorder. Perhaps your friend has shared that they have bipolar, and you want to understand what they are going through. Or you may be a family member learning to find hope and support for a loved one.

Whatever the reason, the most powerful tool we have is knowledge. To keep my story flowing and engaging, let's first review some terms in case you are not familiar with them, as I will use these terms throughout this book.

Bipolar type 1 – Manic episodes that last for at least seven days, nearly every day, for most of the day. Manic symptoms can be so severe that the person needs immediate medical care. Psychosis may be present in mania. Depressive episodes occur as well, typically lasting at least two weeks. Type 1 tends to have more manic episodes and fewer depressive episodes than type 2.

Bipolar type 2 – A pattern of depressive episodes and hypomanic episodes, but not the full-blown manic episodes found in bipolar disorder type 1. Some people may think type 2 is "softer," but people with bipolar 2 often have longer and more severe bouts of depression than those with type 1.

CBT – Cognitive Behavioural Therapy is a form of psychotherapy that focuses on the here-and-now –on the problems that come up in day-to-day life. It teaches us to examine how we make sense of what is happening around us, and how these perceptions affect the way we feel. I think of this as my "toolbox."

DBT – Dialectical Behaviour Therapy is a modified type of CBT. Its main goals are to teach people how to live in the moment, develop healthy ways to cope with stress, regulate their emotions and improve their relationships with others. More tools to put in my "toolbox."

DSM-5 – The *Diagnostic and Statistical Manual of Mental Disorders*, fifth edition. While this is published in the U.S.A., this is the Canadian Psychiatric Association's professional reference book on mental health and brain-related conditions. It is the main guide for mental health providers.

Euthymia – This is our goal: living without the mood disturbances associated with bipolar disorder. In euthymia, individuals typically have feelings of cheerfulness and tranquility and an improved resiliency to stress. Bipolar isn't just mania and depression; euthymia is the in-between state, and it can last days, weeks or even years. Coping strategies, stress and sleep management, and medications can help people remain in a state of euthymia.

ECT – Electroconvulsive Therapy, informally known as "electric shock." ECT is a highly effective treatment used in patients with severe depression or bipolar disorder that has not responded to other treatments. Unlike the procedures we see in movies, it is a brief electrical stimulation of the brain while the patient is under anesthesia...no grand mal seizures or foaming at the mouth.

Form 1 – A Canadian legal document that allows a patient to be held for 72 hours for a psychiatric assessment involuntarily. This is usually done only for patients who are considered a danger to themselves or others. Patients informally say they've "been formed". In the U.S this term is called "5150" and in United Kingdom it's referred to as "being sectioned"

Form 3 – At the end of 72 hours, the patient is either discharged, stays voluntarily, or if still deemed at risk, is put on a Form 3. Form 3 allows the patient to be held for two weeks.

Hypomania – Euphoric and full of energy, or unusually happy or irritable – often all at the same time. These mood swings can affect sleep, energy, activity, judgment, behaviour and the ability to think clearly. This condition is less extreme than mania and may not have a detrimental effect on day-to-day activities.

Mania – An over-the-top level of activity or energy, mood or behaviour that is a change from the person's usual self and is noticeable by others. Symptoms include feelings of invincibility, lack of sleep, racing thoughts and ideas, rapid talking and having false beliefs or perceptions. Psychosis may develop and require medical attention.

Rapid cycling – Four or more episodes of mania and/or major depression per year. However, people can ultra-rapid cycle within the same day or week.

Trusted person – It is not always a family member who is our main support. Our trusted person may be a friend or a health professional. Whoever they are, these are the people in our lives who may notice our changes in stability even before we do. These are the people we trust to intervene if needed and to help with our healthcare decisions.

SOMETHING IS WRONG WITH MY BRAIN

The sterile smell of hospital sheets hits my nose. In the corner of the room I see a young woman, whose name tag indicates she is a student. A look of fear shows in her eyes as she sees me waking up.

Hospital regulations require restrained patients to have continuous monitoring. A perfect job for a second-year nursing student. The room — in fact, the entire hospital — seems eerily quiet.

It's 1996, I'm 23 and I have no idea how I got here.

I'm grateful for the matted sheepskin lining the stiff leather restraints around my wrists and ankles. They almost make me feel as though I'm being embraced by a hug.

Years later, I'll learn that restraints may be effective for some people going through a psychotic episode. The person may naturally calm down when restrained, as opposed to becoming more agitated.

Maybe giving in to the situation is a means of finally feeling safe from yourself.

But at this point in my life, I have neither accepted my diagnosis nor feel safe yet. At 23 years old, this hospital stay is just one of many I've had over the last several years.

Instead of my 20s being filled with college, partying and friends, so far it has been dark caves and brilliant energizing sunshine.

Depression is something I already understand at this point. I have dealt with it a few times. It's a darkness that fills my head until it blocks out any emotion. Its voice is gravelly, deep and slow. With long pauses between words, it says:

"You are nothing."

"You are a waste of space on this planet."

"You will never recover."

Depression makes my body feel so heavy, as if I am tethered to my bed. Only another emotion could rouse me out of the safety of my bed. Anxiety is the other voice in my head, and in its high-strung voice, it screams:

"If you don't get up, people will think you're useless."

"If you don't go to work, you will be shamed and lose your job."

"If you don't have the biggest smile and act like you are the bubbly energetic person they expect, they won't like you. You will be alone."

How did I get to this hospital room? Depression came and went for me throughout high school, mostly passing within days or, at most, a couple of weeks. I also enjoyed lengthy periods of stability, productive energy, happiness and a joy of life. Generally, I'm a likeable person. If you asked 10 people to describe me, I'd guess eight would say, "Bubbly, smiley and warm." (Even as I write this, my anxiety whispers in its high-strung voice, "But what would the other two people say?" However, now I'm 51 years old and I've mostly learned to deal with this. Mostly. I mean – I'm talking about imaginary people.)

At age 20, a new emotion surfaced in me. I didn't understand this one, but I loved it! My own enthusiastic voice now loudly proclaimed:

"You will do amazing things!"

"The world is bursting with rainbows, sparkles and potential!"

"People love to be around you!"

And just as when depression seemed it was seeping into my very pores to reside in my body, the voices now promised me the opposite: "You will feel this way forever as you conquer the world!"

I don't recall a defining moment of being diagnosed with bipolar disorder type 2, rapid cycling. But sometime in 1996, at age 23, that label was stamped on me. I often read of people recalling the exact moment they heard those words – the room they were in, what the doctor was wearing, the chair they sat in. Some people say they feel relief at finally getting a diagnosis, because if you know what you are dealing with, you can treat it properly. Others, like me, deny it: "No, they must be wrong. I don't have a mental illness, I'm just moody." Even now, almost 30 years later, I occasionally question the diagnosis. My meds are working well, I'm using all the strategies I've learned (and will share with you). Life is good. Life is stable. Maybe they were wrong. Then, wham! Bipolar rears its ugly three-headed monster head and puts me in my place. I never know which head is going to be the leader this time: depression, stability or mania.

There are several types of bipolar, as I described in the Glossary. I understand that if you have bipolar and are reading this in an unstable state, you might find it hard to concentrate and may have already forgotten the terms. That's ok, I understand. Simply put, bipolar 1 tends to have more severe mania, sometimes leading to self-destructive behaviour and psychosis. People with this disorder are likely to spend more time in mania and less time in depression, with fewer periods of remission in between.

Bipolar 2 has less severe mania, known as hypomania, generally with no psychosis. The depression, though, can be more intense and more frequent. Remission in between episodes may be longer as well, if the condition is well managed.

"Rapid cycling" means the episodes occur for days to weeks as opposed to months. And I always like to point out that the above symptoms can be relieved or minimized through proper medication, lifestyle changes and therapy.

When someone says, "I would never have guessed you have bipolar!" I respond, "Well, I put in a lot of effort and take a lot of meds to be this way." What I'd really like to say is, "If someone has diabetes but takes insulin, eats properly, exercises and checks their blood sugar regularly, would you guess they have diabetes?" What's the difference? As with any other disease, if mental illness is well managed, it can be invisible.

Before I heard, "You have bipolar 2, rapid cycling" at the age of 23, my life had been a roller coaster — a roller coaster well beyond typical teenage moodiness. I was a late bloomer, and it wasn't until I was 15 that my hormones surged and my emotions swiftly changed — angry, happy, sad and excitable. The needle of my emotional state was wavering back and forth from normal teen moodiness to "Alert! Alert! Danger zone!" That needle got stuck in the Danger Zone when I was 16 years old.

I'm lying on the black leather couch in the family room of our comfortable suburban home.

Two paramedics are standing over me, asking me rapid-fire questions. As I feel the tight squeeze of the blood pressure cuff, I hear the front door open.

It's only 4 p.m. I hadn't expected my mother home for another hour. My mom rushes in with a panicked and confused look on her face, having spotted the ambulance in the driveway.

"What's happened?" are the first words out of her mouth.

I feel a pit of shame in my stomach as I see her scared eyes when one of the paramedics answers briskly, "Overdose."

I am not a drug user or depressed...at least, as far as my mom knows. But in fact I am one of those things.

It's 1988: my family had recently moved from the small town of Woodstock, Ontario, to the big city of Mississauga, a suburb of Toronto. Starting Grade 10 in a new school would be challenging for anyone. But my brain takes this challenge way beyond the normal anxiety a teenager should feel. I feel grey clouds clogging my head. I see them swirling, dipping and diving. I have dark thoughts that scare me. I feel my place in the world isn't deserved. I'm not worthy of the space I take up. I have been given a blessed life, and my mind is telling me to throw it away.

Nighttime is the worst. It's as if when the moon comes out, a beast creeps from out of the darkness and into my head. I hear my own voice whispering thoughts I am not thinking. "You could just kill yourself. Do it." Repeated over and over. I want to drown the words out, to make them stop, but I don't know how to do that. I want to tell someone; I want someone to help me make this stop. Like all teenagers, I don't want to be different, I don't want to be "weird." I am too embarrassed to reveal what is happening to me.

In fourth-period science class, I'm trying to focus on copying the words from the chalkboard. The teacher's voice drones on and on about human cells, and I suddenly realize that I am just cells. Every part of me is just billions and billions of living circles. Cells are survivors. They will fight to live.

I decide that when I get home, I'll swallow some pills, call for help, and let my cells fight to keep me alive. If I do this, I don't need to ask for help.

Someone will recognize my pain and help me. Someone will make these thoughts go away.

When I walk home from the bus stop, I wrap my arms tight around the thin green cardigan of my uniform. It may be to protect me from the cool November air, or it may be my body trying to draw itself inward, away from what I am going to do.

Once home, I realize I don't have any pills to take. As this was not preplanned, it never occurred to me to stop at a pharmacy.

My parents keep a medicine cabinet in their walk-in closet. It's where I usually go for Tylenol if I have a headache or period cramps. Now I pull out all the orange plastic prescription bottles and lay them on the floor. This is a time before the internet, so I don't know what any of them are. My parents are quite healthy, so most of the bottles seem several years old, with peeling, faded labels. I choose the two bottles with the newest dates. It doesn't matter to me what they are. Swallowing this fistful of pills is not suicide. It is a classic "cry for help."

I wash the pills down with a caffeine-free Diet Coke and Fruit Loops cereal. As I don't want to die, I call Andy, the closest friend I have made since moving to Mississauga. His mom is a nurse and will know just what to do.

"Andy," I mumble with a shaky voice.

"What's wrong?"

"I took a bunch of pills. I'm not sure why. But I don't want to die."

I hear the muffling of a hand over the phone, and in the distance Andy's panicked voice yelling, "Mom!"

His mom grabs the phone from him. "Go unlock the front door and lie down," she orders me.

She calls 911, then calls me back to ensure I stay awake. I arrange myself in a dramatic position on the black leather couch and wait for the ambulance. It never occurs to me that they might not come in time. That's the beauty of being an invincible teenager. We think we'll live forever.

I hear a quick knock, the door opens, and two male paramedics in dark blue uniforms come through the open door. I give out a little false groan to let them know where I am.

They seem annoyed to be dealing with me, like I'm wasting their time. Rapid-fire questions: "What did you take?" "How many?" "What time?"

This will be just the first of many times in my life where the medical community treats me like more of a hassle than as a valid hurting patient. Yet emotional pain is just as great as, if not greater than, any physical pain. When is the last time you had dripping tears, snotty nose and uncontrollable sobs from a physical injury? Now, when is the last time you bawled from emotional pain? Through my life, I've had two C-sections, an injured spleen, cracked ribs and two shoulder surgeries, and not one of them brought tears to my eyes. Yet all of those times I was asked about pain levels, was given medication to control it and was treated with respect.

The tall blond paramedic puts the blood pressure cuff on my arm. I feel the squeeze and hear the pump inflate. And this is the moment my mom walks in.

Even now, at the age of 51, I feel an incredible guilt for this staged suicide attempt. As a mom myself now, I can't imagine what she went through. But at 16, I didn't have the words to express what I was feeling – that my brain felt like a tornado. Sometimes I was in its calm eye, and other times I was swirling on its outer edges, spinning faster and faster with it. I knew this wasn't normal but felt I couldn't ask for help. I had loving parents, an upper middle-class life, any extracurricular activity I wanted – ballet, soccer, ski racing. From the outside I had a perfect life. So why did everything feel so unperfect on the inside?

My mom anxiously follows the ambulance in her car. In the ER, we find out that the pills I swallowed were diuretics (water pills) and antibiotics. All they will cause is a lot of peeing, and a tragic death of all the good bacteria in my digestive system. The on-call psychiatrist comes to consult. I'm in more distress now than when I arrived. The bright lights, the beeping machines and the distinct hospital smell aggravate my overwhelmed senses. But the worst is the shame I feel.

After only a 10-minute meeting, the psychiatrist determines that I do not truly want to end my life. He refers me to another psychiatrist, and I get an appointment for a couple of months from now. (Getting in to see a psychiatrist is never a fast process in Canada. Currently, in 2024, average wait times are from 6 to12 months.)

But by the time my appointment rolls around, I am feeling better. I've made friends in school, my mood has improved, and I'm doing well in my classes. At this point I don't feel I need help. Like most teenagers, I now turn up my nose at the guidance of the psychiatrist and my parents. Of course, I know better than them – I'm 16, and smarter than adults! And besides, the darkness has lifted and there is light once again.

These dramatic fluctuations in mood, energy and outlook explain why the average time from symptom onset to diagnosis of bipolar is seven years. Currently, in 2024, there are no MRI or blood tests to diagnosis bipolar (although researchers are doing studies in which CAT scans have shown physical differences in the brains of people with bipolar). Instead, doctors use the DSM-5 (*Diagnostic and Statistical Manual of Mental Disorders*) to diagnose people based on their symptoms. And symptoms can change drastically with bipolar, especially with teens!

Take me as an example. One month, I'm swallowing antibiotics and diuretics, desperately hoping to get help to pull me out from the depths of my despair. The next month, I'm signing up for drama club and the gymnastics team, enthusiastic about everything.

I begrudgingly attend my scheduled sessions with the psychiatrist, Dr. I., at Credit Valley Hospital in Mississauga. I have no way of knowing that nine years later, this very same hospital will dramatically alter the course of my life.

The psychiatrist is an elderly Filipino doctor with a gentle disposition. I'm not sure if she specializes in youth or not, but she never seems bothered by my teenage attitude, or by the fact that in one of my sessions I'm feeling particularly annoyed to be there and sit with my arms crossed, and a scowl on my face. "I wasn't actually trying to die," I insist. "I was just being dramatic. It was a mistake. My parents are overreacting." I roll my eyes to exaggerate my point.

"Don't you think your parents *should* react if you attempt suicide?" "I told you, I didn't attempt suicide,"

I respond, becoming frustrated at her questions. "I just wanted to see what would happen."

"Is this what you wanted to happen?" she asks lightly.

In my head I think, "Of course it was, but now I feel fine. The whispering in my head at night is gone, and I wake up every day feeling the same as the day before." But out loud I respond with a snarky "Of course not. I don't need this."

I figure there are people who need this more than me, and I am taking up their spot. I walk out of that last session and move on with a typical teenage life: enjoying school, working a part-time job at a clothing store, joining the gymnastics team and the drama club. Life becomes normal and steady.

But deep down, I'm aware that I have a dark side that appears from time to time.

Near the end of Grade 10, I meet Mirella. She's beautiful with long brown hair and large, gorgeous eyes. We hit it off right away. We develop a kinship as we slowly reveal our thoughts and emotions to each other. We are surprised that someone else feels the same as we do.

One day after school, I have my head burrowed as deep inside my locker as it can go, like a turtle hiding in its shell. But the sobbing movement of my shoulders betrays my bawling into the darkness of the locker.

"Sandra," Mirella says softly, placing a hand on my back. "What's wrong?" "I don't know," I sob, my voice muffled inside my locker. "Maybe my math test mark?"

She takes both my shoulders and pulls me out. Looking at me curiously, she asks, "Do you mean, you don't really know why you are sad, and are trying to find a reason?"

"Basically. Yah, I guess. I just can't get out of this funk. Something must be causing it."

"I feel that way too sometimes," Mirella admits. "I have no explanation; then a few days later it's gone, and everything is good again."

And sure enough, a few days later, it is.

Mirella and I share a fascination for famous people who are mentally ill or have died by suicide. The next year we make a pact that if we are still alive at 36, the age Marilyn Monroe was when she died, we will kill ourselves together.

After high school we lose touch, but reconnect in our 30s through Facebook. One day, I'm home with my newborn and two-year-old son when my phone rings. It's Mirella, calling me from Iceland, where she had recently moved to get married. I hear sobbing on the other end of the phone. The tears aren't because that marriage is about to end. They are from the depths of a long and dark depression. That's when I learn she had been diagnosed with bipolar in her 20s. Despite the illness, she had managed to be successful in school, even completing a Ph.D. But other aspects of her life suffered – relationships, stable work, and cycles of depression and mania. I can't help but wonder if our attraction in high school came from sensing that we both thought and felt a little differently than most of our other friends.

In Grade 11 on a warm spring night, several of us are in a white contractor van in a city parking lot – the kind of van you imagine kidnappers using. My friend Lisa and I are the only girls. Of the five guys, we only know Ben, the driver. I'm 17, under legal drinking age, and we have several bottles of alcohol in the van. At the time (unlike now), I didn't even like to drink. I didn't like the taste or the feeling, but I wanted to be cool.

Out of the darkness, a flashlight shines a beam into the van, momentarily blinding us.

"Police. Can you open the door?" a deep voice says from the darkness behind the flashlight.

We scramble to hide the alcohol bottles.

I hear two of the guys whisper, "I already have a record! I can't get another charge." My head whips around in shock, my ponytail hitting me in the eye.

Ben, the kid who is driving his parents' van, slides open the heavy door. We are seven people: five boys, two girls.

The cop leans his head inside, takes in a big breath through his nose, and says, "How much alcohol do you have in here?"

"None at all, sir," Ben lies.

"I can smell it, and I see two bottle caps on the floor. I need you all to come outside of the van."

Once we are lined up outside, the officer says he will only charge two out of the seven of us, and we can pick who. This was 1989, and things were a bit different then.

With none of the guys stepping forward, Lisa and I decide to take the hit and get the ticket for drinking underage. I want these guys to like me. This will prove to them I am cool enough to hang out with them. No charge or record, just a fine to pay. I don't even have my driver's licence yet, as I had failed the test the first two times I took it.

The next day, I experience the humiliation of asking my older brother Patrick, to drive me to the police station to pay the fine.

I'm certainly not going to ask my parents. I am still trying to be that perfect daughter for them. They are TV-sitcom-perfect parents. My dad is vice-president of a large company. My mom is in real estate, but she's home most days when I get in from school. She is there to ask how my day went, and to drive me to ballet or soccer or friends' houses. I don't think I've ever seen them argue, even to this day. I've never seen them very sad, or very angry. They are always just...perfect. And I'm not.

However, my desperation to be liked by assholes who cower in a van and let two girls get the ticket isn't the only incident that shows I am struggling more than it appears on the outside.

Trying to cope with my emotions, I start stealing to get a boost to my mood. First, it's just a few small items that are easy to slip into a pocket, like nail polish or makeup from low-end department stores like BiWay or Woolco. Stores that are not even around anymore – maybe because of people like me. In my Catholic school green kilt and innocent-looking face, I don't appear as the type store owners feel they need to keep an eye on. The rush of adrenalin as I walk out of the store, on the edge of getting caught, makes my heart race and my breath quicken.

One Saturday afternoon, I am in a higher-end department store trying on jeans when I realize I can fit them underneath the jeans I am already wearing and just walk out. Impulsively, I exit the change room, my legs a little stiffer under a double layer of jeans. My heart is pounding so loudly it sounds like thunder in my ears. As soon as my feet feel the carpet of the store change to the hard tile of the mall, the adrenalin and dopamine flood my body. I love the feeling...at least for a couple of hours.

But later that night, I'm in bed hugging my pillow to my chest, wracked with guilt. Hating myself, thinking I'm a terrible, shitty person. Why did I do this? I can afford jeans. What if I had been caught? My parents would have been so disappointed. My persona of the perfect daughter would have disintegrated.

I carry around guilt and self-hatred for the next few months, a heavy weight to drag around. Putting on the image of the popular, pretty Grade 11 student exhausts me. My face aches from my fake smile. I'm told by friends and boys, "You are so pretty," but my mind tells me, "Your face is fat and you have no boobs. You are not pretty at all." If a teacher praises an essay, I won't admit how I stayed up late rewriting it eight times because I didn't think it wasn't good enough. At night, I head to bed early with the excuse of needing to get up at 6:30 next morning to catch the bus. Lying in the old-fashioned brass bed that I had begged my parents for, knowing it clashed with the modern style of our house, my mind cannot shut itself off.

Then one day, I suddenly wake up, feeling excited. The sun seems like it is shining just for me. My morning cereal is bursting with flavour. Life has so many possibilities, so much thrill and joy. How could I not have seen this beauty before? I feel power within me. I consider running for school council president. I take on a part-time job at a clothing store. Suddenly, everything seems doable.

I don't know that this is hypomania, but I love it.

School assignments come easily to me now. Normally, I make my patient parents quiz me endlessly before tests, always anxious that I am unprepared. Now, I just glance at my textbook, absorb the information, and ace the test. A stark contrast to my elementary school years, when I would break out in stress hives before tests.

I start feeling frustrated with other students, who seem slower to grasp the concepts that now come easily to me.

In Grade 11 English, Mr. B. asks for a leader for a team project. I immediately shoot my hand up, almost dislocating my shoulder in my enthusiasm to be chosen.

This is unusual, because I'm a natural team player, not a leader. Tell me what to do, and I will execute the task perfectly. Ask me to decide what to do, and I waver until someone takes over. To this day, if I am in a depressive episode, sometimes I can't even decide what to eat or what to wear, so instead just stay in my pyjamas, subsisting on protein bars.

Mr. B. picks out five students to be on my team. I take charge immediately, creating a plan, assigning tasks and setting up an after-school meeting. One week into the project, I'm disillusioned with my team's work. They can't keep up, their work is sloppy, and they don't have the same enthusiasm as I do. Still feeling invincible, I fire them from their roles. I do the entire project myself, put all our names on it, and get an A+.

A few weeks later, I feel "normal" again. My body isn't buzzing with energy, impatient to do flips and bar work in gymnastics that are way beyond my ability. I carry a sense of peace with the world and with those around me. Things are just right. For now.

In bipolar this is called euthymia – the baseline state between depression and mania. I like to think of this as my true self: who Sandra really is. The rest of the population calls it their normal everyday feeling.

Lucky them! Now, with years of therapy and medication, I spend 90 per cent of my time as my true euthymic self. At age 17, I was lucky to get a few weeks of this feeling over the course of a year.

But I miss the buzzing high I felt before. I hadn't even heard of bipolar then, so thought I had just been in a great mood and the world was being handed to me. I begin to crave that feeling again.

I skip school a few times, but that really isn't very exciting, as I truly like school and take pride in being a good student.

I start playing with knives. A friend gave me a butterfly knife (obviously I'm making dubious choices in friends), and I get quite good at swirling it around in my hands. Open, close, open, close, open, close. I like to press it against my skin to just before the point of bleeding. It makes me feel powerful. I can control if I want pain or not. I can make a trickle of blood – and heal. Once again, the billions of cells in my body are doing their job. Surviving. Just like I learned in Grade 10 science.

Like many teenagers, I try smoking cigarettes a couple of times because I think it will make me look cool. I'm going through a punk stage at the time. With Bad Religion blaring in my headphones, I carefully pin the entire inseam of my pants with dozens of safety pins. They are so tight I can't properly bend my knees to walk. My long hair is pulled into multiple braids, which I think makes me look like a Viking. Two drags on my friend's cigarette and I'm spluttering and coughing, leaning a hand on the brick wall of the convenience store for support. I need to vomit, and try running to the bushes, but my safety-pinned pants don't let me run fast enough. With my friends laughing behind me in the background, I realize this is the opposite of cool. A lesson learned and a habit I am so thankful I never picked up. I'm also so grateful I was never offered drugs.

I'm quite sure I would have at least tried them. Or maybe more.

A few weeks later, I find that abandoned pack of cigarettes at the back of my night-table drawer. We have no internet in 1989, but I've heard whispers by the school lockers of girls self-harming.

I know what I want to do. I flick the plastic Bic lighter on and off, over and over. Then, with robotic movements, my hand moves as if on its own. I light the cigarette and press the tip three times against my inner arm. The acrid smell of burning flesh fills my nostrils. It hurts a lot. A whole lot. But in a strange way, that pain makes me feel good. I am only 17 but am already making the connection between how physical pain can relieve mental pain.

That March break, our family goes to Mexico to visit my brother Patrick, who is doing a one-year student exchange. Until now I've been able to hide those three circular burn marks under long sleeves. The scar has begun to fade, aided by lots of vitamin E and a product called ScarFade. In a few years, ScarFade will become a staple in my bathroom.

I wear a long shirt on the first day, sweating in the hot sun. But before the day is done, the beautiful blue water of Acapulco lures me into my bikini.

My mom's eagle eyes spot the three light pink, almost faded circles. She grabs my wrist. "What is that?" I don't even remember what excuse I told her, but I remember her response: "I don't think so."

I prepare for a heated conversation, but then a loudspeaker blares, "Join us in the main pool for a salsa dancing lesson!" "I'm going to do the salsa," I yell as I take off.

And that's it! She doesn't ask me anything else.

I look back and wonder – was it denial on her part that a seemingly happy honour roll student could self-harm? It was only a year ago that I had taken that "overdose" of water pills and antibiotics. Or perhaps she couldn't process what she was seeing on the white sand of a tropical beach beneath the shade of a palm tree. How can a parent imagine that their child would do this? My mom likes good. She likes happy. She likes the world to be a cheerful place. And a family vacation is supposed to be all those things.

I run to the salsa lesson to avoid more questions, and the stress of the encounter begins to dissipate as I focus on the dance steps. I have no answer as to why I pressed that cigarette into my skin. Now, as I mambo and cha-cha-cha, the thought of burning myself seems crazy to me. So I find other means to harm myself.

I begin to date a boy, a bad boy, Emil. All these years later, I still don't like to say his name. But at the time, he's what I am looking for. He flunks half his classes, comes from the wrong side of the city, and has an abusive father. As often happens in families with abuse, what the parent does, the child repeats.

It isn't long before he becomes jealous. He starts coming to my gymnastic meets, because he thinks guys are looking at me in my tight leotard. He randomly shows up at my part-time job at a clothing store, because he thinks one of the guys there likes me.

At first it feels nice to be wanted so much.

I remember the first time he hit me. I'm in the driver's seat of my father's new car. A Burgundy Bonneville. We are parked in the lot outside his apartment building. I don't know what I said, or what he said, to make it happen, but suddenly he slaps me across the face. My tooth bites into my lip and blood drips from my face onto the armrest of the new car. I'm more concerned about the fabric of the car than with what just happened. I don't want my parents to know. I'm embarrassed and ashamed that I put myself into this position.

Yet, I don't break up with him.

A month before that incident in my dad's Bonneville, the universe put out a giant red flag. Yet, I completely ignored it.

Grade 11 law class is one of my favourites. I love the criminal side of law class, and when we learn the political side of law, I let my mind wander out of the room. My enthusiasm for the criminal side is thrilled to learn we will be having a field trip to the local court.

The morning of the field trip, I wander through the large halls with three friends. The maximum number of students allowed per courtroom is four. The first case is a breach of bond over petty theft. Interesting, but not exciting. The next case listed is domestic assault. I want to attend that case. What does an abuser look like? What does his victim look like?

My friends decide to attend another case. I quietly tiptoe into the courtroom and take a seat on the back bench. The plaintiff is already being addressed by the judge. I see almond-coloured skin on his neck above his shirt. His shirt still has the creases, as if fresh out of the package, bought to impress the judge. I notice his short black hair is freshly cut. The judge asks him how he pleads.

"Guilty" is his somber answer. His voice seems familiar, but I can't quite place it.

As he turns his head sideways to look at his lawyer, I get a brief glimpse of his face. My breath catches. I slump down in my seat, hoping to become invisible.

I'm only about 15 feet from the door. I can't stay here. I can't be recognized. I slowly slide out of the bench, curl my spine small, tucking my chin to my chest. Once out the door, my hand reaches to the wall for support.

The plaintiff is Emil's brother. The victim is his sister-in-law.

My adult self cries now for my teenage self. Over the next year of dating Emil, there would be a few more incidents of abuse. Statistically, people with mental illness are more likely to be the victim of violence than to commit violence. Yet media depicts people with mental illness as volatile and dangerous.

One month before I finally break up with him, my period is late. I've still been chasing some kind of dopamine hit, a high, and risk-taking was part of that hunt. We had never been too careful with contraception.

There's no question for me about needing to terminate the pregnancy. I know I cannot stay with Emil.

This spurs other adult decisions. Ending the abusive relationship. Spending less time with people who are heading down a path I should not follow, and more time with those I should. I get accepted to a nursing program in college. I feel happy. My life is on track, and the future is mine to discover.

It might seem like I'm rushing through my pivotal teen years. I'm not pretending they are not important – they are. They are the first indication of bipolar brewing in my brain, and the first symptoms of what will become a heart-wrenching few years.

This part of my story is what I have struggled the most with writing. I see the potential I had: friends, good grades, loving family. Yet I know that what lies ahead of me is dropping out of schools (yes, plural), suicide attempts (plural again), job loss and multiple hospitalizations. My 51-year-old self wants to reach out to my teen self, hug her and say, "It's going to be really, really tough. But it's not your fault. You have an illness that you will struggle with, but eventually will manage. Life will be good once you get through a few rough years. Hold on."

The first symptoms of bipolar often appear in the teen years, yet the average age of diagnosis is 25. I've always been a keener, so my diagnosis at just 23 puts me in the high achiever category. Teacher's pet = Doctor's pet. I still try to impress my doctors with the efforts I make, the programs I attend, my punctuality for appointments – until one psychiatrist told me my constantly being early for all my appointments was a sign of anxiety. "Well, yeah," I thought. "After all, there are so many things that could go wrong on the way to an appointment that might make me late, and therefore a bad patient, and therefore a bad person."

The U.S. National Institute of Mental Health states that "bipolar disorder, previously referred to as manic-depressive disorder, is characterized by dramatic shifts in mood, energy, and activity levels that affect a person's ability to carry out day-to-day tasks. These shifts in mood and energy levels are more severe than the normal ups and downs that are experienced by everyone."

Anyone who has been a teenager, or knows a teenager, understands that shifts in mood, energy and activity levels are a weekly or daily occurrence.

It's easy in the teen years for teachers, parents and doctors to label the teen as "moody" or "anxious" or "sensitive." Teenagers guard their privacy, and often share more with their friends than their parents.

Health Canada states that one per cent of Canadians have bipolar. The statistics vary for youth mental health, but anywhere from 2.8 to eight per cent of 15- to 19-year-olds have experienced at least one major depressive episode (not bipolar). In 2022, Ukraine had the highest rate of youth depression in the world. We can all agree that the youth in Ukraine are experiencing trauma, fear and anxiety. It's understandable that anyone who lives in a war-torn area would be depressed.

But what about a girl like me? Loving parents, honour roll, a fluffy white puppy, vacations, and a swimming pool. What right do I have to feel depressed? When your life appears blessed, but you feel the world is a dark place weighing down on you, it's hard to understand that the chemicals in your brain aren't right.

I didn't know then that brain imaging has shown differences in the limbic area of the brain in people with bipolar, and shrinking grey matter in the frontal and temporal regions. The limbic system regulates emotion and memory, while grey matter enables control of movement, memory and emotions. The temporal region centres around auditory stimuli, memory and emotion. Hold on, I've forgotten what I was writing about - my memory must not be that good. :)

In my research for this book, I have learned that lithium, the first-line medication for bipolar, has been shown to increase grey matter volume after just four weeks of treatment. Numerous studies have found that people with bipolar have a three times higher risk of dementia and that the risk increases with each manic episode. I'm hoping my years of lithium therapy are building my grey matter and lowering my dementia risk.

Yet at age 18, I don't know any of this. I'm just a girl, in a world where I seem to feel everything too strongly. When I'm happy, I grin from ear to ear, excited to experience everything the world has to offer. When I'm sad, I want to hide from that same world, which is now bleak and depressing. My peers have the same stressors as me, and I see them work through it, while I crumble. Why is that? A quote by Robert Horry, a pro basketball player, says it best for me. "Pressure can burst a pipe or pressure can make a diamond." We all respond differently. My pipe bursts, water exploding everywhere. According to the International Bipolar Foundation, "people with bipolar disorder are more prone to stress than the average person; they have more difficulty adjusting to and recovering from stressors. Stress can trigger symptoms and relapses. When you're experiencing stress, you're more likely to become depressed, manic/hypomanic, anxious, or angry."

I've been planning to go into nursing school once I graduate, but just before high school graduation, I defer my nursing program for a year. I'm scared to move forward. I need an extra year to get on track, to grow, to heal. I figure a year should do the trick. If only I had known then that it would be another 10 years before I could get on track.

Reflections and Resources

List five experiences/symptoms you remember having that were early indicators of bipolar.

When was the first time you had medical help? Did you seek out the help or was it suggested for you?

Daily Mood Chart

Mood charts are especially useful during times of medication adjustments, major life events, and mood changes. They are also an easy "at a glance" tool that you can share with medical practitioners. I've switched to using an app for mood charting, but sometimes there is nothing like pen and paper in front of us to help us visualize our patterns. Ideally when you map out your own mood chart, you will see less "Roller Coaster" and more "Kiddie Ride."

This Mood Monitoring Chart from The Centre for Clinical Interventions in Australia is specific to bipolar.

(With print books you can get the link by scanning the QR code with your phone. With e-books simply click on the QR code to be brought to the website.)

Suggested apps: eMoods Bipolar Mood Tracker, How we Feel (my favourite) and Daylio Journal Mood Tracker.

I also like to track sleep and exercise using my Garmin watch, as lack of either of those can start me spinning.

Life Chart

This is an "at a glance" autobiography of symptoms, treatments and life events. I first completed a life chart in 2018 while I was attending a 12-week bipolar program through my local hospital. I found two valuable benefits:

1. Upon reflection, I noticed a pattern. There was often a trigger before an episode. Usually it was a stressful event, but sometimes positive changes in routine, such as a busy vacation, could start a spiral. While it's impossible to eliminate all stressful events and routine changes, I now pay closer attention to practicing self-care during these times.

2. My life chart was invaluable during a hospitalization in 2023. Rather than having to repeat my history to unfamiliar doctors in the ER, I simply handed them my life chart. This single, homemade sheet summarized medications, treatments, relapses and stability over 30 years, allowing them to provide the appropriate care. It offered me the relief of not having to repeat traumatic history to multiple strangers in a moment of crisis.

Simply draw a straight line lengthwise across a paper and start with your first episode you remember. Put in major life events such as marriage, job loss, etc. Episodes of depression go below the line; episodes of mania above the line.

I transferred mine to a Word bullet point document to make it easier for others to read.

If you want to take it more in-depth, *Bipolar News* has an excellent article about life charting, at

Songs: I'd also like to share a song in each chapter that I hope will resonate with many of you. I have a Spotify playlist called "Headf**k". I listen to it when my thoughts are f**cked. The music makes me feel less "weird," more understood. It reminds me that there are others out there feeling exactly what I am.

Song: "Manic" by Coleman Hell. He is open about having bipolar, and his words sum up the roller coaster beautifully.

My Grade 10 Yearbook photo. A great example of how looks can be deceiving when we are struggling with our mental health

A SPARKLING TORNADO

Only four years after my high school graduation, at the young age of 22, I'm standing on the bow of a yacht, my father's arm around me. We are slowly pulling into the Port Credit Yacht Club, to the clapping and cheering of 50 people. One of those people is Tim, my fiancé.

My white dress and veil are billowing in the wind. (Two years later, Rose and Jack will reproduce that same scene in the movie *Titanic* – but I did it first.)

Looking back, I'm thinking that 22 was young to get married. Tim and I loved each other, but I'm not sure why I had such a desire to get married just three years into this relationship. I think I craved stability. For the previous three years, my sparkling tornado had built up momentum. I had dropped out of nursing school after two years. Tim and I had left our respective parents' homes and moved to London, Ontario. I had attempted suicide again and had my first hospitalization. I'd been diagnosed with rapid cycling bipolar 2. I'd been fired from a job, experiencing mental health stigma for the first time.

I thought getting married would mean a normal life. A life of stability and domesticity.

Tim and I meet on a hot, humid July night. My friends and I are enjoying one last summer together before everyone heads off to university or college. A friend's band is playing at a local bar; we are underage, but make our way there anyway. We giggle as the bouncer turns a blind eye to three girls in short skirts with wide smiles.

Across the smoky bar is a tall, lanky guy in a brown suede jacket. His long curly hair appeals to my "looking for a bad boy" side. He must feel my stare, because when the band takes a break, he approaches me. I see soft kind eyes behind his glasses and think, "Maybe I should give a good guy a chance."

We only manage a short conversation before the band starts up again. It's too loud for us to talk besides yelling into each other's ears, but I piece together that someone in the band is a friend of his as well. And the sexy part – Tim is a drummer in another band.

This is 1991, before cellphones. I scribble my parents' home number on a napkin. He calls the next day. That's a good sign.

A respectful sign. Tim makes me feel safe. His long arms wrap me in a hug that tunes out the rest of the world. His demeanour is calm, patient and devoted – the complete opposite of Emil. And, most importantly, he makes me laugh with his quirky impressions and imaginative thoughts. A couple of months into dating, we go on a camping trip with friends. With the cool morning air filling the tent, he asks me, "What would you do if you woke up and a mushroom was growing out of your forehead?" Who can't laugh at that?!

Routine is a key factor in minimizing bipolar episodes. Francis Mark Mondimore, MD, author of *The Concise Guide to Bipolar Disorder,* states, "BD [bipolar disorder] is a 'stress-sensitive' disease. Lifestyle changes that reduce psychological and physical stress are a vital aspect of staying well."

As I have deferred my nursing school admission for another year, I'm working full-time at a mailbox service store. At this point, I have no idea that this will be the only full-time job I will ever have in my life. Still undiagnosed, I'm not yet aware of my vulnerability to stress. Without realizing it, my low-stress gap year is delaying the bipolar bubbling below the surface.

My gap year is all about routine. Every day, Monday to Friday, I leave the house at 9:45 a.m. sharp, walking 10 minutes through the green, forested park behind my parents' house. I arrive five minutes early to my job at mail service store. It's a low-stress job. I simply receive packages, serve customers and assist some to use a "new technology" called a Fax Machine to send things like business documents or letters to loved ones overseas. This consistent routine contributes to my stability that year.

My only stress comes once a month, when I help the owner, Ken, with his handwritten bookkeeping. Ken is in his 60s, a slight man who carries the stale smell of cigarettes. As we stand side by side at the waist-height counter, he calls out numbers and I input them into the calculator, reading back the totals. Inevitably, his hand makes its way to rest lightly on my butt. Just slightly cupping it. My heart races with anxiety, but I say nothing. "He's just an old man," I tell myself; I naively think, "This can't be on purpose." I lack the confidence to say anything. I just mutely keep inputting numbers into the calculator, constantly aware of the heat of his palm.

My evenings are mostly spent hanging with Tim. We listen to music, watch TV, walk to Little Caesars Pizza for bread sticks. Nothing exciting, but our time together feels special. It feels peaceful. I'm 18, and he is 22.

I like that he's older and more mature than the high school boys I knew. Most of my friends have headed away to college or university, but Tim lives only 10 minutes away. He is studying film and TV production at a local college. Like all young lovers, we are in the blissful state of a new relationship.

Toward the end of my gap year, the anxiety of starting nursing school creeps in. The "what ifs" dance in my head. "I don't know anybody. What if I don't make any friends?" "What if the science and math classes are too hard and I fail?" "What if I make a mistake and kill a patient?"

However, as is usually the case, the "what ifs" don't happen. By the second semester I've made friends, completed days of clinical practicums in the hospital without killing anyone and mostly aced my classes. Yet I still feel overwhelmed. At night I lie awake, thoughts of self-harm calling out to me. Visions repeat in my head. I can see the layers of my arm cut open. The pale white forearm skin slit wide. The bubbly, yellow layer of fat. The pink layer of muscle with thin capillaries like spiderwebs. I don't want to be thinking this or seeing these things, but I can't make them go away.

The first time cutting myself is the hardest.

It's a cool October afternoon, and I'm staring at the dead leaves swirling in the wind and collecting in corners of the yard. Trying to replace the self-harm images in my head with something else. Anything but that. But it's impossible.

My parents have a set of three self-sharpening knives – the kind where you return the knife to its case each time, and it sharpens itself as you pull it out.

I pick the smallest knife of the three. The first cuts are hesitant, barely making a mark on the top of my left forearm. The slight sting makes me focus on the task. I feel present. My mind is concentrating on only one thing. I realize I must go deeper. The next cut splits my skin open, maybe an inch long. I stare at the blood seeping out, and a sense of calm comes over me. I continue to stare, wiping it with my other hand, now mesmerized by the blood on both arms. Anxiety seems to seep away with each drop of blood.

It may be hard to understand, but people who cut often describe a specific type of high, relief, connectedness or sense of calm. The euphoria may be attributed to endorphins that the body releases when injured. Endorphins energize us so we can take actions to avoid the hurt. This impacts not only the physical pain but the emotional pain.

I now feel calm as I reach for our kitchen phone (it's the old landline, still anchored to the wall). Its long, curly cord is twisted from years of me walking as I talk into the receiver.

I dial, not sure what I expect Tim to do. But I want him with me.

Fifteen minutes later, I hear the muffler of his old Datsun as he pulls into the driveway.

The cut is still bleeding, obviously needing stitches. While I have kept my repetitive, intrusive images of cutting a secret from him, he later tells me he is not surprised. My stress has been showing and my mood has been low.

Credit Valley Hospital is the closest. It's the same place where I went in Grade 10, and the same hospital that in a few years will get me on the road to recovery and change my life.

Three stitches later, I am sent home. No psych consult, no follow-up.

I wear long sleeves to cover the stitches, hiding them from my parents and the school.

A month later, I cut again. I crave the sense of calm it gave me last time. This cut is bigger and more visible on the top of my forearm. I drive myself to the hospital, feeling ashamed that I've done this again. I tell the ER staff I cut it on a fence. As the nurse sews in seven stitches, she asks me again how it happened. I stick to my story. Based on my last experience, I feel they don't really care anyway. They have "real" patients to tend to.

This time I tell my parents. Their instinct is to want to help, to take action. My dad arranges therapy through his Employee Assistance Program at work.

A week later, 2 a.m. Again my brain is filled with the visions of my forearm cut deep open. It's as if some unknown dark person inside of me is daring me to do it.

I know I am not hallucinating, but I am seeing things I don't want to see. Over and over, my head replays images of my forearm cut wide open. I don't see the knife. I don't see who does it. I just see the flesh, the muscle, the blood. If I am not wanting to see this, who is putting it in my brain? There must be someone, something. This will only end if I do what it is asking.

I quietly tiptoe in the dark to the kitchen. When I open the knife drawer, the knives are gone. I search through several more drawers. I'm overcome with shame when I realize that my parents must have hidden them, trying to protect me from myself.

In my second year of school, the pressure becomes higher as we move into clinical rotations working in the specialized areas of the hospital, with higher expectations and responsibilities.

It feels unbearable for me. My stomach is in constant knots on the drive to the hospital. I feel like a fraud, trying to exude confidence I don't have. The number one rule for nursing students is to never let a patient see that you are nervous; shaky hands during a procedure make patients and staff very tense!

One month before the end of the school year, a patient my age dies. Sheryl had multiple sclerosis and I had been her caretaker the week before. She had a sudden stroke. While it's not uncommon for someone with MS to die from a stroke, she was quite young, and it was unexpected.

When our teacher tells us, my reaction is different from the other students. They feel shocked and sad. I, on the other hand, feel envious of her. Her worries are over. Her pain has stopped. She has no stress or pressure. I say nothing, recognizing that my thoughts are not normal. I'm ashamed to be thinking this. I imagine how I would be judged and labelled.

The next week, I'm changing an IV bag for an elderly man with lung cancer. My back is turned but I spin swiftly around when I hear gurgling and coughing. Blood is spewing from his mouth with each cough. I'm briefly frozen, unsure what to do. After a few critical seconds, I run into the hall, shouting – probably too loudly – for help. He dies too.

I go home, utterly drained. I can't seem to do anything but drag my heavy body. Though I'm 110 lbs, I feel like I weigh 200. Every day I still think of Sheryl. I wonder what she feels now. Anything? Darkness? A brilliant new world? Reincarnation? These all seem like better options than how I feel. I can't continue with this. I'm just not cut out for this world. I see others around me handle with ease the same things that are drowning me. I know now I don't want to be a nurse, but I don't know what else I want to do...or can handle doing. The next day I stay burrowed in my bed, telling my mom I don't feel well. It's not a lie.

It can be challenging to explain how clinical depression feels to someone who has never felt it. It is so much more than sadness. In the essay collection *Voices of Bipolar Disorder*, one of the authors, Gareth Allen, tries to explain it. *"Like all people, I have had occasion to feel deep unhappiness: at the ending of a relationship, the death of a close relative. These feelings are very real and would be very painful to anyone. But to compare these feelings with depression is simply not appropriate. Comparing unhappiness to clinical depression is akin to comparing a stubbed toe with a broken ankle. Not only is depression different from unhappiness, it is not even measured along the same scale."*

With my teen years just behind me, this depression is heavier than anything I have felt before. I feel I have no future. I drag myself out of bed in the mornings and go about my day with a smile plastered on my face. My cheek muscles ache from that fake smile. Then I get home and smile a little longer for my parents. All I want to do is to close my bedroom door and curl up in the bed with my dog, Bisou, and cry tears on his soft fur. I can't stop thinking of Sheryl, and how easy things are for her now. I think about Tim. The kindest thing I can do now is to end our relationship, so I don't drag him into this darkness with me. I think about my parents, but I struggle to justify how they will be better off without me. I can't see any future for me where I will ever be happy or successful.

I am nothing more than a useless crumb on the floor. I twist thoughts around and around until I convince myself that my parents have a very full life of their own, and a messed-up daughter is just in the way. They will no longer need to hide knives.

I've gotten through the "why" of killing myself. And figured out the "how": pills to lull me gently to oblivion. But I don't want to die alone. No one wants to die alone.

To this day, I still think how unfair it is that people who are in extreme emotional pain are forced to die alone, in shame and guilt. One in five people with bipolar die by suicide. And I'm sure most die alone. In Canada, Medical Assistance in Dying (MAID) for mental health reasons has just been delayed approval...again. I understand both sides. Proponents argue that mental pain often causes more anguish than physical pain, and in some disorders is lifelong. Mental health is the fourth leading cause of long-term disability. This can mean a lifetime of suffering. Yet our healthcare system in Canada is broken, particularly when it comes to mental health. Many who are suffering and considering ending their life have not been given access to all of the treatments that might greatly improve their quality of life. Only once all those treatments have been tried with no improvement should MAID be an option for them to end their pain – surrounded by their loved ones in a place and time of their choosing.

At age 20, my favourite spot to be is wrapped safely in Tim's arms. His hairy chest blocking my view of the world. The smell of his shaving cream. That is where I want to die. Many nights I stay at his house.

With my decision made to end my life, I stop at the pharmacy on my way to Tim's place one day and buy a 12-pack of an over-the-counter sleep aid. I don't know how many I need. It's not exactly the kind of thing you can ask the pharmacist. I'm quiet throughout the evening, but that hasn't been unusual the last few weeks. My lungs feel tight, like I can't get a full breath. I keep needing to sip in more air. I begin to wonder if I should hold off for a week. My mind goes back and forth with it. Our evening passes as usual: dinner with his parents, walk his dogs, TV. It should have been a pleasant, relaxed evening, but all evening I'm trying to drown out a voice – my own voice, whispering over and over in my head, "You could just kill yourself. You could just kill yourself. You could just kill yourself." It is relentless.

According to the study "Characteristics of Impulsive Suicide Attempts and Attempters," published in the journal *Suicide and Life-Threatening Behavior*, "Of 153 case-subjects, 24% attempted suicide impulsively. Attempts were considered impulsive if the respondent reported spending less than 5 minutes between the decision to attempt suicide and the actual attempt."

This may seem like an incredibly short amount of time to people who have never seriously considered ending their life or been plagued by suicidal ideation, but it's important to remember that the pain and despair have likely existed for a long time. (Suicidal ideation is when thoughts of suicide ruminate incessantly in your brain.) Actor and comedian Stephen Fry, who is very open about his diagnosis of cyclothymia (a milder form of bipolar), says, "As long as I can remember, the thought of ending my life came to me frequently and obsessively."

Does it take me even five minutes to swallow the pills once I stop wavering back and forth? No, more like one minute. I go through the process of brushing my teeth and washing my face. Then I swallow the pills, two at a time.

Afterwards, I crawl into the warm bed. Tim is already there. I turn to face him so I can burrow my face in his chest. This is my safe space. My heart beats loudly in my ears. I feel adrenalin running through my veins. I had thought I would start to relax and get sleepy, but instead tears start to stream from my eyes. I'm suddenly wracked with guilt and anxiety. I imagine Tim waking up to my cold, dead body. My mom crying after receiving a phone call that her daughter is dead. I can't do this to them. Tears and sobs wrack my body.

Half-asleep, Tim mumbles, "What's wrong?"

"I did something bad. I'm sorry." My words come out between ragged breaths. Even as I tell him, I beg him not to take me to the hospital. But he doesn't give me the option.

Without waking his parents, we rush out to his car. It's a quick five-minute drive to the hospital.

By now I am getting sleepy, and he keeps touching me on my shoulder to keep me alert.

I'm a little unsteady as we walk up to the triage desk at the Emergency Department.

Immediately I'm taken to a cubicle and laid down on a gurney; the curtains are loudly whisked closed on both sides.

I'm alert enough to drink the coal-black charcoal drink a nurse brings me. Activated charcoal adsorbs or holds drugs and poisons onto its surface, preventing their absorption from the gastrointestinal tract. The drink is as thick as a milkshake, smells earthy and tastes like dirt. I struggle to drink it, the black liquid running down my chin.

A few hours later, the on-call doctor flies in. "You're lucky you got here so quick. Your vitals and blood work are stable now. Physically you are good to go, but Psychiatry isn't in until morning. You're going to need to wait for a psych consult." I sleep fitfully, always aware of the beeping of machines, the groans of injured patients and the bright hospital lights. Early the next morning, I hear Tim's mom's voice in the hallway. The curtain is whisked back, and Jennie is there, standing with open arms, ready to give a hug.

Tim and I look at her, shocked. No one knew we were here. We hadn't purposely hidden it but we had never made it to a payphone to call my parents or his.

"Mom?" Tim says with a shocked voice. "How did you know we were here?"

Jennie, always a smart one, says, "Mother's intuition. You guys weren't there when I woke up, and something told me to come here. I felt something was wrong."

Even now, as a mother myself, this still amazes me. While she knew about the cutting and that I was struggling with anxiety in school, I have no idea what made her think to come to the hospital. But that day in the ER, her hug fills me with warmth. I ask her to call my parents. I feel too ashamed to do it myself. They are such good people, and in my depressed brain I feel I am a terrible daughter.

Soon, a young psychiatrist rushes in, clipboard in hand. All I want is to go home, and all he wants is to free up the bed for another patient. Perfect: we have the same goal in mind. The charcoal drink still sits heavy in my stomach, and the hospital smell adds to my nausea. I answer all his questions in a way to appear regretful and with no future thoughts of harming myself – whatever the right answers are to get me out of here. He tells me I will be discharged, and a nurse hands me a folder with pamphlets and mental health resources, a brochure with community resources and crisis line number, as well as a note to give my family doctor, whom I'm supposed to call as follow-up.

Tim and I silently drive to my parents. It's 10 a.m. I'm exhausted. I climb into my bed and burrow under my duvet. My mom comes in, tucks the duvet around me and leaves me to fall into a deep, dreamless sleep.

That night I have a long conversation with my parents. I confess how stressed the nursing program makes me. I love the classes and the learning, but the clinical days fill me with dread. I'm terrified I am going to do something wrong and kill a patient. At night all the scenarios go through my head – a bubble in the IV line, the wrong medication, not responding in time to an emergency.

I feel I will be viewed as a failure if I quit the program with only one year to go. A waste of money, a waste of time, a waste of learning. And a waste of space on the planet.

But my parents' concern is for my mental health, not my education. It had always been assumed I would go to college or university and have a successful career. We agree we can put that on pause for now. Only as I grow older will I recognize how fortunate I am to have the kind of parents I have. At the moment, I am just relieved to have gotten it off my chest.

The next day, with a pit in my stomach and a trembling voice, I call the college office to say I will not be coming back.

Today schools make a variety of accommodations for students with learning disabilities and mental health challenges. In 1993, you either made it through or you didn't. Looking back, I'm disappointed that they didn't question my withdrawal from the program. My marks were excellent and the fact that I was always anxious in clinical classes probably made me a better nursing student. I double or triple checked everything.

Not completing this program is one of the biggest regrets in my life. I think I would have made a fine nurse – and a compassionate one, certainly.

In the meantime, having quit my nursing program, I go to work part-time at the mail service store again, still getting my ass grabbed at the end of the month. But the part-time work allows me to focus on therapy and manage my stress levels.

In the next few years, I will go back to college again, yet I will never complete a program. Repeated hospitalizations, side effects of medication and memory loss from ECT (Electroconvulsive Therapy) will make it impossible. But at this point I am still naive about what is ahead.

A month after that overdose, I wake up with a brilliant idea.

"Tim," I say excitedly, "let's move! We can go to Edmonton and get a fresh start! It's a quieter lifestyle, and you say it's a great city!"

"I don't know," Tim says reluctantly. "That's a big step. Our families are here." While he is originally from Edmonton, he moved to the Toronto area with his parents a few years ago.

But I barrel ahead. "I'll apply for the Nuclear Imaging program, and you can start your Bachelor of Science."

I barely give him a chance to speak as I chatter rapidly about the details I have planned.

His face shows bewilderment. "We need to talk about this more. There's a lot involved in moving. And it's already April – most school programs have closed applications."

Just two weeks ago, I was doubting everything about myself and the future. *Will I ever be able to complete a degree? Can I handle anything beyond a job opening letters and sending packages? Why do I hate myself so much?*

But now I'm full of self-confidence. "That's not a concern! You have a college diploma and I have a part diploma. Why wouldn't they accept us?!"

I'm so excited I don't sleep all night; I'm thinking about our new life in Edmonton. I'm at the mall 30 minutes before it opens: I know the province of Alberta is very cold, and I want new clothes.

Being April, winter clothes are hard to come by: just the few leftover items from last season. I find a pair of boots rated for up to -40°C temperatures. Perfect! (Fun fact: I still have these boots.) There's a rack of winter coats marked down 70 per cent: a ski jacket for all the skiing I imagine us doing in the Canadian Rockies, and a glamorous dress coat that is completely impractical. In 1993, you could still pay for items by cheque. I don't know whether or not I have the money in my account to cover all these purchases, but I'm not thinking that far ahead. I need to be ready for Edmonton. I carry my heavy bag full of purchases through the mall, having spent money I'm sure I don't have.

Ahead of me is a Sunglass Hut. I need sunglasses! Apparently, it is cold but always sunny in Edmonton. A beautiful pair of Ray-Bans displayed in the window catches my eye. I try them on and look amazing in them. One more purchase, all with money I don't have.

Back at home, I hide my purchases. I really want to show them off, but I recognize it is an excessive shopping spree.

Once my bags are tucked at the back of my closet, I call the Northern Alberta Institute of Technology and the Southern Alberta Institute of Technology, two Alberta colleges. They are at completely opposite ends of the province, but geography means nothing to me. I explain that I'm moving to Alberta and am interested in studying Nuclear Imaging or Respiratory Therapy.

"Well," the man from the registrar's office says slowly, "we have already sent out acceptance letters to all students for September. But it is possible that not all of them will accept and there will be spots available. I suggest you put in your application, along with your transcripts. You will receive our application form in the mail in three to five days. Try to mail it back as soon as possible."

Things didn't move as rapidly then as they do now, which in a few days would turn out to be a stroke of luck for me.

I still haven't convinced Tim, but in my mind we are almost on our way. I feel like I have future success burning through me.

A week later I open my eyes, and immediately close them again. The unfilled college applications are on my desk. The sun coming through my blinds seems too bright, hurting my eyes. I try to get out of bed, but my legs feel so heavy, unable to move. I think I must have the flu to feel so terrible. Even my chest feels heavy. I can't take in a full breath, only small sips, then a sigh.

My mom knocks on my door. She is going to the cheese store and wants me to come. We are Swiss, so we go to the cheese store a lot, but I think her real motivation is to get me out of bed.

I drag myself out of bed and pull on some clothes, then get out to the car, teeth unbrushed.

My mom is a very bubbly and chatty person. She rambles away in her slight Swiss German accent – about the dog's upcoming vet appointment, about a house she is selling, about the cheese she is buying. Then... "How are you going to move across the country? You are up one week, then down the next. I know you try to hide it, but I see it."

"Umm," I stammer. "Actually, I think I've changed my mind. I don't know anyone there, we don't have a place to live, and we don't even know if we will get accepted to any school. I don't know what I was thinking. Tim already has a place at the University of Western Ontario in London. It's only two hours from here. That makes more sense."

My parents jump right in to help. They purchase a house in London so we can live rent-free, and in exchange we will oversee renting out the other two rooms to students. They view it as a financial investment and a way of helping us out.

Still to this day, my parents are always willing to step in, and make my life simpler. Everyone recognizes that a stressed Sandra quickly becomes an unpredictable Sandra, either crawling into bed or thinking of moving across the county. A decade later, after my divorce, they will again jump right in to help me with housing.

I decide to study Medical Administration – still in the medical field, but working in an office will mean much lower stress. I can't get into the program until January, and we moved to London in August.

In the meantime, I find a job at another mailbox store, within walking distance of the house. Not quite full-time, but it gives me time to redecorate the house. It's an old military base house, so in need of some TLC.

A month into the job, sadness is building. I miss my Mississauga life. We don't know anyone. Tim is often away long hours at the university. He has attention deficit hyperactivity disorder (ADHD) and finds it difficult to study at home, so spends a lot of evenings in the library where there are fewer distractions. I'm lonely and still disappointed in myself. My friends have started their third and final year of nursing school. Their "real" lives will be beginning soon.

Soon sadness turns to depression. For the lucky people who have never experienced clinical depression, I imagine that they think depression feels like sadness. I've felt both. They are not even close to the same.

In the book *Voices of Bipolar Disorder*, H. Rachelle *Graham writes an essay, "Bipolar Buried under Water,"* in which she describes the feeling. *"I am at the bottom of a dark ocean with a hundred pounds of concrete on top of my body. My friends and family are snorkeling nearby. I can hear them call out to me, but I cannot see them. They tell me, 'The plants and fishes are so pretty and the water feels so warm.' I feel nothing but ice cold water and heavy concrete. I cannot move my arms and legs to join them. I am drowning. I cannot breathe. I feel dead. This, for me, is depression."*

This feeling is so familiar to me. Those around me say, "You are so lucky; you have x, y and z good things." "But you love skiing – why are you unhappy?" or "You just need to appreciate things." These statements just add to the guilt I already feel when I'm depressed...and make me feel like an even more shitty person.

Soon the intrusive self-harm thoughts return. I know if I cut, the thoughts will stop. I didn't know the science behind it then, but I knew from experience that I would feel better after. Physical pain releases endorphins to minimize the feeling of pain. These same endorphins also release mental pain. At this young age of 22, I don't have any coping tools to stop my mind's plea to hurt myself. I have never even heard the term CBT, let alone had the opportunity to learn and practice it.

So I take the step. No hesitant cuts this time. No feeling of shame. Just a task that needs doing. I'm ready with a sharp kitchen knife, paper towels, a cloth and Band-Aids. Enough experience to do it over the sink so I can just wash the blood away. From the kitchen I hear a repetitive guitar verse as Tim practices his new instrument in the basement. The music adds a strange element to my task.

I cut my upper arm twice, quickly rinse it, pat it dry, and hold a cloth on the still-bleeding wound. Without any emotion in my voice, I go downstairs and let Tim know in a matter-of-fact way that I need to get stitches.

Tim is calm. He stops playing mid-strum but doesn't overreact or get upset. This isn't his first time either.

He gets a towel from the bathroom, wraps it over the bloody cloth on my arm. As we walk to the car, he drapes one arm protectively over my shoulders.

We drive to University Hospital, where I get 10 stitches and a referral to Psychiatry...in three months. Yes, three months. Meanwhile, I'm spiralling into the darkness of the tornado. I don't want to get to the bottom of it – I can't imagine being able to ever climb out.

Along with the referral to Psychiatry, I am given a prescription for Prozac, an antidepressant. If the thoughts become overwhelming, I also have lorazepam, a mild sedative. This is my emergency pill to take to stop from spiralling.

With no insurance, I worry about the cost of the medication. And the weight of depression is still making it hard to get organized, so it takes me three days to fill the prescriptions.

When I swallow my first Prozac, I feel hope. Maybe this green-coloured pill will make the grey clouds in my eyes go away.

All week I try to stop myself from drowning. Nothing helps. I walk outside in the autumn leaves, but the colours seem dull and the air feels cold. I try to practise gratitude, but it only makes me feel guilty: I have all this goodness, yet I still want to die. I go to my job and give fake smiles to customers while my internal voice tells me, "You are a fake. Everyone is better than you. You will never get out of this darkness."

It's dinnertime. I'm alone. I can't bother to make anything to eat. I don't want to die but I don't want to live. I can't even decide on this.

The bottle of lorazepam keeps tempting me. This will be easy, painless.

I think about whether to write a note, but nothing seems worth saying.

I take a glass of water to my bedroom. The childproof lock on the pills comes off easily, which I take as a good sign. A sign that I am making the right decision. If I had struggled to get the lid off, I probably would have given up and gone back downstairs to watch TV.

Lorazepam pills are small, so I swallow the handful with one gulp. I curl up into the safety of my bed and wait to fall asleep. Then, I'm not sure how much time has passed, but I hear my name.

"Sandra! Sandra! What did you take? Wake up!"

The voice sounds distorted. Tim is shaking me, and I want him to leave me alone. I can't open my eyes; they feel full of sand.

He rushes me to the car, half-dragging me as my feet stumble.

I'm jolted out of my semi-conscious state only when I feel a tube being inserted in my nose. I am not alert enough this time to drink the charcoal. I try to shake my head to stop it. As the tube passes through my throat, I feel like sandpaper is painfully scraping me all the way down to my stomach. It's hard to breathe, and panic sets in. The outer end of the tube is taped to the end of my nose, and I oddly feel embarrassed by how I must look. Like an elephant. Charcoal is pumped into my stomach through the tube.

The rest is a blank, until the next day when a psychiatrist comes in to do a consult. Dr. L. is young and good-looking with longish wavy hair. But I'm angry that I'm still here, still alive. I have no regrets about this attempt. My only regret is that I didn't add alcohol to increase the lorazepam's efficacy. (I didn't drink at the time, so didn't have any alcohol available in the house. Another thing I am now thankful about.)

I tell Dr. L. I am ok; I will not do this again – thinking it will be as easy as the last time to be discharged. I ask for lorazepam or sleeping pills, telling him I'm just stressed. But I know that I plan to use them again, this time with vodka. Dr. L., with his 10 years of medical school, sees through this.

"I consider you at high risk of hurting yourself. The history I hear from the last few years shows repeated self-harm, and a second suicide attempt. It doesn't sound like you have ever had more than a few months' stability at a time. I can't let you go home. Here we can help you work on a plan to feel better." His voice is quiet and gentle.

I laugh loudly, an inappropriate reaction. "I can't stay, but I'll come to a follow-up appointment."

He opens his folder and shows me some papers. At the top is "Form 1." "I've placed you on a hold for 72 hours, so we can evaluate you and create a plan to help you."

I angrily respond, "You can't make me stay, I'm an adult." I start to get up. Dr. L. holds up his hand, indicating I should stop. "It's my duty as a doctor to keep you safe. If we consider you at risk of harming yourself or others, we need to place you on a Form 1. It is a legal document that allows us to keep you in the Psychiatric ward for 72 hours, or until we determine you are no longer at risk."

"I can't stay!" I beg. "I have a job! I promise, I'm not going to hurt myself. I don't want to stay. Please believe me."

"How about we discuss this more tomorrow? On the ward. You still have stitches in your arm from last week. One of the nurses there can take them out for you tomorrow as well."

An orderly pushing a wheelchair and a nurse with a tag indicating she is from Psychiatry appear and ask me to come with them. I'm reluctant to sit in the wheelchair, wanting to walk. Thinking about running.

"It's just protocol," the orderly tells me. "For all patients. Don't worry, it's just a quick elevator ride."

When the locked doors open on the 10th floor, I don't know what to expect. I've seen *One Flew Over the Cuckoo's Nest*, and that is my only knowledge of Psych wards.

But here, the halls are quiet. No people rocking back and forth with blank stares. No out-of-control patient being restrained and injected with a sedative.

I smell food. Vague with no defined smell. Nothing appetizing about it. My room has two beds, with an open curtain between them. One bed has a colourful comforter, books on the night table and photos taped to the wall. The other has a thin, pale pink blanket with folded grey hospital pants and a short-sleeved shirt placed neatly in the middle. These will be my clothes for the next three days – along with large red socks with a white rubbery pattern on the bottom. I would soon learn the expression, "I got the grippy socks."

As I get undressed, the nurse puts my clothes in a large plastic bag with my name on it, explaining, "This will be stored for you until your discharge. The other patients are finishing lunch in the lounge. Because you have just arrived, I can bring a tray to your room. Normally all meals except breakfast are eaten in the lounge."

I'm glad to avoid the other patients for as long as I can. I'm not crazy like them.

Lunch is pale white bread sandwiching runny egg salad. On the side is a watery salad where I can't taste the difference between the lettuce, the carrots and the radishes. After a few bites, I move on to the chocolate pudding. At least something with flavour.

I've been given no instructions, so I sit on the edge of the bed, not wanting to get too comfortable. I don't have any belongings, as they were put in a plastic bag labelled with my name and locked in the nurses' station.

An hour later, the owner of the photos and colourful bedspread arrives. Approximately my age, she starts talking in a quiet voice with a slight Vietnamese accent.

"Hi, I'm Linda. What's your name?"

"Sandra."

"My last roommate was discharged today. She was probably 60. I'm glad to have someone my age."

"Uhh, yah," I stammer. "I'm going to be discharged on Monday, though. My Form 1 is three days."

"That's what they start with," Linda says. "After that, they can add a Form 3. Fourteen days. Or they can lift it, but 'highly encourage' you to stay voluntarily. That's me. Ten days and counting. Anyways, I'm just grabbing my notebook. I'll be in the hallway. I don't like to stay in my room too long."

I flop back on the bed and stare at the wall. I feel more depressed than before.

At 4:00, visitors start to trickle in. When Tim knocks on my door, I jump up and run to his arms. Tears burst out of my eyes.

"Please take me home. I don't want to be here. I'm not crazy."

He reaches into a backpack and pulls out lip balm, hand cream and books. The items I asked for.

"I tried to bring you a couple of other things, but the nurses said they weren't allowed. They looked through the bag."

Linda soon comes back into the room. The curtain doesn't give Tim and I privacy to talk, but I still don't want to leave the room. I haven't learned yet that privacy is non-existent in the Psych ward. Showers don't lock. Toilets don't lock. Medical conversations happen in front of other patients. Hourly night checks shine a flashlight onto your sleeping or fitful body.

At 5:00, a nurse comes to tell me it's medication time and to come to the nurses' station.

Tim promises to be back tomorrow and to bring me my favourite pillow. A few patients are milling about the nurses' station. Some look haggard in hospital clothes and grippy socks like me, eyes darting around anxiously. Others are in their own clothes and slippers or flip-flops. They have a different air about them. Calmer and resigned.

I don't know what I am supposed to do. I spot Linda walking toward the nurses' station.

"What are your meds?" she asks.

"I don't know. I don't think I have any. I was on Prozac."

I hear a female voice call out my name.

"Sandra? Nice to meet you. I'm Stephanie and I'll be your night nurse. Dr. L. wants you to continue with Prozac. He'll talk more about it with you tomorrow."

She hands me a Styrofoam cup with water and a small plastic cup with the familiar green pill.

I take the cup and swallow the pill. As I turn to leave, Stephanie calls out, "Please open your mouth."

Feeling insulted, as though she is treating me like a child, I purposely exaggerate the movement, opening my mouth wide and circling my tongue. She doesn't even react. I'm sure I'm not the first to do this.

I hear a rattling sound and see a guy pushing a large trolley with trays. He calls out "It's dinner time; the lounge is on the left. You will find a tray with your name on it." Patients start to follow him. It makes me think of the story of the rats following the Pied Piper.

The lounge is divided into two sections. One half has round tables with chairs, and I see people eating. Some eat in silence, head down, staring at their plate. Others converse with other patients, even occasionally smiling or laughing.

The second half of the lounge has a couple of couches, some worn-looking chairs and an old TV.

I find my tray and go to the only empty table, still avoiding the other patients. When I try to pull out the chair, it yanks my arm. It must be three times the weight of a normal chair. "Do they make these special for Psych wards?" I wonder. Harder for an angry patient to throw around. Other patients trickle over to my table, but we say nothing. Maybe they sense my depressed state, or maybe they feel as depressed by this place as I do.

The food has the same bland taste as at lunch. I return my tray to the trolley and walk back to my room, unsure what to do. Many patients still have visitors and are sitting with them in corners of the lounge. I overhear bits of conversations. Some families are tearful. Others are trying to be upbeat, bringing crosswords and jigsaw puzzles.

At 9:00, we all shuffle back to the nurses' station for medication. There is no rush to go anywhere here. We have nothing but time on our hands. My nurse, Stephanie, is there again with a Styrofoam cup of water. This time the small plastic cup has a white pill in it.

"Dr. L. has prescribed medication to help you sleep. It can be tough in here to relax. We do hourly checks in rooms, so you may hear us open the door and see our flashlight shine in."

I gratefully accept the pill, thinking sleep will be better than anything else in here.

For the first time all week, my sleep is deep and dreamless. A loud male voice wakes me by poking his head in: "Linda, Sandra, time to get up. Breakfast trays are here."

Immediately after breakfast, I'm called to Dr. L.'s office. It's a tiny, windowless room used just for meetings with in-patients. The same heavy chairs.

There is no small talk. He jumps immediately into it. "Last week when you were in Emerg after cutting, Dr. S. started you on Prozac. How has that been going?"

His voice is quiet and calm, which soothes me, but my stomach is still filled with anxious butterflies.

"It took me a few days to fill it. We don't have any insurance. So I just started three days ago."

His hand strokes his beard, a move I will learn is his thinking move.

"We can get you a meeting with a social worker who may be able to help you access resources if finances are an issue. It will take at least two weeks to see an improvement from the medication. In the meantime, our goal here in hospital is to ensure you feel safe. Think of this like a reset. It also gives us an opportunity to see how you respond to the medication, and adjust it if needed. Your day nurse will take your stitches out today as well."

The day passes with not much happening.

My stitches are removed from my upper arm, and I realize it will be an ugly scar. I don't care.

I sit in the lounge with the other patients and watch *Wheel of Fortune* and *The Price is Right* all morning. The minutes drag by.

At lunch, an older woman with scraggly long grey hair sits next to me. "First time, right?"

"I'm just here for three days for a reset."

She throws her head up in the air and cackles like a witch, then proceeds to separate each item of food, creating tiny piles on her plate.

While I wrestle to cut the dry meatloaf with a dull plastic knife, I watch her eat each pile, one by one.

The afternoon is quiet except for an optional group program which I choose not to attend. Some patients can go off the floor for Occupational Therapy or Art Therapy. Several have "privileges" to leave to have a smoke or go to the hospital cafeteria. Those of us in grippy socks enviously watch them head out the door.

"Grippy socks" is a self-deprecating humorous term used by psychiatric patients.

"I got the grippy socks" means you have been put on a Form 1. Your shoes are taken away and replaced with non-slip socks in a generic size. Mine are too big for my size seven feet, and they flop around as I walk.

I stare at the clock, waiting for Tim's visit. University Hospital is on the University of Western Ontario campus. I look out the window and watch students scurrying back and forth, moving quickly to avoid the autumn chill. I feel envy. They are there, free to do as they please, getting an education, laughing with friends. I am locked up in the Psych ward, with red grippy socks flopping off my feet.

Tim arrives promptly at 4:00, the beginning of visiting hours.

"I'm not allowed to bring in flowers, but thought you might like this guy." It's a plush husky. We had recently adopted a husky/German shepherd cross named Chico, and I already miss him. Tim also holds a pair of slippers that pass hospital criteria, so I can get out of the grippy socks. I can't strangle myself with a soft slipper, and it's too light to hurt anyone if I throw it at them.

"Your parents will be here soon, too. I let them know what is going on."

I look up at him, my eyes tearful. "Are they mad?" "Of course not. The opposite. Really concerned." I want him to see the lounge. It's nice to be out of the room. He seems nervous, and I realize he has the same views of a Psych ward as I did – the craziness that movies like to show. But it's quiet. A few people visiting and a few staring, bored, at *The Young and the Restless*.

After an hour, the nurse who started the 3 p.m. shift comes to me. "Your parents are here to see you. You are only allowed two visitors at a time, though." I look at Tim. Reluctantly, he says, "They drove two hours to see you. I'll be back tomorrow after class."

I stare after him as he leaves, but quickly jump to my feet when I see my parents. I hug my mom hard and start sniffling, then sobbing. My dad hugs me too, and I cry louder as we walk to my room. Linda is not there, as she has privileges and likes to go out with the smokers even though she doesn't smoke. Anything to get off the ward.

My mom, always the optimist, comments on the fluffy husky plush toy, the lounge and the nice nurse she met.

None of it seems nice to me. I don't want to be here.

My dad is an organizer. He is good at collecting facts and getting things done.

"Are you able to do anything? Maybe tell them you will take me to your place?" I plead.

"Honey, I think this is the right spot for you to be," my dad responds. "It's just for three days. Things have kind of been leading up to this."

With too much enthusiasm, my mom chirps, "But we will come back to London to visit as soon as you are home."

Two days later, I have another meeting with Dr. L. to discuss my discharge. It's been six days on Prozac. I'm feeling optimistic that things may change. The thought of going outside into sunshine, eating good food and sleeping in my own bed perks me up.

I promise to keep taking the medication and to attend a follow-up appointment with him three days later.

Beds are always at a premium. Other patients are revolving through Emerg – suicidal, psychotic and delusional. I'm happy to give them the bed. I'm not experiencing the same level of distress as when I first came, and I have a discharge plan that includes follow-up and a safe home to go to.

When Tim comes to collect me, I'm bubbling over with excitement. I feel free!

The next day I call Sheryl, the owner of the mailbox store where I work. Tim had let her know I was in hospital and couldn't come in. I don't know how I feel about going back: I know we need the money, but I also don't feel I have my thoughts together enough yet to work. My mind is constantly returning to the last few days. Being hospitalized is traumatic enough, but when it is against your choice, that adds a new level of trauma.

"What happened? Are you ok?" Sheryl's voice seems to express concern. I mistake concern as caring. At that age, I was an open book. I've always been a sharer. As a social person I love deep conversations, honesty and connection. So it doesn't occur to me that anything bad would happen by being honest. I explain that I've been dealing with depression, and it became bad enough I had to be hospitalized. I leave out the suicide attempt.

There is a long pause before Sheryl says, "Why don't you take a couple of more days off, and I'll see you on Monday next week."

"Umm, actually I have a doctor's appointment Monday. With the bus, it will take me most of the morning. Is noon ok?"

In a flat voice, Sheryl says, "Whatever you need to do." And hangs up. Two days later, my phone rings. The Prozac has really started helping. I feel much better. My head feels less cloudy, almost lighter, as if a weight has been lifted. I am ready to go to work.

"Hello," I answer brightly.

"Sandra. It's Sheryl. I'm sorry, but I've made a decision that unfortunately affects you. I need someone reliable. I'm a small business, and I need someone who will be able to do the job."

I'm stunned. "But I never called in sick before this. I always did the work properly, and customers liked me."

"I've already hired someone else. I'm sorry."

A SPARKLING TORNADO

I didn't know it at the time, but a double storm was brewing for me. When I look back at my Life Chart (which I talked about at the end of Chapter 1), I see that each of my depressive or manic episodes had a trigger before it. Being fired was embarrassing and shocking. I knew that if I had needed time off for a broken leg, accommodations would have been made. This experience would be only the first of many where mental health is treated different from physical health.

The second part of the simmering storm was the Prozac increasing the serotonin levels in my brain. Simply put, serotonin is a chemical that your nerve cells produce and is responsible for mood regulation and happiness. Serotonin levels are lower in depressed people, and that is why antidepressant SSRIs (selective serotonin reuptake inhibitors) help. But for someone with undiagnosed bipolar, SSRIs can have dangerous consequences, taking the person beyond a healthy baseline and into mania or hypomania. It was first noted in 1958 that "in individuals who are predisposed," the drug could give rise to manic-like states or even a manic state." It is now recognized that the predisposed individuals are people with bipolar. In Marya Hornbacher's memoir, *Madness: A Bipolar Life*, she describes the effects of taking the incorrect medication. *"Because I'm not, in fact, depressed, Prozac makes me manic and numb – one of the reasons I slice my arm in the first place is that I'm coked to the gills on something utterly wrong for what I have."*

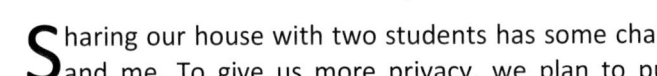

Sharing our house with two students has some challenges for Tim and me. To give us more privacy, we plan to put drywall and flooring in the unfinished basement and use it as "our space." With no experience (and no YouTube at the time), Tim learns how to do the work himself from a well-worn *Reader's Digest Home Renovations* book.

Unaware that I am entering a manic episode, I feel my body vibrating with energy. My thoughts feel fast and brilliant. My world is suddenly a beautiful sparkling tornado. I see every colour more vibrantly. Blades of grass are bright green, and I see a shimmering glow in my skin. As I walk the dog, even the air seems fresher. Life is amazing. I can't believe that two weeks ago I tried to kill myself.

Late one evening, I wander down to the basement, leaving Tim watching *Seinfeld* upstairs. Creativity is surging through my veins. The drywall is primed, a blank canvas ready to paint. We have several buckets of paint of different colours, all bought in the half-price "mistint" section at the hardware store. I line up the buckets, analyzing each one. I have a vision of horizontal stripes, each one a different colour, one shade blending perfectly into the next.

With my thoughts moving rapidly, I have no time to plan it out. I need to start painting!

I grab a brush and dip it into the navy-blue bucket. Being only 5'3", I start at the bottom. I see no need for painters' tape. I drag the brush along, the line wavy with carelessness. No worries – we haven't put up trim yet! Next comes a bright plum burgundy. As the navy paint isn't dry, the two colours bleed into each other in a crooked line.

It is about this time that I hear Tim's voice call from the top of the stairs.

"Sandra? What are you doing?"

With pride in my voice, I yell up, "Painting!"

He walks down and sees me with brush in hand.

"I wanted to use all the colours to make it unique. No one uses multiple colours – but we are!"

This isn't usual behaviour for me, and Tim doesn't know what to think. It's only months later, after another suicide attempt, that we would learn of the term "hypomania."

The next few days, I can't sleep. I don't feel tired and don't seem to even need sleep. I still have a couple of months before starting school, and I want a project to occupy my time. Although I have no artistic skill, I decide to start a craft business: "Hot Pot Designs." (Fortunately, cannabis wasn't legal at that time or people would have thought I was selling something completely different!)

I'm determined to be professional. First stop is to the printing store to get 500 business cards printed. Nothing says "I'm official" like business cards. Next stop: the Service Ontario government office to legally register the business name. Now on to the craft store to buy paints in every colour, along with brushes, sponges, stencils and clay pots. My plan is to paint and sell pots. Not sure where – online shopping doesn't exist yet. But I haven't thought that far ahead. Now is the time to create!

Tim thinks it is better for me to be painting pots than painting walls, so I spend days painting pots. I go to community centres, stores and restaurants to leave business cards. I have the pots; now I need the customers. The week before this, I had attended my follow-up appointment with Dr. L. I'd been filling out a Depression Rating Scale daily, and the numbers were dropping. And low is good.

The goal is 0. I assume this drop means the medication has worked and I don't need it anymore. So I stop taking it and cancel the next follow-up appointment.

What a mistake this would prove to be.

Reflections and Resources

What is a regret of yours that you believe is a result of your bipolar? (e.g., my regret is not finishing school)

Was there a positive that came later from that situation? (e.g., in Chapter 5, you will see that I end up with a career I love in a completely different field)

Plan of Action

A Plan of Action is a plan to help you and your loved ones recognize signs and symptoms before they become severe. In this plan, you also detail what steps you can take to help yourself, and what your trusted person can do to help you. The time to create this plan is during a time of stability, when you can logically think through the steps. The Plan of Action should be kept easily accessible to both you and the trusted person.

Online and printable resource: The Australian Centre for Clinical Intervention has a free online bipolar course, with worksheets, including a Plan of Action. Click on 'courses', then click 'bipolar'.

Youtube: Mental Health Action Plan, by Heads Above the Waves

Song: "Voices in my Head" by Falling in Reverse. The line "The voices in my head keep on telling me I'm going to die" hits home. Intrusive thoughts are something that I have yet to be able to get rid of. I've learned to push them aside, but during times of distress they still whisper, "You could just kill yourself, you could just kill yourself, you could just kill yourself." It's hard to explain to those who are fortunate enough to have never experienced this, just how difficult it is to ignore these whispers. They push themselves in, and I push just as hard to let them out.

My dad and I on a yacht, floating toward the altar, and a marriage that would become my lifeboat through the upcoming storm.

FREQUENT FLYER POINTS (WITHOUT THE CHAMPAGNE)

For the next week, I focus on painting pots and handing out business cards anywhere I go. I'm confident I'm going to make a huge success of this! My enthusiasm is bubbling over, and I imagine people are looking at me – seeing a powerful Bossgirl.

Then, a few days later, I wake up tired. Really tired. The lack of sleep has caught up to me. I don't want to paint pots anymore. I don't want to create a crafting empire. I don't want to do anything but lie in bed and stare at the wall. The sparkles have swirled out of my tornado.

Poet Emma Bleker says it well. "You are a hurricane of a girl; remember to breathe every once in a while, do not drown within your own storm." I'm drowning in my own storm.

I can summarize the next few months leading to my diagnosis of rapid cycling bipolar type 2.

Week 1 – Cry, sleep and hate myself.

Week 2 – Another suicide attempt: overdose and cut both wrists.

Week 3 – Hospitalized on a Form 1 for three days, then Form 3 for 14 days. Lithium added to my meds.

Week 4 – Still on Form 3, grippy socks and "psych patient" scrubs.

Week 5 – In hospital as a "voluntary" patient. Lithium is beginning to slow the tornado down to a small dust storm.

Week 6 – Diagnosis of bipolar type 2, rapid cycling.

Week 7 – Discharge from hospital with prescriptions for lithium, Tegretol and Ativan. Lithium is typically the first medication tried with a bipolar diagnosis. It is a mood stabilizer that has been used since the 1970s. It is still my main medication to this day. Tegretol is an anti-seizure drug that helps stabilize moods. Anti-seizure drugs are frequently used in bipolar; they reduce "excitability" of nerve impulses in the brain. Ativan is a benzodiazepine, or "sedative," to be used as needed.

Week 8 and the next two years – Several more hospitalizations, medication trials, long-term disability, ECT...and a basic total disaster of my life. The first diagnosis that was considered for me was borderline personality disorder, because of my self-harm cutting and the mood swings. But those were the only two diagnostic criteria I had. The other symptoms typical of borderline disorder are unstable relationships, explosive anger and fear of abandonment, none of which I exhibited.

The medical field is quick to look at self-harm and suicidal behaviour and label the patient as borderline, especially in young women. With borderline personality disorder, the symptoms are relatively constant. However, in bipolar, symptoms vary greatly, from the euphoria of a manic episode to the deep despair of a depressive episode, and balanced "life is normal" euthymic periods in between.

The DSM-5 criteria for bipolar require symptoms of both mania and depression.

DSM-5 Symptoms of Hypomania in Bipolar 2

(My answers below are based on the unstable decade of my 20s – things have improved since then!)

1. Exaggerated sense of well-being and self-confidence, euphoria, grandiosity *(Yes: I would be the entertaining life of the party, the powerful business owner and the brilliant student.)*

2. Decreased need for sleep *(Yes: Me to psychiatrist: "But if I'm not tired, why do I need to sleep?" His brilliant response: "Because your husband beside you needs to sleep.")*

3. Unusual talkativeness *(Yes: I'm always chatty, but in hypomania my speech is fast, with my mouth trying to keep up with my racing brain.)*

4. Rushed/scattered thinking, racing thoughts *(Yes: Sometimes I feel like I'm on top of the world, managing everything that comes my way. Then, other times, the thoughts are too quick for even me to make sense of.)*

5. Attention/focus issues, distractibility *(No: At the time, I lived with a husband who had ADHD, so I was actually the more focused one in the household.)*

6. Psychomotor agitation, which is an increase in purposeless physical activity (e.g., restlessness, pacing, tapping fingers or feet, abruptly starting and stopping tasks, rapidly talking, and moving items around without meaning) or increase in "activity toward goals" *(Yes: I've been told I'm "buzzing.")*

7. Impulsivity, poor decision-making, and risk-taking *(No/yes: Because I'm actually a logical person, that slows down the typical manic impulsivity. Then again, just last year, in a hypomanic episode, I found myself at the pet store about to buy a guinea pig....)*

DSM-5 Symptoms of Bipolar 2 Depression

A major depressive episode involves that last at least two weeks and are severe enough to cause significant emotional and occupational distress. An episode of must involve a depressed mood or loss of interest and pleasure, in addition to at least four of the following symptoms:

1. Significant changes in weight and/or appetite *(No: For me, only the meds caused the scale to climb, not depression.)*

2. Sleeping too much or too little *(Yes: I lean toward insomnia.)*

3. Restlessness or sluggishness *(No: Any sluggishness I had would have been related to the meds.)*

4. Loss of energy *(Yes: I hadn't gained physical weight in depression, but my body felt too heavy to lift itself out of the bed.)*

5. Feeling extreme worthlessness or guilt *(Definitely yes: Shame and guilt are something my therapist and I still work on to this day.)*

6. Attention difficulties, indecisiveness *(Yes: Even a simple decision, such as deciding on breakfast, seems insurmountable in depression.)*

7. Thinking about, planning or attempting suicide *(Yes to all three.)*

My bipolar diagnosis was also confirmed by the medication I was taking. My mania was brought on quickly after I started taking Prozac. If a person with bipolar takes an antidepressant like Prozac on its own, it will typically flip them into mania. Someone with unipolar depression (meaning only depression, not bipolar), or borderline personality disorder, will be brought out of depression to (hopefully) a healthy baseline.

With bipolar, if someone is prescribed an antidepressant like Prozac, a mood stabilizer must be added to avoid mania. In the upcoming years, I will try, and go off, many different medications. Lithium is a medication that's used solely for bipolar. It won't have much of an effect on any other mental illness. I respond quickly and positively to it, which confirms the bipolar diagnosis.

There is a genetic component to bipolar as well. I'm not too familiar with my birth father's side of the family, so I only have bits and pieces of the Steiner family history. When I've been writing about my dad, I'm talking about the wonderful man who raised me. I was a lucky six-year-old girl when he came into our lives and married my mom.

There isn't a better dad out there than him. My birth father I have rarely seen. When I was two years old, we moved to Canada from Switzerland with him. Shortly after, my parents split up and he left for Montreal. From there, he remarried, moved to Venezuela and started a new family. In high school, I had the opportunity to spend a couple of summers in Switzerland, traveling from relative to relative, staying a few days with each. My birth father was still in Venezuela then, but I spent time with his side of the family, the Steiners. I saw alcoholism in my aunt, who had always been unmarried and childless. I heard stories of odd behaviour and alcoholism in my grandfather, whom my grandmother had divorced many years previously. Psychcentral.com says having bipolar disorder is linked to a 22 to 59 percent higher rate of addiction to alcohol or drugs.

Perhaps my aunt and grandfather were self-medicating with alcohol. This was the 1980s. Mental illness was rarely discussed. Odd behaviour was explained as "moods" or "melancholy." Women were often prescribed sedatives for "hysteria."

But these behaviours were not spoken of outside the household. It's because of this shame and stigma, which remains today, that information about the family genetics of mental illness is often not passed down correctly. And I'm guilty of this myself. Here I have published this book about my bipolar disorder, yet I have still never told any extended family about this diagnosis.

After many years of having no contact with my father, we received a telephone call from his wife in Venezuela. He had been hit by a truck while jogging. It was touch and go. When my mom told me, I didn't feel any emotion about it, one way or the other. He eventually healed physically, but I heard that after the accident he developed odd religious convictions. Years later, I would connect with my half-sister in Switzerland.

She said he would read a page of the Bible every day, out loud in five different languages, insisting they listen to it all. Though, to give him credit, he actually did speak five languages. He soon divorced again and moved back to Switzerland, taking my half-brother and half-sister with him because of the dangerous political and human rights situation in Venezuela. I haven't seen my half-brother in two decades.

I hear he is living as a shaman in a commune in Tulum, Mexico. I mean, it's possible – maybe he really is a shaman? My father is now remarried for the third time, living a quiet life. I have minimal contact with him, and that is ok with me.

His life seems to have settled down, but the chaos it created around his family seems like a tornado too.

My cousin, Carine, and I bonded as teenagers during those summers in Switzerland. Now in our 50s, we still keep in touch. Her two kids are the same age as mine, and we've traveled there to visit her three times. In their younger years, the kids would play happily together without even understanding each other's language, while Carine and I catch up, chatting in French over a crisp glass of Swiss white wine. Unfortunately, both her teen kids have recently developed mental illness.

During Covid, her 17-year-old daughter was hospitalized for four months due to an eating disorder. I've met several people with eating disorders during my hospital stays, and I know it is an illness that requires a lot of therapy and time to manage. It can take years. Four months is just the beginning of the healing.

Carine's son went to do his military service at age 18 (as is mandatory for males in Switzerland), but was dismissed early due to clinical depression.

I hear he is improving, but I can't help but wonder if this is the "Steiner gene" beginning to show its face.

During this same time, Carine's 73-year-old mother died from suicide by jumping off a bridge. (Saying someone "committed suicide" implies that the person did something wrong. People commit adultery, commit a crime, commit a robbery.

When someone dies from suicide, their illness is causing so much pain and suffering that suicide is the last stage of the illness.) I can't imagine dealing with all those things at once, especially when Covid was isolating the world.

This shows my cousin's strength and resilience. It also demonstrates that genetics can increase your vulnerability to certain illnesses but doesn't predetermine the outcome.

While I don't know my full family history on the Steiner side, I recognize that shamans, alcoholism, depression and eating disorders indicate there may be some problems. The Canadian Association for Mental Health states that children have a 10 percent risk of bipolar if one parent has it (though I have also heard higher statistics).

To compare, one percent of the population has bipolar. At the time of writing this, my boys are 20 and 22. I may be biased, but I think they have grown into wonderful men. In their teen years I watched them closely, always with fingers crossed. I have seen no signs of depression, mania, anxiety or mood disorders. I often wonder how I got so lucky. My older son dealt with his first heartbreak with unusual devastation, and I worried it might lead to more.

"Is this the first sign? Is this his trigger?"

I wondered. However seeing a therapist gave him some perspective and coping tools – enough that he moved on to study psychology in university.

I think I can finally breathe a sigh of relief for both of my boys.

It takes an average of seven years from the onset of symptoms to receive a bipolar diagnosis. We can only hope that will change soon, as more studies are looking at brain imaging and their results show physical differences in the brains of people with bipolar.

I don't remember the actual moment of being told, "You have bipolar type 2, rapid cycling." Many people say they felt a sense of relieved at finally getting a diagnosis. If you know what you are dealing with, you can start to work on healing.

In 1996, when I'm diagnosed at age 23, the internet is just starting, and there isn't much information about bipolar to be found. Dial-up connection is so slow that I sit at our large desktop computer with a magazine beside me to flip through as I wait for each page to load. I want to learn more, but the only information I have about my new diagnosis is in pamphlets from the hospital: "So, you've been diagnosed with Bipolar" and a bright yellow book called *Bipolar Disorder for Dummies*. (Yes, that's a real book.)

I also learn from other patients on the ward. There is an odd but comforting fellowship among psych patients. You are in the same trenches, battling the same war.

My mom brings me self-help workbooks on her weekly visit. Her thoughts are in the right place, but my mind can't focus on things more complicated than rug hooking or word searches. My head and my heart aren't in it.

I recognize that in writing this book I am preaching the exact same thing to you.

"Do these exercises! They will change your life!"

"You can feel better if you have a toolbox of coping strategies!"

"You need to get up, go outside, exercise!"

I also recognize that in depression or mania, or with the side effects of some meds, it may be cognitively difficult to work through anything. I personally know the challenge of understanding and accepting the benefits of putting in work that won't always be pleasant.

At age 23, I don't yet recognize that I need to be responsible for myself. So my mom's workbooks remain blank. Unfilled pages that have so much potential.

In hospital, every decision is made for you. Every hour is planned. Breakfast at 8:00, meds at 9:00, Group at 10:00, lunch at 12:00. The routine continues until Lights Out at 10:00. The only change in routine is on weekends, when lights can stay on until 11:00!

Once I'm discharged home, I have no one to keep me on a routine.

The antipsychotic med Seroquel has recently been added to my cocktail of drugs. A side effect is fatigue, and I feel exhausted all the time: I sleep from 10 p.m. to 11 a.m., then need another nap in the afternoon.

In three months, I gain 20 pounds on Seroquel. Antipsychotics are notorious for weight gain. It's not just because of the lethargy they cause; they also affect the metabolism.

Researchers at the University of Pittsburgh School of Medicine found that "blocking inhibitory dopamine receptors with antipsychotics causes a vicious circle – the brake comes off and insulin and glucagon release become unchecked, quickly desensitizing the body and further propagating hyperinsulinemia, hyperglycemia and, eventually, obesity and diabetes."

That's a lot of words – but simply put, it's not just the lethargy and extra sleep lowering your metabolism, it's actually a change in hormones. As someone who has always been athletic and fit, the weight gain devastates me emotionally.

Even in my high school days, at 110 lbs I still viewed my 5'3" body as not thin enough and not strong enough. In high school I actually wished I had an eating disorder!

I loved the way my stomach looked in the morning before food, so I tried not eating. That just meant I became cranky and starving until I scarfed down a large serving of steaming poutine at the school cafeteria. I thought bulimia might be better: I'd get to eat what I want, then just throw it up.

After several attempts to purge with a toothbrush down my throat, I could only gag and cough. So, anorexia and bulimia were out for me. Thankfully. Now, gaining 20 pounds in three months lowers my self-esteem to nothing. I hate seeing myself in the mirror. High-starch hospital food makes my face greasy. My long curly hair is dull and frizzy from lack of care. And I detest my body.

Because of the constant fatigue, my doctor takes me off Seroquel and puts me on olanzapine, another antipsychotic. I gain another five pounds. But I'm still not 100 percent, or even 50 percent, stable. Then again, I'm still not 100 percent compliant with my meds either.

Dr. L prescribes trials of medication cocktails, which together have side effects ranging from mental numbness and exhaustion, to weight gain and even eye issues.

I'd much prefer a gini cocktail, but alcohol is out of the question at this point.

One medication actually causes my pupils to jump and affects my depth perception. In one single day, I rear-end three cars! All happen slowly at stop lights, with no damage. But three on the same day! Each time, I need to get out of the car, walk anxiously to the front and hope the other driver isn't going to scream at me. I silently beg that there won't be any damage that we can't afford to fix.

I am taken off that medication the next day.

I can't remember all the meds I try, but I still cycle up and down. Earlier, I said my biggest regret was not finishing post-secondary education.

But the regret of never taking my medications properly and consistently is a close second.

Their side effects were so brutal that I'd go off them without telling the doctor or Tim. Then I'd have an episode and be hospitalized. With consistent medication in hospital, I'd stabilize. Go home; periodically take my meds. Episode, hospital, stabilize, repeat.

The first medication I was put on after the diagnosis was lithium. While it doesn't work for everyone, I now know that it is the most effective medication for me.

I often wonder, if I had taken it as prescribed back then, could the turmoil of my 20s been avoided? Would my life have been totally different? Would I have an education and a high-level job? Lithium, discovered in 1949, is considered the "gold standard" for bipolar. Not all patients can tolerate it, though.

From 20 to 30 percent of people on lithium will develop hypothyroidism, meaning they have an underactive thyroid gland. I have been on thyroid medication for 22 years, as the benefit of continuing lithium outweighs the health risks of taking Synthroid to keep my underactive thyroid functioning properly.

Shaky hands are experienced by 65 percent of people on lithium. It was a side effect that was mostly just embarrassing to me, but once I took up mountain biking, it became a safety issue.

So then a beta blocker had to be added to stop the shaking. The cocktail gets larger.

A couple of years ago, my creatinine blood levels were too high. This meant lithium was impacting my kidneys, another common effect of long-term use.

My doctor lowered the lithium dosage and added another mood stabilizer, Lamictal, which turned out to be a brilliant combination for me. Both meds are low dose, so I had no side effects, but each medication supports the other. And it meant I could stop the beta blocker since I no longer had shaky hands.

A pretty good cocktail! Not as good as my favourite gin and tonic, but something I can tolerate and that works. Bipolar episodes can also sometimes include psychosis. I have two distinct memories of psychosis.

One happened in 1996, and the other was a "stopped just in the nick of time" episode in 2023.

I've had different psychiatrists diagnose me with either bipolar 1 or bipolar 2. I prefer to say bipolar 2, though sometimes I think – who cares? What difference does it make? The medical field is now starting to recognize that there is a spectrum to bipolar, similar to the autism spectrum.

It is not as black and white as it had once been considered. Bipolar 1 has fewer depressive episodes coupled with more severe mania with episodes of psychosis. Bipolar 2 has more depressive episodes, with hypomania and no psychosis.

Both have periods of stability in between. The stability can last days, weeks, months or even years. After my children were born, I had relative stability for a good decade. But in 1996, my psychotic episode built quickly.

I've been feeling extra wired for a few days and have an appointment with Dr. L. at his outpatient clinic at St. Joseph's Hospital.

Since Tim and I share one car, I often take the bus to my appointments. I'm still not working, so have more available time than him.

I arrive early and am sitting in the waiting room. St. Joseph's has a hospital newspaper, the type you pick up for free to browse through while waiting. Community events, hospital announcements, local businesses advertising, that sort of thing.

I'm flipping rapidly through the newspaper, tapping my foot impatiently on the linoleum tile. No time to read this page, I need to read the next! Flip, flip, flip. Nothing can keep my attention – until page 4. I see an article about me! It praises me for being an ideal patient. Doctors worldwide are studying how I successfully cured my bipolar. I realize I am a role model to others!

I hear the secretary call, "Sandra, Dr. L. is ready for you. Head on in."

I walk with quick, energetic steps down the hallway to his office.

The day before, I had impulsively walked into a low-end hair salon and asked them to cut my long curly hair short – so short it's almost a buzz cut.

A buzz cut will immediately get a psychiatrist's attention. (Britney Spears wasn't the first one. It's common in mania to drastically alter one's appearance. I follow a Facebook group "Women and Bipolar," and I can't count how many posts of changes in hair colour or style, or impromptu tattoos, I've seen.)

Tapping my fingers, legs swinging, I excitedly tell him about the article that features me – important, amazing me!

"Did they interview you for it?" I ask him. "They never interviewed me. I don't know how they knew this stuff, but it's great. I can be a role model. Did you see my new haircut? I was tired of long hair. It gets in the way. I don't think I need any more appointments. I can stop my meds too. My cat got its paw stuck in a tiki torch last week and we had to take it to the vet...." I would have kept rambling if he hadn't stopped me.

"What made you decide to cut your hair? Tell me more about it." (You'd think he would have started with "You saw an article about yourself in the newspaper?")

I jabbered on about my hair, my new job search, the person I saw on the bus with the scar across their neck who I'm sure tried to slit their throat. "Can you show me the newspaper?"

"I'll go get it from the waiting room!" I say, rushing off.

I grab the newspaper, flipping through it as I walk back down the hall to his office. I simply can't find the article now.

I give it to him, looking over his shoulder impatiently as he slowly turns the pages.

"Is it possible you saw something that was similar, but not about you? Or that was not there at all?" he asks as he hands the paper back.

I grow frustrated, even hostile, that I can't find it.

After a few more questions, he suggests a medication change to bring me back to baseline.

"I think that as we adjust your meds, we should monitor this in hospital. I don't want to see you get to the point of psychosis. Will you agree to stay a few days?"

I'm not a danger to myself or others, so he can't legally put me on a Form 1 to keep me in for 72 hours. He needs to convince me to stay.

"You saw something that isn't there," he says. "You drastically changed your appearance. You are talking so fast I can't follow your conversation from one topic to another. I believe you are close to psychosis. We can stop that. I'm sure you understand that it is not fair to ask Tim to handle that responsibility. We can call him to bring whatever you need, but I'd like you to stay now."

Whether I'm at baseline or experiencing mania or depression, I always still have the motivation to not burden others. Dr. L. knows this and uses it to his advantage to convince me.

He makes a few phone calls, while I try to sit still to prove that I can. But the frenetic energy in my body means I need to move.

My hands fidget, my feet tap, I shift my weight. I stand up, then sit down.

The door opens and one of the nurses I recognize smiles at me. "Hi, Sandra. Dr. L. asked me to come and walk with you to the ward."

I'm still convinced about the article. It just wasn't in the specific paper I gave Dr. L.

My grandiose thoughts think that maybe I am on the ward to help other patients, to inspire them. I don't see myself as the patient.

But it only takes a few doses of Ativan and some antipsychotics for me to realize that I am not an inspiration to anyone.

Having been in and out of hospital over the last few years, I was now known as a "frequent flyer." Frequent flyer points are a great thing. We all like free flights. Frequently flying into the Psych ward is not so great. I was also known as a "runner."

My goal was often to escape. I attempted escape four times, and three of those times I got out of the ward, out of the hospital and quite a distance away. Psych wards are typically locked.

Visitors need to get buzzed in and out. If you are not on a Form 1, you can earn "Privileges," meaning you can wear your own clothes, go down to the cafeteria and, if you are on a longer stay, even get day or weekend passes to go home short term.

My favourite thing to do is to go to the cafeteria and get an Oreo yogurt: sweet vanilla yogurt, with crumbled Oreos to sprinkle on top.

A wonderful change from the bland, unseasoned hospital food. Any money we have is kept at the nurses' station. You ask for it, fill in a sign-out sheet and head down to the cafeteria.

I get off the elevator and turn left toward the cafeteria. I have no plan to keep going; it just happens. My feet walk past the main floor cafeteria.

I hide my hospital bracelet under my long-sleeved shirt. I walk out the front doors, and directly onto the bus that is waiting out front.

I don't even know where the bus is going, just that it is going away from here. I open the window, and inhale diesel fumes combined with fresh outdoor air. A few stops later, I see the Mongolian Grill restaurant and know that I am downtown. I ask for a transfer as I get off. I still don't know where I plan to go. In fact, I have no plan. I wander downtown for an hour, zigzagging up and down the main street.

I decide to go home. I know the transit system and where to wait for the correct bus. As the bus rumbles on, my stomach starts to fill with butterflies and dread. Anxiety creeps in, and I can feel prickly stress sweat on my underarms.

I suddenly feel unsafe. While no one wants to be in hospital, you are safe there. Things are predictable and calm. People don't judge you. You have no responsibility other than to rest and get better.

The people on the bus are strange and chaotic. A pack of teenagers, still in their school uniforms, laugh loudly. A disheveled man mumbles to himself, and I wonder if that is how I appear as well.

A frazzled-looking mother tries to calm her crying toddler. I feel mayhem around me.

When I see my stop, I exhale a deep breath I didn't even know I was holding. I quickly hop off and walk in the direction of my house. It's only a three-minute walk.

There is no sidewalk, so my hard-soled slippers shuffle loudly on the gravel curb. I'm almost at my house when I hear the crunch of gravel behind me and sense a car slowly pulling up.

I turn and see a blue and white police car. Fight or Flight kicks in. Do I run? A short blonde female officer exits first. "Sandra?" I'm frozen. No words come out. "The hospital and your husband are concerned. We want to check if you are ok." A male officer also exits the car, and they come to either side of me, about six feet away.

I'm speechless, afraid to say anything. I consider bolting. They must have picked up on my body language, which is coiled and ready to sprint. They move closer.

"Can we just have a chat and make sure everything is all right?" The male officer still hasn't said a word. I nod, accepting that the jig is over.

After a few questions, the female gently asks, "Will you come with us? We've been asked to take you back to the hospital so you can continue working on feeling better."

By nature, I am a people pleaser, always eager to do what is expected of me. Worried that if I don't, people won't like me.

I want even the officers to like me. So, I obediently take a seat in the back of the cruiser and apologize to them for the inconvenience. Once back on the ward, my clothes are taken away and I'm given scrubs.

The light shade of blue indicates I am a patient, not a doctor. It's a little harder to run away when you are wearing patient scrubs. But two days later, I try anyway. I've been here three weeks now and am desperate for good food, for sunlight on my face, and a TV where I can pick what channel to watch.

I want to be able to lock the door when I shower and to shave my legs. I want to go to bed any time that suits me.

During the day, the locked doors are constantly opening and closing as various staff come and go. I walk up and down the hall, partly out of boredom, partly figuring out the timing of the doors. There's no chance – the staff quickly pull it closed behind them.

But the visitors aren't that smart. I linger by the door at visiting hours. At this point, I have no friends who come to visit. I've been the "crazy girl" for too long. My parents come once a week, making the two-hour drive from Mississauga.

Tim comes most days, but he has class Wednesday nights. I know tonight I'll have no visitors. Single visitors are quick at the door, but families hold it open for each other. I see two worried-looking people in their 60s with a pretty woman in her 30s.

As the younger one holds the door open for the other two, I dart under her arm into the hallway. Then I freeze. My mind can't think what to do. Just like on the bus, leaving the safety of the ward without a plan causes immediate anxiety. I stand there for a minute, waiting to see what happens.

Over the speaker blares "Code Yellow, 10th floor, Code Yellow 10th floor."

They say humans have a Fight or Flight response. But I think I have more of a Freeze or Flight response. If I'm crossing the road and a car comes toward me, I'll literally freeze in the middle of the road. Most people would either run across or run back. I have the "deer in the headlights" response.

I remain frozen until I see two security guards. Unlike the cops who used gentle coaching to get me to come with them, these guys mean business. "Hey! You!"

Now I practice the Flight response. I take off for the staircase. I sprint the first two flights, but my level of fitness has dropped significantly because of lack of exercise and the weight gain from the antipsychotic meds. By the third flight of stairs,

I'm gasping for air. I turn and put my back against the wall, accepting defeat. Once again, I do the walk of shame back onto the ward. Some of the patients raise their hand in the air, a high-five for my efforts. This time, we walk past my room. Past my cozy blanket and the pillow Tim brought me from home.

Our walk stops at a room at the end of the hall. It has only a bed and two chairs. I quickly turn and take a few steps away from the room.

The two burly security guards are still beside me and each grabs an arm, spinning me back toward the room.

Cathy, one of my favourite nurses, steps in and guides me toward the bed. In her hand is a small plastic package with two pills, and a Styrofoam cup of water. The rest gets fuzzy here.

This is where I started my story. The book's first paragraph takes place right here, in this bed, my wrists and ankles in restraints.

The scared-looking student nurse, sitting by the door in one of those heavy, unthrowable chairs made especially for Psych wards.

Apparently, I tried to bolt out of the room whenever I was let up to use the washroom. I believe I was in restraints in the solitary room for two days. I'm not sure.

I have some extremely vivid memories of those two days, and a lot of blanks. In fact, much of my 20s is either big blanks or big memories.

That's partly due to the ECT that I will soon be treated with, and partly due to the meds. I'm also sure my brain has blocked out parts of that decade it didn't want to remember.

Rachel Graham's essay in *Voices of Bipolar Disorder* tells a similar story.

"*Mania is even worse. It is as if I am locked inside a bare room, unable to sit still. The nurses wait on guard outside my door, afraid I will hurt myself, more afraid I will get out and hurt them. My thoughts are speeding and my limbs are out of control. 'Help me,' I scream to the nurses. As soon as they come in, I dash like the Energizer Bunny to the exit. At the door, I throw a pitcher of apple juice at one nurse and scratch the other one until she bleeds. The emergency intercom blares that there's a dangerous person on the loose. Two security guards grab me and throw me back into the tiny room. And my hell begins again."*

That time spent locked in restraints – two days – is one of the most traumatic memories I have. But like all trauma, there are also good parts. Kay Redfield Jamison, a prominent author, manic-depressive (her preferred term for bipolar) and psychiatrist, says,

"For each awfulness in life, however, I seem to have been given an offsetting stroke of luck." In my future, I will be fortunate to have several offsetting strokes of luck.

Resources that many aren't offered. The first one comes in the form of a social worker named Karen. She is the highlight of my long days in hospital and a break from my lonely days when discharged home. Through sessions with her, I learn coping skills to short circuit the ups and downs as soon as I start to feel thought and energy shifts.

I begin to acquire life skills that I missed learning when my days were more focused on staying alive rather than actually living life. At this point, I have lost every single friend I had in my "before life."

They have moved onwards and upwards, while I'm still moving backwards and sideways. There wasn't as much understanding of mental health then as there is now.

There was stigma and fear. But it's also my own mind that is telling me I am beneath everyone else. The only friends I have now are the other Frequent Flyers in the hospital.

We understand each other, comrades stuck in a life we don't want to be in.

By November, I've been in hospital long enough that I have weekend passes. Sometimes Tim and I go back to Mississauga to stay with my parents.

Other times we drive to the beach to play in the waves with our dog, Chico. Christmas season rolls around, and I'm still in the hospital. I get an extended pass to visit my parents for the holidays.

The Psych ward will be empty except for only the sickest patients. Staff want time off too. Family traditions, good food, presents and yuletide joy lift my spirits.

I feel love. Once back at the hospital, I add photos from Christmas to the collection taped above my bed – a reminder of the world waiting for me. My social worker, Karen, puts her all into helping me become a healthier self.

Her attitude is very different from those unforgettable words Dr. L. once said to me:

"You have to remember you have a very serious illness. You will never be able to do what other people do."

But Karen disagrees. I'm now doing occupational therapy in the hospital. I paint a lot of birdhouses and cook pancakes in the supervised kitchen. That may not sound like much, but it's baby steps. Soon, we progress to societal expectations and job suitability testing.

Karen readies me for the outside world. She helps me apply for Ontario Disability Support Program payments.

Not only will I get a modest income, but it will cover my very expensive medications. Cost is one of the reasons I have not been consistently taking them.

Who wants to spend $150 a month on something that makes you fat, tired and shaky?

Once I'm discharged, Karen says, she will put me in touch with an organization to find volunteer work to keep me busy. She secures a discounted membership at the YMCA so I can exercise. She will even get me bus tickets to get to and from appointments.

However, as an in-patient, even on consistent medications and with colourfully painted birdhouses, my depression deepens. Hospital Psych wards are not meant for long-term stays.

They are meant to keep people safe from harm, for monitoring, medication adjustments and perhaps diagnosing. Then out you go into the world. There is someone else in the ER waiting for that bed. At three months, this is my longest stay ever.

In 1996, London still had a residential psychiatric hospital for long-term care: the London Psychiatric Hospital, and that's where I'm to go next.

In Canada, most of these residential hospitals have now been closed. Newer medications that give more patients the ability to live independent lives are one reason for the closure; budget cuts are another.

London Psychiatric Hospital's last patients were released in 2014. The streets and the jails have picked up many former patients who were unable to adapt to independence or were uncompliant with their medications.

The final thing for me to try before I'm transferred to long-term care is ECT – Electroconvulsive Therapy, informally known as electric shock. It sounds terrifying. Images in the media are of a patient restrained, mouth gagged, back arching in a seizure. Wheeled back to the ward drooling and numb afterwards.

I feel like I have no other option. I desperately want a normal life.

Reflections and Resources

Who has made a difference to you in your mental health journey, and how?

Think of a negative experience you have recently had, or a problem you are currently working through. Complete the below Thought Record to rework it in a different point of view.

CBT – Thought Record

I often use Thought Records to work through emotions or thoughts creating a negative thinking pattern. It's one of my favourite CBT tools. The basic premise is that you isolate the event or thought that is troubling you. List the beliefs attached to that thought and the emotions those beliefs create. Write down all the Unhelpful Thinking Styles you use (see the resources below). Now weigh the evidence For Your Thought and the evidence Against Your Thought. Dispute Your Thought – what are other ways of viewing the situation? How realistic is it? For The End Result, replace your original thought with a more balanced and helpful thought.

Working through a Thought Record can take 30 minutes, so give yourself a quiet space and focused time.

YouTube: Best Way to Reduce Negative Thinking: CBT Thought Record

This cartoon video explains it simply.

There are many versions of the Thought Record available online. The detailed version I like can be found under bipolar worksheets.

Unhelpful Thinking Styles

Certain emotions, such as depression and anxiety, are usually preceded by unhelpful thoughts.

Through practice, I've learned that my instinctive Unhelpful Thinking Styles are "Shoulding," "Ignoring the Positive" and "Mind Reading." It's hard sometimes in the moment to recognize these patterns, but looking back, or in a Thought Record, I see it in hindsight. Changing our thinking styles is a big aspect of CBT.

Which of these Unhelpful Thinking Styles do you recognize yourself thinking?

Mental Filter – When we notice only what the filter wants us to see, and dismiss anything that doesn't 'fit.' Am I only noticing the bad stuff? Am I filtering out the positives? What would be a more realistic view?

Judgments – Making evaluations or judgments about events, ourselves or others, rather than describing what we actually have evidence for. How we interpret the world doesn't mean our judgments are always right or helpful. Is there another perspective?

Prediction – Believing we know what's going to happen in the future. How likely is it that what we envision might happen?

Emotional Reasoning – I feel bad, so it must be bad! I feel anxious, so I must be in danger. Just because it feels bad doesn't necessarily mean it *is* bad. Our feelings are just a reaction to our thoughts – and thoughts are just automatic brain reflexes.

Mind Reading – Assuming we know what others are thinking (usually about us). What's the evidence they are actually thinking that? Is there another, more balanced way of looking at it?

Mountains and Molehills – Exaggerating the risk of danger or the negatives, and minimizing the positives. Am I exaggerating the bad stuff? How would someone else see it? What's the bigger picture?

Compare and Despair – Seeing only the good and positive aspects in others, and the negative in ourselves. This sets us up to get upset when comparing ourselves negatively against others.

Catastrophizing – Imagining and believing that the worst possible thing will happen. What is realistically most likely to happen?

Critical Self – Putting ourselves down, self-criticism, or blaming ourselves for events or situations that are not (totally) our responsibility.

Black and White Thinking – Believing that something or someone can be only good or bad, right or wrong. Things aren't either totally white or totally black – there are shades of grey. Where is this thought on the spectrum?

Shoulds and Musts – Thinking or saying 'I should' (or shouldn't) and 'I must' puts pressure on ourselves, and sets up unrealistic expectations. Am I putting more pressure on myself, setting up expectations of myself that are almost impossible? What would be more realistic?

Memories – Current situations and events can trigger upsetting memories, leading us to believe that the danger is here and now. In fact, the memory is just a reminder of the past. That was then, and this is now. Even though this memory makes you feel upset, it's not actually happening now.

Song: "My Mind & Me" by Selena Gomez. I love this song because I applaud her bravery. She uses her fame, and her struggles with bipolar, to educate others. This will especially help any of her young fans who are going through similar challenges.

A SPARKLING TORNADO

My brother Patrick and me. My hair has had a couple of weeks to grown in, but what on earth was I thinking?

BZZ, BZZ

As scared as I was when Dr. L. suggested ECT, once he explained it, I felt it was worth a shot.

Johns Hopkins Medicine explains the procedure like this: "ECT is given to depressed patients, under general anesthesia and muscle relaxant. It sends electrical impulses to the brain through electrodes applied to the head. This stimulates a seizure. Repeated a few times a week for a short period of time, it has been shown to relieve depressive symptoms in 80-85% of patients, for an extended period of time. The seizure caused by ECT leads to alterations in brain chemistry."

My non-scientific explanation would be that the brain is somehow "reset." Like rebooting your computer.

I underwent about a dozen treatments, and contrary to what the media shows you, my experience was mostly positive. Thanks to the general anesthesia and muscle relaxants, there is no full-body seizure or pain. In fact, if someone was watching, they would only see toes moving or slight tremors in the body.

Movies like *Shine* and *One Flew Over th e Cuckoo's Nest* portray patients strapped to a metal table, a rubber gag in their mouth and terrified eyes wide open. The angry-looking doctor pushes a button and the patient's body arcs and convulses. Through it all, the patient is trying to scream through the gag in his mouth. Then we watch the sedated patient get wheeled back to the ward drooling and seemingly short a few brain cells.

This is great dramatics to keep moviegoers entertained, but a far cry from the reality of modern medicine.

From my dozen treatments, I only have one negative memory. Actually, it's the only treatment I remember at all – the day the anesthetist was running late.

In-patient procedures are in the morning and outpatients in the afternoon, so I'm the first to be sent down. Two orderlies arrive at 8 a.m. to collect me from my room. I'm hungry, as I can smell breakfast arriving. Normally the bland eggs and plain oatmeal don't tempt me, but it's as if my stomach knows I can't eat before the procedure, and now wants something it can't have. I climb onto the gurney, embarrassed as always to be wheeled around when I have perfectly good legs. ECT happens in the bowels of the hospital – the basement. I feel the elevator descend and descend. With the orderlies on either side of me, I wonder what they think of me. Do they think I'm crazy? Or lazy? Do they pity me or scorn me?

Once in the ECT treatment room, I see only three nurses. A nurse wearing colourful scrubs with a pattern of smiley faces informs me that the anesthetist is running late but will be here any minute. They have other patients after me, so the nurses start to prepare.

I have never seen the preparation before, as I should already be under anesthesia when they start. The metal table beside me looks like a Grade 6 science fair experiment. Wires are hooked up to a machine that seems left over from 1955. Beside it are long metal tongs with circular pads on the ends. I see a black rubber mouthguard, similar to a hockey mouthguard but with a knobby handle. Several needles are already filled with a clear liquid, ready for injection into my IV. I shiver in my thin hospital gown. Not from the chill in the room, but from fear they are going to shock me while I am still awake.

Just then, the anesthetist rushes in, mumbling something about traffic. A mask is placed on my mouth, and I inhale the smell of rubber and chemicals. Anesthesia is pumped into the IV, and I begin the countdown from 10. I wake up an hour later back on the ward, with the usual intense headache. I'm a little groggy and tired for the rest of the day, but by evening the headache is gone and I'm ready to receive hugs and chocolate chip cookies when Tim arrives at 5:00.

I'm having three treatments a week, and in only two weeks I feel quite a bit better. In fact, well enough to leave the hospital and continue the treatments as an outpatient for two more weeks.

But my memory is affected – greatly affected. Memory loss is a main side effect of ECT. A recent review shows that 60 percent of patients report memory problems, with 40 percent of those reporting that these problems lasted from several weeks to several years. I have huge gaps from the two years around the procedures.

Ever the comedian, Tim uses the term "Bzz, bzz" whenever I have no recollection of something he is talking about.

With not much to do, I sometimes walk to Blockbuster to rent a VHS cassette for us to watch together in the evening. "I think you'll really like the movie I rented today. It's an action with Bruce Willis. It looks really good," I say when Tim gets home. "What's it called?" he asks. "I forget, I'll go get it."

I return and show him the video case. "It's *Last Man Standing*." "You rented that a couple days ago. Bzz, bzz,"

He laughs. I vaguely remember that at some point in this time frame I went to the local college, Fanshawe, to study Medical Administration.

This was the program I had never ended up attending when I was first hospitalized a couple of years earlier. In my efforts to write my story as accurately as possible, I text Tim to ask him to confirm I actually went there. At this point he doesn't know I am writing this book, so I'm a bit concerned about what to say if he asks why I want to know if I ever went to college.

I get a quick message back. "I kind of remember something like that." My response is jokingly, "Bzz, bzz." "Lol," he writes. "I mean I literally laughed out loud reading 'Bzz, bzz.'"

I WhatsApp my mom. "Did I ever go to Fanshawe College? Like a semester or something?" My parents know I'm writing this book, so won't be too surprised by my questions about something so many years ago. Three hours later, she replies.

"That seems familiar. Let me ask Dad. He'll know." She quickly texts back: "Yes, you did. One semester. He remembers because he paid." With everyone else having forgotten as well, I feel a little reassured that maybe the memory gaps are not solely due to the ECT. The passage of time puts what is important and worth remembering into perspective. My mind says, "Does it really matter?"

You attended, you left, you moved on to better things. Forget about it." During my month of ECT treatments, I notice a big improvement. My mood is stable. My sleep schedule is regular.

I'm able to accomplish everyday tasks that I struggled with before: sweeping the floors, cooking dinner, doing my hair. I even have the confidence to apply for jobs. I'm thrilled when I get an interview at a clothing store – and even more excited when they offer me the job! I ask for part-time, which is all I have the confidence to handle right now.

It's always in the back of my mind that this "normalcy" won't last. That the tornado will whip up into a storm again. This job gives me a reason to get up, to get dressed in the cute clothes I buy with my discount and to put on makeup. I feel pretty and purposeful.

No one there knows I swallow more pills daily than a 90-year-old. It's my secret that I just had my brain zapped with electricity. Conversations with the other salesgirls are about normal everyday things: weather, clothing, boyfriends, school. The things I've been missing out on.

But reminders are never far away. One afternoon, I'm hanging the store's bohemian-style dresses on a rack, my back turned to the entrance. "Sandra! It's so nice to see you! I didn't know you work here. I love the clothes." A girl my age is talking to me with bubbly enthusiasm. I look at her blankly.

"How are things?" she continues, fingering a tank top on the nearby display shelf. "Tim still at Western?" "Yeah," I answer slowly. I have no idea who she is.

"I haven't seen you out with Chico lately." She looks at me strangely. I try to think of what to say.

We obviously know each other; she knows my dog. I nervously shuffle my feet on the store's scuffed wooden floors. She starts to clue in that I don't recognize her. "It's Amanda. From the dog park. Our dogs are best buddies..." her voice trails off. It still doesn't help me, so I fake it.

"Of course, Amanda. I was just thrown seeing you out of the usual place." I'm mortified. And frustrated. At this point I'm on five different medications, all of which affect my brain. Because of their various side effects, my cognitive processing isn't great, and now ECT has added memory gaps.

I feel like my brain is moving in slow motion. External stimuli pour in, then my brain trickles them down to molasses and eventually filters them back to the world.

Having been out of the "real world" for so long, I need to make an effort to respond in a way that I imagine is the appropriate reaction. I'm fortunate to have a pretty upbeat, dynamic personality when I'm healthy, so this carries me through a lot of situations.

I bring up these cognitive issues with Dr. L., and he agrees that this would be a good time to taper down the meds. I've been stable since the ECT, and the side effects are having an impact on me being able to function in the way I want to. I'm moving away from survival mode and toward recovery mode.

A group of mental health survivors, Culture of Recovery, defines recovery as "the hard work a person does him or herself, with the kindness and compassion of the people they choose to support them – in an environment that acknowledges and believes in their potential for wellness.

" As I was writing this book, my friend Kate sent that definition to me. My response to her: "OMG! I feel like that's me!"

In 1997, the year I underwent these ECT treatments, I wasn't quite in recovery or thriving. But I was moving toward thriving-ish.

Tapering down, then stopping, the antipsychotic makes a huge difference. The constant fatigue disappears. The numb flatness gives way to emotions again: joy, love, sadness, excitement. Normal feelings. Not too high, not too low. The normal gentle wave of human emotions.

I start going to the YMCA daily with a girl, Michelle, that I met in hospital. A gym membership is a luxury I can't afford, but I'm able to receive a financially assisted membership. Michelle is another Frequent Flyer my age. She's been in a deep clinical depression for two years now. We'd crossed paths twice as in-patients and exchanged phone numbers.

Keep in mind that this is almost 30 years ago. Awareness of mental illness was very low. My friends from the "before years" were busy with their own lives, moving forward: finishing degrees, starting careers, buying houses. I'm sure there was some fear and ignorance on their part, some trepidation of getting dragged down into the mess of my life. I don't blame them. There was no "Bell Let's Talk" Day or "International Bipolar Day" being spread all over social media. No famous people posting about their mental health. No TikToks giving 30-second bits of insight into depression or anxiety.

Instead, I made friends with the people who understood me. People going through the same thing. Which is ironic, because I shamefully admit that I'm now a mental health snob. I'm now the one hesitant to become friends with someone I meet through my Canadian Mental Health Association (CHMA) bipolar group or through the hospital. For a different reason, though – I've learned I don't have the capacity to support them if they need help. I can generally hold myself up –sometimes with Scotch tape and glue, but I can stay put together. However, I don't always have enough Scotch tape and glue to share with others. I selfishly need to save some supplies for myself.

Some days, Michelle doesn't show up at the Y for our usual class. On those days I go to a payphone, put in a quarter and dial her number. I want her to know I will wait here if she will come. I want to encourage her that it will be worth it. I've never left a workout feeling worse than before I started.

One day she doesn't pick up, so I leave a message. It's not uncommon for people in depression to turn away from the outside world. Simple tasks like getting dressed or answering the phone can be insurmountable. During step class my thoughts keep drifting back to Michelle, hoping she is ok.

My feet are trying to V-step, Around the World and Grapevine, but my mind knows the danger of a depressed person not answering the phone. I call her again when I get home, but the phone still rings to voicemail. The dopamine hit I was riding from exercise has now worn off with worry. Michelle has talked of suicide in the past.

We both feel comfortable sharing our thoughts, curiosities and, sometimes, desires. It feels good to express these thoughts without fear of judgment. Contrary to what many people believe, most people communicate, either directly or indirectly, their desire to die.

More than a desire to die, it's a desire for the pain to stop. Ignoring someone who's expressing thoughts of suicide can be dangerous. I contemplate going to her house, but I'm scared of what I will find. What if she's dead? I imagine different scenarios, each one worse than the one before. Late that afternoon, my phone rings. I don't have call display, but I hear sobs and know it's Michelle.

I know she is in pain, but my heart is filled with relief. "I'm so sorry," she says between sobs. "I feel like a shitty person. I heard you on the answering machine, but I couldn't make myself pick up. I've been pretty much catatonic all day. I can barely get out of bed to go pee." I'm still concerned. "Michelle, when is your next appointment with Dr. L.?" "It's a couple of weeks away."

"You need to call and get in sooner. I think you've been sliding down for a few weeks now." "I only called back because I felt so guilty. But I don't really want to talk about this right now. I just wanted to let you know I'm still alive. At the moment." She hangs up. If a loved one talks of suicide, it's scary. You may think that telling them,

"Don't do anything stupid," or downplaying the situation will make it go away. Death is an uncomfortable topic, especially in regard to suicide. NAMI, the U.S.-based National Alliance on Mental Illness, suggests how to speak to someone expressing thoughts of self-harm.

*Do you have a plan in place?
*What might make you act on these thoughts?
*What holds you back?

I wish Google had existed back then and that punching in "what to say to someone expressing thoughts of suicide" would have given me the words to help. Fortunately, her story ends well.

I still go to the YMCA every day – I need it for stress relief – but now I'm by myself. I love the dopamine hit that exercise gives me. Exercise had always been a part of my "before years."

In high school I'd go with my mom to her aerobics classes, or pop in a *20 Minute Workout* VHS cassette and move along with Jane Fonda in the family room.

As I work out, I have no idea that in a few years, the YMCA will become the jumping-off point for my career in fitness. But at this moment, it's a place to move my body, be around other people, and have a purpose in my day.

Thanks to the exercise and dropping the antipsychotic, I quickly lose the 25 pounds I'd packed on my previously small frame. The weight gain had deeply affected my self-esteem, so this is a huge confidence boost for me. I feel healthier inside and out. I feel like Sandra is back! While I enjoy working at the clothing store, I now want something more challenging. A chance to use my brain, which once gave me straight A's in high school.

I remember that Karen, the social worker, had mentioned an agency that helps people who have been on disability find jobs, so I reach out to her. She's delighted to hear I am doing well and sets up an appointment with the job agency.

They help me polish up my spotty resumé and suggest a few companies that are hiring.

When I get an interview at a life insurance company, I feel I have a shot at getting the job.

As I begin to feel more confident in myself, I also begin to realize that my quick smile and pretty looks open doors. People really do form a first impression in 10 seconds. The impression I gave off in my interview was of a likeable, happy girl. No suggestion that behind that bubbly surface are so many scars, inside and out. The impression must have been good, because I get the job.

When I look in the mirror, I see someone I like. While beauty does come from the inside out, I'm sure we can all agree that how we look can affect how we feel. My impulsive buzz cut of last year has grown back to shoulder-length curls. My body is becoming toned by my daily workouts. My skin even has more of a glow now that I am taking care of it. In hospital, my hygiene would take a back seat, due to both lack of supplies and lack of motivation. If I washed my face at all, it was with the harsh antibacterial hospital soap. The medical-smelling moisturizer provided was thick and greasy, meant for skin infections or bedsores. Most people assume that hospital food is healthy, but it is carb-heavy and processed, meant to feed hundreds of people. During the last two years, I developed acne that I hadn't had before. With a cleaner diet at home, my skin has begun to clear up as well.

Appearances are not the only reason I see someone I like. As I walk past a shiny store window on my way to work, I see the reflection of a smiling girl with a new job, contributing to society and being a partner in a marriage. And that makes me feel good.

The simple act of putting on "real" clothes and interacting with people makes me feel like a normal person.

That's one of the reasons why, to this day, I still try to get dressed and out of the house when I'm feeling down. I keep plans I have made, knowing that no matter how much I want to stay home, I'm a natural extrovert. People lift me up. If I can drag myself there, I will always feel better afterwards.

My job at the insurance company is simple. I match the receipts people are submitting for reimbursement to what they claim on their health expense form – medications, massage, physio, etc. Then I input those claims into the computer.

That's it. But it is perfect for me: consistent routine, low stress, minimal expectations and three days a week. My mom still comes weekly to London to visit me. We go out to dinner, a treat that I normally can't afford. Sometimes we just go for a walk at the small lake a short drive away.

It feels great to spend time together as mother and daughter in a way we couldn't the last few years. I'm sure as we feed the ducks at the lake, she has concerns that I will be able to keep the job, but she doesn't say it. I'm alive.

That's good. She probably wonders if another episode is lying in wait around the corner. I'm sure she worries about whether my marriage will survive, or whether I will remain stable and able to support myself.

Those are all thoughts I have myself, but I don't express them and neither does she. We each pretend to be confident in the future. When I lie awake at night, I wonder if my parents have ever discussed if I will even live to see my 30th birthday. What a horrible thing to have to wonder about your child! Shame again rears its ugly head as I imagine all the things they go through. When I ask them, though, my parents tell me they are grateful that I am alive, out of hospital and enjoying each day. Eventually, my mom admits she has a different worry now. "Every time I see you, I see less of you. You've lost so much weight."

I laugh. "Mom, remember how quickly I put on weight with that one medication? I'm off it. It's great! I've lost 25 pounds in two months! I feel amazing." My mom still looks unsure. "You remember my friend Gretta? You remember she has a daughter? She's your age and has an eating disorder. She's 97 lbs. Her mom comes home every day at lunch to make sure she eats. The whole drive up, I've been thinking you might be doing something like that. Not eating." "Mom, I'm actually enjoying food. I can choose what I want to eat, and when. I can cook healthy. The hospital food was terrible."

These are the simple pleasures in life that someone who has never spent time in a Psych ward can't imagine not having. The first sip of a hot coffee in the morning, instead of the lukewarm, powdered, instant decaf imposter served alongside cold toast and dull eggs.

Fresh fruit instead of precut apple slices in plastic packaging. Now that I am feeling better, I begin to question the diagnosis. Am I actually bipolar? Were they wrong? I'm doing just fine. I can't accept that I am going to have to take medication for life "just in case" of another episode. I'm resentful. Every day I look at the plastic prescription bottles and feel a lump in my throat at the thought of swallowing my cocktail of four pills daily. So often, I don't.

Tim's nightly question is, "Did you take your meds today?" "Yup" is my consistent answer, looking in a different direction from his eyes.

I'm still feeling the benefits of the ECT treatment. My roller coaster has fewer highs and lows. No steep climbs and quick descents. More of a gentle roll up with a nice flat roll before the next dip. The kind of safe amusement park ride that gets five-year-olds squealing with delight. With the inconsistent administration of meds, the added time commitment of work, and the loss of the sheltered environment of the hospital, the improvement from ECT is starting to wear off.

Mania starts to add shiny multicoloured sparkles to my tornado. It starts with an excited feeling.

I want to do everything: apply for new jobs I have no qualifications for, go back to college and finally finish something. I bake muffins for all the neighbours.

My body has an energy to it, as if every cell is vibrating. My nervous system is on fire, but in a brilliant, fantastic way. There is a difference this time, though – I think I can control it. I practise the exercises Karen taught me to try to ride out the wave. I fill out my daily mood log, which shows me I am definitely heading up the rollercoaster.

I pull out my Plan of Action (from Chapter 2). The worksheet is filled out with my messy, multicoloured printing:

*Write out a Schedule

* Avoid caffeine and alcohol

*Take a sleeping pill

*Get outdoors

I take it one step further and use a Weekly Activity Diary (at the end of this chapter) to plan my activities for the week, and rate my mood before and after the activity. If I stay on top of these things, I tell myself, I seem to be staying on top of moving any higher into the surge of mania. Pride bursts out of me as I realize that for the first time, I am in charge of myself.

I have the tools to deal with my thoughts, my actions and my feelings.

Overspending is an extremely common symptom during mania. With the feeling of euphoria and grandiosity, people often believe they will soon be making lots of money through their new job, business, relationship or impending fame. I could insert really anything here. My flowerpot painting empire was only one of many I was sure would be my future success. I also planned a furniture refurbishing business. Of course, I got business cards to make me look professional. Registered the business legally. Then bought a bunch of furniture at the Goodwill thrift store and sponge-painted it all in shiny, bright blue paint. Then lost the motivation to try to sell them. And eventually donated it all back to Goodwill. I wonder if they ever realized that these were the same pieces they'd had a month ago, now covered in bright blue splotches?

And then there was my hat painting business. Let's be clear: I can't paint. I don't have any artistic skill. Yet I thought I could paint wide-brimmed hats, and people would buy them as decorations for their walls. In mania, we believe everything good will be great. I ended up hanging 15 painted hats on my own walls and eventually donating the rest to...you guessed it – Goodwill.

Years later, in 2007, I decided to become a bookkeeper. Math and numbers are probably quite low on my list of talents and aptitude, but that didn't stop me. I hastily signed up for a correspondence bookkeeping course. After the third of 20 units, I quit. I can't imagine what I had been thinking! My personality is so not suited to bookkeeping.

Some people get into a lot of debt if their mania goes on unchecked for months. They can spend thousands on shopping, new business plans, gambling. This creates a cycle of financial instability as people blow through savings, incur bad credit and harm relationships. I was lucky in two ways. Firstly, I have type 2 rapid cycling bipolar, meaning episodes may only last a few days – less time to get into trouble. Secondly, in my 20s, we didn't have much money.

In the 1990s you paid by cash or cheque. I didn't even have a credit card. There was no online shopping in the '90s. There was no way I could go on a shopping spree. Until...I received an envelope with a greeting card. I'm at my parents' house for the weekend, visiting from London. Tim has stayed back to study for an exam.

My parents have an excited look on their faces from the moment they open the front door. There is the delicious smell of my dad's pork tenderloin in the oven.

On weekends, my dad is usually the cook. Weekdays my mom takes over, as my dad gets home later. My mom has never been interested in cooking gourmet meals – cooking meals in general, actually. However, we always eat dinner in the dining room, no matter how simple or gourmet the meal is. Breakfast and lunch take place casually on our white circular kitchen table. After dinner, I'm sitting at the table, looking at my parents' dog, Bisou, thinking how much I miss him. We got him when I was in Grade 10; he is a friendly, caramel-coloured mixed breed.

Bisou isn't allowed in the dining room while we eat. But he's a smart dog. He starts with his body on the kitchen tile, and his paws just over the line to the dining room carpet. Inch by inch, he creeps discreetly forward. By the end of dinner, only his fluffy rear end is on the kitchen tile; the rest of him is in the dining room.

Technically, though, he is still in the kitchen and following the rule. I'm about to get up to clear the table when my dad hands me an envelope. I'm surprised, as there is no special occasion. I've been stable a few months, so I think maybe it is a "You are doing great" card. When I open the card, a pink $1,000 bill spills out onto my lap. I've never seen one of these before (and never will again, as they stop making them in 2000). "What's this for?" I gasp.

My dad grins. "I received a bonus at work, and thought you and your brother deserve a little bonus as well." Until my recent new job, I'd been on disability payments for two years.

Tim is a full-time student with a part-time job. $1,000 is a fortune to us. On Monday, I drive excitedly back to London in our beat-up red Jetta, my hands tight on the steering wheel. I've only done the two-hour drive a couple of times by myself, and the busy highway makes me nervous. I feel the whoosh of semi-trucks as they consistently pass me. Each time I hear their heavy engines behind me, I feel my shoulders hunch higher to my ears.

I have an appointment with Dr. L., so my plan is to go directly to his outpatient office at the hospital, the $1,000 bill tucked safely in my purse. By the time I arrive for my appointment, I'm revved up from the stress of driving on Highway 401. Revved up is never a good way to arrive for an appointment with a psychiatrist. For some reason, I tell him about the $1,000 bill I have in my purse.

I'm still buzzing with energy from the building mania that I'm trying to outride. A symptom of hypomania is "pressured speech," meaning the person feels the need to get all the words that are in their head out of their mouth and into the world.

"What are your plans with it?" he asks, his face unreadable as always.
"I don't know. It was a gift from my parents. I can't believe it's so much!"
"Does Tim know you have it?"

"Of course he does. I called him from my parents' house."

"Where are you going after this?"

I pause, open my mouth to speak, then close it again as I see him reach for the phone. As if speaking to a child, he says, "I'm going to give Tim a quick call just to ensure he knows you have this." This infuriates me. I'm an adult who can make my own decisions. I'm tired of being treated like a child.

What do I have to do to prove I'm done with this whole "bipolar thing"? I sit there feeling both angry and foolish, my head slumped with embarrassment as I listen to him talk to Tim.

And then, a few days later, like the flick of a switch, depression claws its way back into my tornado. I feel the weight of my brain change. I understand this isn't physically possible.

All I can say is, I still feel it happen all these years later. My mind feels heavy, clogged and full. My thoughts are all negative. Intrusive images flood my mind, and I hate myself for not having the control to stop it.

Other times, I sense my brain getting lighter, lifting higher in my head as if it wants to burst out of my skull with happiness. I feel electrical impulses buzzing in my brain.

With my heavy, clogged brain, I start calling in sick to my job at the insurance company. I don't care about anything. Not really wanting to die, but also not wanting to live. Which I guess is an improvement from a year ago.

A month later, my supervisor approaches me as I'm at the photocopier. "Sandra," Mark says, talking more to the photocopier than to me. "HR asked for you to go up to see them."

This is probably everyone's nightmare, when you can anticipate why you are making the trek to the big boss's office.

It's kind of like being called to the principal's office in high school. The HR director is a kind, plump Irishwoman. The kind who lets me down gently and with true regret.

"Sandra," she says in her gentle Irish lilt. "We've been catching a lot of errors on your inputting.

Claims going through that don't match the form total or aren't valid."
"I'm sorry,"

I mumble, looking down at my lap. "I've had some things going on and maybe haven't been as focused as I should."

I know that I am still having memory difficulties from the ECT.

Mine tends to be in gaps. I have whole chunks of time from before, after and around the ECT that I don't remember. "You have also missed seven days in the last month," the HR director continues. "If you need time off to sort things out, we can arrange that. But the current situation isn't working."

I'm struggling too much to maintain my mental balance to fight to keep the job. I don't want to explain the truth. I wrestled as much then as I still do now with shame and guilt.

"Actually, I need to resign," I lie. "I'm having some family issues and need to return to Mississauga."

I can't even look at her in the eye, I feel so ashamed. Ashamed for the lie and ashamed for another failure. Even as the words come out of my mouth, I recognize I'm making a mistake.

This job is probably the best opportunity that I will get without formal education and with a resumé full of gaps. I'm sure that had I stayed, I could have worked my way up over the years.

My dad thinks so as well, and that resigning will be a missed opportunity for me. He calls the company on my behalf.

I can't imagine what they think about a grown adult's dad calling. I don't know what he explains, but he probably uses his HR director experience to explain some vague aspect of a medical condition. Of all companies, one that processes medical claims should understand. Mental illness wasn't talked about much then, and companies didn't have policies regarding stress leaves like they do now. They again offer to keep the job waiting for me, but I never go back. My confidence is shattered. I feel I fail at everything I start. I can't do anything. I can't keep a job. I can't finish school. I can barely manage my fair share of household responsibilities.

In her memoir *The Other Side of Me*, Julie Kraft writes, "Often, feelings of unworthiness came from my inability to deal with the mundane – package deliveries, paying bills, school pickups, birthday parties, and even trick-or-treaters at my door.

Shame and embarrassment would overwhelm me. Why were such simple things so stressful? Why couldn't I cope?" I understand Julie's words completely. Small talk can be fraught with dangerous possibilities to bring out the shame.

"So, what do you do?"

"Well, if I'm not having my brain zapped, I'm probably at the pharmacy picking up my gazillion prescriptions. Or you may find me at my psychiatrist's office. Sometimes, I'm just lying in bed trying to block out the world." "Are you in school?" "Yeah, I've tried that a couple of times. Not for me. Too stressful. And suicide attempts tend to get in the way." "Those are some rough scars. What happened?" "You know those tiny plastic swords that come in bar drinks? I got into a fight, and those were the only available weapons. But you should see the other girl."

I feel like I'm at my rock bottom. I can't see a future existing of anything more than this. I now have no job, no completed education and no friends.

My parents probably think that having me staying alive and out of the Psych ward is the best they can hope for. I have a husband who must act more as a babysitter than as a partner.

Tim has just finished his science degree and is applying for jobs. In my mind, I'm just dragging him down as he goes forward. When we are at the bottom, we don't see the light at the top even though logically we know it's there.

I have no idea that just ahead is a job offer, a move and a new psychiatrist, that together will pull me out of the dark eye of the tornado. My life as an unstable bipolar patient is about to change. I just need to hold on.

Reflections and Resources

What was your rock bottom? What did you think and feel at that moment?

How did you get out of your rock bottom?

Weekly Activity Planning

Routine is an important factor in bipolar stability. We don't do well with changes to plans we have made, or to unpredictable circumstances and overstimulation. Keeping a schedule and planning your day and your week is important. If you are not working, days can be long and seem purposeless. Plan activities, even as simple as: 10 a.m. vacuum house, 12 p.m. eat lunch, 2 p.m. read *A Sparkling Tornado*. Rate how you feel both before the activity and afterwards. It may have been difficult to push yourself to go out for a walk, but if you felt like a "2" before and an "8" after, that will encourage you the next time.

I went into a deep internet rabbit hole to try to find you the best planner. One hour later decided that there are dozens of ways to plan your schedule and rate your mood. My mood was a 7 going into the rabbit hole and a 4 coming out. Amazon, Pinterest and Etsy sell lots of planners, but you can simply use your phone calendar or a printed version as well.

Song: "In My Blood" by Shawn Mendes. This song has more hope than some of my other recommendations. The line "Sometimes I feel like giving up, but I just can't; it isn't in my blood" shows the strength we can have to overcome our negative thoughts.

A beautiful day spent away from the hospital on Grand Bend beach, playing in the waves with Chico. When I was an in-patient, day passes from the hospital, like the one I had this day, allowed me to re-enter the world in a slow and gentle way. Some days I would return to the ward happy and stress free, desperate for a quick discharge. Other days I'd be raw with anxiety, overstimulated and fearful of leaving the protective shelter of the hospital.

24 HOURS IN A WEEK

Just after his graduation, Tim has an interview with a pharmaceutical company.

I feel a sense of jealousy as I watch him head to the car. Briefcase in hand, crisp new suit, beginning a crisp new life. Will my life ever be crisp and new? Or am I stuck with soft and sludgy?

A few hours later, I hear a car pulling onto our gravel driveway. I'm watching a TLC reality wedding show without paying any attention to it at all. My head is too full of thoughts of a new life in a new city. I jump up and run over to our front door, pulling it open just as Tim is reaching for the knob.

"So? How did it go?"

He smiles. "I think really well. They've asked me to go to their Mississauga office next week for a second interview."

Tim tells me the job is as a pharmaceutical rep. He doesn't know what territory yet, but that we need to consider the possibility of a move.

"You have no idea how much I'd love to get out of London!" I jump in. "I feel like here I'll just drift in and out of the psychiatric system. I can't seem to accomplish anything. I'm at least surviving now, but I'm not thriving. A fresh start might change that."

I feel hopeful that a change of location will do good. I want a new beginning. I want to be where no one knows my history. A city where I can become whomever I want to be.

Tim gets the job, and it requires daily commutes within his sales territory of southwestern Ontario, so we have some flexibility with living location. No matter where we move, we will be closer to our parents again...which is both good and bad.

Good because we will have some support as we set up our new life — people who love us. Bad because while we were living in London, I was able to protect my parents from the really tough days. Phone calls were still charged for long distance then, so I always kept things brief and tried to sound positive.

I still do this now today. I mostly text with my parents, so I just put a bunch of exclamation marks in my texts to sound happy.

"We went out to dinner yesterday!"

"I had an awesome bike ride with friends today!"

"The weather was beautiful at the cottage!"

Tim's job starts in two weeks, so we need to pack up and move quickly.

House shopping is really stressful for me. Truthfully, any decision making is hard — I do much better when given just a few choices. Someone once told me, "You make a great soldier, but not a general." And that's ok. The world needs all types. Give me a task to do, and I will do it efficiently and with care. Ask me to decide or direct others in the task, and I will waver, afraid to make the wrong choice. I can't even shop on the Wayfair website because there are too many choices. Looking for a desk lamp? Here are 200 you can choose from!

To alleviate my stress, Tim goes alone with the real estate agent to view multiple houses. He narrows it down to just a few, and then I go along to make a decision. We find a townhouse in Burlington that looks like it hasn't been decorated since the 1970s. It still has shag carpeting and brass banisters. But it is in our price range and has a backyard for the dog to run around in.

In London we had modernized our house on the cheap, so we figure we can do the same here. Nothing a little paint and creativity can't fix. As long as I don't paint horizontal lines of wavy, differing colours again...

In 1998, you could buy a fixer-upper three-bedroom townhouse for $134,000 with a $10,000 down payment. Twenty-five years later, the average house price in Toronto is $1,026,000. I wince as I write that number, wondering how my kids will ever afford a house.

My grandmother in Switzerland had died a few months earlier, and my parents share $10,000 from her inheritance so that we can have a down payment. This won't be the last time they help me with housing:

they will step up again in a few years when I become a divorced single mom. I recognize how lucky I am. Many people with mental illness live below the poverty line with unstable housing.

As I write this, payments under the Ontario Disability Support Program (ODSP) are $1,200 a month, and the average rent in Toronto is $2,634. How can these folks possibly afford food?

The Canadian Mental Health Association (CMHA) says about 40 percent of ODSP recipients have a psychiatric or developmental disorder as their primary diagnosis. Even when I was on ODSP, I never needed to worry about being able to afford food or shelter, thanks to my family's support. And that makes me very fortunate compared to many with mental illness.

Our new house has a three-month closing, so we need somewhere else to live until then. We do what many adult kids do – we move into my parents' basement.

I have no job, no friends and nothing to do. My thought that a new city would bring a new me isn't happening. I sleep late in the mornings, not having the motivation to get out of bed.

My medications make me tired, but at least I am taking them regularly now. It helps that we now have health insurance through Tim's work to cover the cost. But the biggest motivator to take them regularly (or to "be compliant," as the doctors say) is that I desperately want this new life to work. I see a glimmer of hope that my life can be more than ups and downs – more than feeling "less than" my peers.

My mom, recognizing that my sleeping in and having nothing to do all day is not helpful for my recovery, starts taking me with her on errands. I join her wherever she is going, especially to her YMCA fitness classes. I rarely make the morning classes, but I love going to the lunch aquafit and step classes.

The music, the people and the movement always elevate my mood. Is it weird to say I even like the smell of a gym? It's a month before I have my appointment with a new psychiatrist, and that is only because of the referral from Dr. L. in London. Ironically he is at Credit Valley Hospital – the same hospital that had stitched my arms and pumped my stomach after my suicide attempts in high school and nursing school.

My shoulders, neck and stomach are in knots on the drive there. My fear of hospitals, Form 1s, restraints and ECT swirl in my head. As my heart pounds in my chest, I feel tension in my neck creeping higher into my skull.

The Psychiatric department is on the ground floor, at the far end of the hospital. As I pass the gift shop filled with bright multicoloured flowers and stuffed animals, I see a young, good-looking guy pushing a janitor's cart. I quickly jump behind a rack of gift cards. Peeking out between the rows of Get-Well cards, I see Rocco. Rocco was one of the cool kids in high school.

He was Puerto Rican and hung out with the Hispanic kids, smoked cigarettes in the parking lot and drove a rusted Camaro. You could smell Paco Rabanne cologne floating out the window as he drove past. Rocco had a rotating stream of pretty girlfriends. And now he is working as a janitor. He was the guy every girl swooned over. He was the one sitting at the back of the class, rocking on the legs of the wooden chair making funny (or sometimes crude) comments. And now here he is mopping floors. I laugh at the irony. I guess I'm not the only who hasn't landed where I want to be. One wheel of the cart squeaks, and I wait until the sound is far off in the distance before I reappear.

I don't want Rocco to recognize me. I can imagine the conversation. "Sandra!" Rocco would say. "Where have you been?

I haven't heard anything about you." I'd have three choices: 1. Lie – "I was studying nuclear imaging in Alberta and just got a job working at this hospital. In fact, I'm on my way to pick up my name badge now." 2. Tell the truth – "I've been completely beaten down by bipolar. Life sucked, but I'm getting better.

I'm here to see my new psychiatrist." 3. Feign ignorance – "I'm sorry, I can't remember you. You say we went to high school together? That was so long ago. We must have hung out in different crowds." I'm a terrible liar, so option 1 would be too obvious. I'm still carrying so much shame about my diagnosis, so being honest with option 2 won't work either.

I'm an empath, so with option 3, I'd be thinking all day about how hurt he would feel to just be forgotten as he pushes his mop and bucket around. Truthfully, I wouldn't know what to say.

Hiding behind the greeting cards has taken up five minutes, so I pick up my pace to make my appointment on time...which for me always means early. I'm not sure if it's my Swiss background, running on time like a Swiss train, or my people-pleasing mentality, but being on time makes me anxious. I need to be early and have a moment to relax. Especially for a first appointment with a psychiatrist.

A heavy-set, older man, Dr. S. flips through my thick file that had been faxed to him. He reads in silence. I sit awkwardly, waiting. At this point in my mental health journey, I know that the assessment starts the moment you walk in the door, before you even sit in the chair. Your posture, your gait, your eyes, how early or late you arrive – it all means something to them.

Finally, Dr. S. clears his throat, lifts his head and looks at me. His face is neutral. It's impossible for me to guess what he is thinking. I wonder what my file says. How much does he know? "You've had a pretty tough go the last few years," he says.

"Definitely!" I don't know what more to say. "It's a big file. How would you sum it up?" I've never been asked my opinion on anything. I'm nervous to say the wrong thing. "But didn't they send all that?" "They did. I want to hear what you think has helped and what hasn't. Don't worry, though, I have some thoughts."

After a few more questions, he shocks me. "I don't like your medication cocktail. You are on too much. It's no wonder you have a hard time working or studying. These meds all affect your thought processing, memory, mood lability and energy. Lithium seems to have been your one consistent medication. Let's try just lithium and Depakote. We'll see how that goes and adjust as needed."

Decreasing my meds is something I'm desperate to do. Every Sunday, I pull out all my pill bottles and line them up like plastic soldiers. One by one, each soldier gets knocked down as I place the pills into my clear plastic "days of the week" pill box. I'm finally at a stage where I don't want to forget and have a setback.

This keeps me on track. Each Sunday, as I hear the "plink" when I drop them into their daily box, I feel a pit in my stomach looking at all the rainbow of capsules my body is consuming. I feel them stick in my throat, not wanting to go down.

My mind imagines my intestines clogged with capsules of pills. "I'd also like you to consider a four-week outpatient program. It will be a lot of Cognitive Behavioural Therapy, Dialectical Behaviour Therapy, life skills, meditation, etc. We have a new session starting in two weeks. Monday to Thursday, 10 to 4. We can arrange bus tickets if needed."

"Um, I don't know. I was planning to look for a job."

"You might not be ready for a job at this point. Part of this program is to prepare you for work or school: things like working on stress management, job skills and interview techniques." "Does it cost money?" "Not at all.

It's an OHIP-covered program with the goal to prevent relapses and decrease hospital admissions. Have you ever learned CBT or DBT?" (OHIP is the public health insurance plan in Ontario.)

The hospital I was at in London didn't have a lot of therapy. It seems like their treatment involved mostly meds. And ECT. But I did have Karen, a really good social worker. Dr. S. describes a bit more about the program. CBT focuses on the link between your thoughts, feelings and behaviours, then teaches you to replace the unhelpful patterns with more helpful ones.

DBT is a type of CBT, but is more about regulating emotions, mindfulness in the present and creating effective relationships. We are fortunate in Canada to have free access to resources like this. However, the downfall in our mental health system is that you must be "sick enough" to be allowed to access them. I hear stories of people struggling with depression or anxiety who are unable to get help through government programs because their situation is not viewed as dire or life-threatening.

Many are forced to pay out of pocket for therapy, and and wait times for psychiatry are months long. A piddly seven percent of the Canadian healthcare budget is for mental health.

Bipolar, schizophrenia and suicidality are seen as urgent and chronic and are likely to use up much of that seven percent. I've always been fortunate enough (or crazy enough??) to get help when needed.

Free or not, I don't agree immediately to the program. The thought of being in hospital, even as an outpatient, brings anxiety. In my mind I imagine a nurse jumping out from behind a corner: "Hey, what are you doing here?

Get back on the ward!" In my imagination this nurse is wearing a 1960s-type hat, starched white dress and chunky white shoes – even though the only psychiatric nurses I have known have always worn regular street clothes and been rather kind. At dinner, I'm asked how my appointment went.

Tim and my parents look at me expectantly. I hesitate and look wistfully down at the line between the kitchen tile and dining room carpet where our dog, Bisou, used to lie. He'd passed away from cancer a year earlier. "I liked the doctor. He really took time to read my chart.

He was surprised by how many meds I've been on, and how often I was hospitalized. And he thinks that I should have had more therapy along with it. It kind of seems like he feels Dr. L. over-treated me." "That's awesome! You have been wanting to take less meds," Tim jumps in. "Yeah, that part is good."

I say hesitantly. "But what?" my mom says. "He wants me to do a program. Four weeks at the hospital. Outpatient,"

I rush to add. "But I feel like this move is my chance to get a job or school or something. No one here knows I'm the crazy girl." My real hesitation, though, is the thought of going back into the psychiatric system. I want to put London and bipolar behind me.

This irrational fear of hospitals will stay with me for life. Years later, when I bring my beautiful baby boys home from the hospital, I'll be relieved to have escaped the possibility of lock-up. On my way to visit my dying mother-in-law, panic tears will pour out of my eyes, making it difficult to see as I drive. While I'd like to say it was tears about her dying, it was also the irrational fear of a nurse jumping out from around the corner to drag me away.

After I show them the program brochure I'd been handed on my way out of Dr. S.'s office, they have me convinced this is a good thing. That this can be my new start. Two weeks later, I sit with a dozen people in a chilly meeting room just off the Psychiatry ward. I sniff the familiar smell of unseasoned hospital food drifting from a few hallways down. That means the in-patient unit is close.

The room feels electric with our various anxieties. The elderly woman next to me clutches her purse tightly on her lap and twists the decorative leather tassel over and over. A young kid, maybe 18 years old, stands in the corner as if embarrassed to be seen as part of this group. I perch perfectly still on the edge of my chair, my backpack under my seat. I'm a seasoned pro. I know the staff are already assessing us. If it weren't for their hospital badges, we wouldn't even know they work here. Generally, the Psychiatry department doesn't wear scrubs or white jackets. Street clothes give more of a "Hey, relax, I'm just like you" vibe.

We learn that the program will be run by an occupational therapist, a psychologist, a psychiatric nurse and a social worker, all overseen by a psychiatrist. Rachel, the occupational therapist, claps her hands lightly and enters the centre of the room.

"I'd like you all to close your eyes." Small nervous giggles are heard all around. "It's ok if you don't want to. We are going to do a guided visualization together, and if you can close your eyes, you will find it easier to concentrate.

Just sit comfortably, and I'll take you through it." We are all on edge, anxious about what's ahead. Closing our eyes and wandering our mind into a spring meadow covered with flowers is exactly what we need. Rachel's voice is soothing, and I'm just beginning to mellow when a tall guy in his 30s walks in. He looks a little disheveled. I notice that he wears two different socks, and every zipper on his backpack is open.

"Sorry, man. I totally forgot today was the start date," he says. "Oh, shit, you guys are meditating? My bad."

"Just come in quietly and take a seat," whispers Rachel.

"Yah, yah, ok."

We hear the loud scrape of him moving a chair, and his backpack dropping to the floor. The mood is lost. No getting the chill vibe back today. For the next four weeks, though, we begin every morning with a meditation/visualization. I begin to understand why people do this.

Whatever feelings I arrive with mellow. My breathing, my heart rate, my thoughts...all...slow...down.

I'd like to say that I still practise meditation daily, but the honest truth would be that I practise intermittently. Being 2024, I now use an app called Calm to help guide me and keep my thoughts focused. It's also one of my favourite sleep tools.

Between each session there is a 15-minute break. Many of the participants (we aren't called patients) have difficulty focusing for more than an hour at a time. Most of us haven't worked in some time. We are all on varying medications and struggling to get our thoughts and moods regulated.

That 15-minute break gives our minds a chance to rest and process what we were learning – and to get to know each other.

The break also allows the smokers to go outside for a quick puff and return a little less jittery. Smoking is more common in people with mental illness. At that time, in 1999, 36 per cent of people with a mental illness smoked, compared to 21 percent of the healthy population.

The rates are thankfully lower now for both populations. The rest of us take a few days to figure out what to do with each break, awkwardly making small talk, or spending our time hiding in the bathroom. Nowadays everyone would grab their phones, bend their head over their screen and ignore the other people in the room, using the phone as a social crutch.

Back then, we had no choice but to talk to each other.

Over the next four weeks, we have sessions focused on education about various mental disorders, CBT exercises, DBT, physical exercise, medication, etc.

We also discuss how to deal with family, how to prepare for work or school, and stress reduction techniques. It's a mental health boot camp. During the last week, we create a W.R.A.P. – a Wellness Recovery Action Plan. This is similar to the Plan of Action I mentioned in Chapter 2, but in much greater detail.

This plan itemizes the steps we and our trusted person can take to stop a spiral from turning into a crisis. Our discharge plan is the hardest one to do.

We are "highly encouraged" to do volunteer work, schooling or paid work. And part-time is actually encouraged to help us ease into these new roles.

"What can I do? I have no diploma, nothing. Barely any work experience,"

I whine to Shelly, one of the other participants I've grown fond of. She has bipolar as well, and while she has had more stability than I have, she hasn't been able to work for the last year.

"Well," she says, "what do you like to do?

You always talk about how much exercise helps you." "That's not really a job." One of the therapists, Rhonda, is in the room, helping people with their discharge plan, and Shelly calls her over. Rhonda listens to me and assures me exercise is indeed a career. Fitness instructors, personal trainers, yoga. There is lots I could do.

I look into the qualifications needed to become a personal trainer. The same YMCA where I am taking fitness classes is offering a certification program next month. All it will take is two full weekends and a 10-hour apprenticeship. With my biology knowledge from nursing school lurking somewhere in the back of my brain and my love of fitness, I'm somewhat confident I can do it.

When I fill out the registration form and pay the money, I feel something I have never felt before. I am making a decision. I am choosing a new career. Not with the influence of mania whispering my superpowers in my ear, but having weighed the pros and cons, consulted with the psychologist, and spoken with Tim. I took time to ask questions of the front desk staff at the Y before rushing into it. I did this logically and responsibly.

The library is right beside the Y, so I go there to flip through biology books, kinesiology books, sports and fitness magazines. I'm worried that everyone else in the class will have more knowledge than I do. One of the things that I learned in the group program is to control the things we have control over. I have the control to prepare for this course, and being prepared makes me less anxious.

The first Saturday of the course, I park at the far end of the parking lot, always trying to get in that little bit of extra exercise. I haven't dressed appropriately for the windy October day, so the cold bites through my thin leggings. I focus on the feeling of the cold as a distraction for my nerves dancing in my stomach – again, a DBT technique of mindfulness I just learned.

Pick something from all five senses to focus on. I feel the cold on my legs. I hear the police siren far off in the distance. I taste the toothpaste in my mouth. I see the yellow lines of the parking spaces. I smell the fabric softener on my hoodie.

With a deep breath, I pull on the door to the room – but the handle doesn't turn. Immediately I worry that I mixed up the date or location. I always assume I did something wrong.

I pull out the crisply folded registration paper. Session starts at 9 a.m. Crap. It's only 8 a.m. The door to the room is still locked. I stand outside, watching gym goers walk briskly by on their way to the locker rooms. Nowadays I'd whip out my phone and scroll social media. No one just stands and people-watches anymore.

Just before 9 a.m., an Asian-looking guy arrives with a key and unlocks the door. He's short, not much taller than me, but his shoulders are wide with muscle. His biceps strain against his red YMCA T-shirt. Ten of us enter the classroom. I'm surprised to see all ages. The youngest is a university student studying kinesiology. I learn the oldest is a grandmother of five, finally having the time to do what she has always wanted to do.

Two weekends later, I am ready to begin my apprenticeship. I shadow a personal trainer, learning how he creates his clients' programs. The most important thing I learn is not the exercises, but the aspect of the trainer-client relationship: building rapport, keeping them entertained and having fun during their workout. That's what people are really paying you for. I realize that this is what I want to do.

I want to work in a gym. From our group of 10 who started the program, only eight finish. Two of us apply for the job of floor staff that is available. When I first put on my red T-shirt saying "YMCA" on the front and "Staff" on the back, I feel so proud. I feel important. I imagine strangers thinking,

"Wow, she's a personal trainer."

Being new, I'm given the grunt work and the early-bird shift. Three days a week, 6 a.m. to 2 p.m. After a month of cleaning gym equipment, putting away weights and telling members not to run backwards on the treadmill (yes, it happens), I get promoted.

I lead an eight-session group program where new YMCA members learn the basics of exercise. At the end of the eight weeks, the participants give my supervisors great feedback about me. I run a few more groups through the program.

During this time, my supervisor asks if I have interest in the Group Fitness Instructor certification. For years I'd been in the background, following bubbly instructors. Now I can be one of them!

After the Group Fitness Instructor course, I have my apprenticeship. Each class, I lead more and more of the class until eventually I'm teaching the entire class.

I get such a rush of endorphins from the energy the participants bring. They give it their all, sweating on the gym floor as I shout encouragement into the microphone. I remember my love of being on stage in dance recitals in middle school, and drama club in high school.

Give me a microphone and an audience, and I'm in heaven. Teaching fitness gives me the same feeling.

It's also an ideal job because everything happens in one-hour increments. One-hour personal training session. One-hour fitness class. No matter if my mood isn't 100 percent, I can always get through one hour. It's easy to fake anything for one hour.

Good thing is, I don't have to fake it much. The Y is really happy with my performance, and pays for me to attend a yoga instructor course. And then Spin, and then aquafit...

Within one year, I've gone from a spotty resumé to a full list of certifications and various positions within the Y.

So now, the work side of my life is on track. But there is something else I still want — a baby. I've always known that I want to be a mom.

I've been stable a couple of years. I'm 27, Tim's 31.

We decide to start a family. It's a big decision. Bipolar has a genetic component, and I'm not sure I'd want to inflict the last 10 years of my life on anyone else. One percent of the Canadian population has bipolar. However, if one parent has it, statistics show there's a likelihood of 10 to 30 percent for their child.

I've been stable long enough that I've only been seeing my family doctor for prescription refills. To get pregnant, I will need to go back to see the psychiatrist at Credit Valley Hospital. We switch my medication to a different mood stabilizer that is proven safe for a baby. I'm not too concerned about my mental health. In fact, I actually question the diagnosis. There is still the little thought at the back of my head: "Am I really bipolar? Maybe they were wrong. Maybe it's all over."

Two months later, we are ready to start trying. I assume that with all my body has been through, it might take a while.

In a few weeks, I'm too excited to wait, even though I know it's technically too early to do a pregnancy test. But, I figure, what the heck? I'm sitting on a toilet, peeing on a stick, with Tim waiting anxiously outside. I watch one line appear. Slowly, a second line becomes darker. "Positive!" I gleefully shout out to Tim.

I'm a person of extreme emotions, and I don't mean bipolar emotions. Human emotions. When I'm excited, I'm hopping from foot to foot in anticipation. If I'm hurt by someone's words, I carry it inside me for days. If I have a gift for someone, I'm more eager for them to open it than they are. Human emotions have a reason and have control. Bipolar emotions come without any reason and without any control.

Many people wait until the 12-week "safe" time to tell people they are pregnant. But I can't. I want the world to know that I, Sandra Steiner, am creating a life inside me. Soon, a beautiful baby will arrive!

Naturally, our parents are thrilled they will be grandparents. A job, a baby; life is seeming normal for everyone, with so much possibility for the future.

I had recently reconnected with Christina, a friend from nursing school. She is pregnant as well, just four weeks ahead of me. We chat about our growing bellies, our hopes for the baby, maternity clothes. It's wonderful to have someone to share the excitement of pregnancy with. Work is the only place I wait 12 weeks.

When I tell Pete, my supervisor, I assure him I am fine to keep teaching my classes, and that I plan to work as long as I can. I know fitness is good for the baby. I'm also very worried about weight gain during pregnancy, and plan to exercise and eat healthy so I can stay within the recommended weight gain of 25 to 35 pounds. I remember how my self-esteem plummeted with the weight gain from antipsychotics. I didn't have control over that, but I have control over this.

At 16 weeks I go to my family doctor, Dr. R., for a standard checkup. One of her first questions is always about my mood. I'm great. I'm happy. I'm working. I'm creating life.

I'm decorating my new house. I'm using skills from the Credit Valley program to catch things before they go too far. Now let's move on to how my baby is doing.

I squirm a little as Dr. R. squirts the cold ultrasound jelly onto my belly. She moves the Doppler around to pick up the baby's heartbeat. At 16 weeks, it should be loud and strong. I'm smiling as I wait to hear the amazing whoosh-whoosh heartbeat that I heard at my 12-week appointment.

"Ok, he is being tricky. Hiding a bit. Give me a minute to move around and get his heartbeat."

Dr. R. tries for a couple more minutes. The room is silent as she concentrates. My smile disappears as she squirts on more gel and tries again. She stops moving the wand.

"Sandra, I'm sorry, I can't hear a heartbeat."

I sit straight up, the gel dripping down my tummy. My voice creaks as I ask, "What does that mean?"

Her voice is gentle and quiet. "It could be a variety of things. I'm going to call your obstetrician and ask her to see you tomorrow." I still don't understand what "no heartbeat" means.

She never said the baby was dead. I never miscarried.

Everything I read in *What to Expect When You're Expecting* says there is bleeding and cramping in miscarriage.

I've had none of that. I assume her machine isn't strong enough and the obstetrician can do an actual ultrasound. Then I will be able to see his wiggling toes and tiny hands.

Tim is out that evening, hosting his first work event since starting his new job. He is on a charter bus with a bunch of doctors on the way to a football game in Buffalo, NY, one and a half hours away. I don't call him.

I don't see any urgency, as I have an appointment tomorrow where my obstetrician's more specialized machine will confirm everything is ok.

It is amazing what we tell ourselves when we are in denial. As I drive home, I begin to wonder if I would know if my baby was dead inside me. I feel fine. There has been no cramping or bleeding.

I just purchased maternity clothes for my newly expanding waistline. Tim and I had our first prenatal class last week. I eat leftovers for dinner while watching TV, trying to distract myself.

But I can't focus on the show. My thoughts begin to wander and worry. "What does Dr. R. mean, no heartbeat?"

Christina, my pregnant friend from nursing school, works as a labour and delivery nurse in Guelph, an hour away. I call her and explain what the doctor said.

"Sandra, don't wait for the obstetrician to call you tomorrow. On Labour wards we have ultrasounds. If you walk right into the ward and tell them what the doctor said, they will do an ultrasound. No matter what happens, it will be ok."

"I can just walk right in?"

"Depending on the nurse, they might give you a hassle at first, but they will take you. Say the words 'The baby has no heartbeat at 16 weeks.'"

As I drive to the hospital, I feel like I'm in a dream. Not a nightmare, but definitely not a good dream. Nothing seems like reality. The ward is surprisingly quiet.

I thought I would hear screams of labour. I'm basing my assumptions of Maternity wards on what I see on TV. Kind of like how people imagine what Psych wards are like based on TV.

My running shoes squeak loudly on the linoleum flooring. I feel a pit in my stomach at the similar-looking hospital hallways. It doesn't matter that this is not a Psych ward.

It's still a reminder of too many months spent walking up and down long hallways, watching the minutes on the clock slowly tick by. The nurse behind the desk has her head over a chart, her pen rapidly scribbling notes.

She comes out immediately when I explain the situation. I had been ready to have to fight a bit, but she guides me directly to a private room. Looking at the bed and the equipment, I realize this is a Labour and Delivery room.

"Honey, I'll be right back. I'm going to get the portable ultrasound machine." Some people hate being called "Honey," but I love it. I feel comforted, like everything is going to be ok with those words.

The nurse returns, moving the ultrasound wand around my belly while we look at the screen. I see him! A boy! He's there! "I'm going to call the obstetrician who is on call.

She's just finishing up with another mom."

"She called me mom," I think. "She said, 'another mom,' like me." As she is walking toward the door, she turns around.

"Honey, is there someone we can call for you?" I want Tim here, but I know I won't be able to reach him. I ask them to call my parents. The ultrasound screen is shut down, so I look around the room, thinking about how many babies came into the world here.

After waiting 15 minutes, I pull my shirt over my exposed belly. The room is cold and sterile-looking. It's another 15 minutes before she returns. A tiny woman in dark scrubs accompanies her.

"Hi, Sandra. I'm Dr. F., the on-call obstetrician. Let's have a look." She speaks quickly, as if she is trying to get in as many words as she can in as little time as possible.

As the screen lights up again, I see my baby boy floating in his little swimming pool. But he's not swimming; he's not even moving. Dr. F. is talking to me, but I barely hear her words.

"I'm very sorry, but your baby has stopped growing." Her face shows no emotion.

I still don't understand what this means. "What does 'stopped growing' mean? He's too small?" "There is something called a 'missed miscarriage,'" she tells me.

"The body doesn't recognize that the fetus has passed away and continues to produce pregnancy hormones. Your body still thinks it's pregnant and doesn't expel the fetus." I try to speak through the lump in my throat.

"So he's dead?"

"Unfortunately, yes. Judging by the size, the fetus stopped growing at about 13 weeks." My body kept him an extra three weeks.

This oddly comforts me. My body loved him too much to let him go. "We will need to perform a D&C to surgically remove the fetus.

You should receive a call tomorrow with a time to do the procedure in the next two or three days."

Tears are streaming down my face as she exits the room. To her, I'm just an unknown patient. Another miscarriage in her day. To me, this is my world shattering.

My parents arrive, my mom in tears. Only then does it occur to me that they lost a grandbaby today too. They take me back to my house and we watch a *Friends* rerun, trying to distract ourselves until Tim returns. I rush to the front door when I hear the squeak of the hinges, which have been in need of oil for months.

Before I can open my mouth, Tim envelops me in a hug. Seeing my parents' car in the driveway at 11 p.m., he knows something is wrong. "We lost the baby," I murmur into his chest.

He holds me tighter. I hear him start to cry as well. Two days later, we are back at the hospital for a D&C to remove the fetus. This is my first time as a patient for non-mental-health-related care.

I'm holding together better than I would have expected. While I feel deep sadness, grief and even guilt, these are logical emotions to a miscarriage. Logical emotions have control. They make sense. There is a reason for these feelings.

Bipolar depression and mania have no logic.

They don't make sense. There isn't a reason for these feelings. I have survived that. I can survive this.

The hardest part is telling others, especially those not close to me. Those I haven't seen at the gym for a couple of weeks and who now ask how far along I am.

Ask if I know yet if it's a boy or girl. I'm surprised by how many people tell me their own story of losing a baby. Research shows that 10 to 20 per cent of pregnancies end in miscarriage. Why don't we talk about it more?

Everyone says there is nothing I did to cause this, and nothing that could have been done to prevent this. Just bad luck.

But I still question the medication. Even though it's deemed safe for babies, I wean myself off it against the advice of the doctor. I tell myself, "At the first sign of sliding into an episode, I will go back on them." Tim and I decide to wait only the three months recommended to let the body heal from the miscarriage.

I'm eager to try again. I've just finished teaching an aquafit class, the smell of chlorine still on my skin, when my cellphone rings. I flip it open and the tiny screen displays "YMCA Susan." I had shadowed Susan during my fitness instructor apprenticeship.

If you scroll through my phone, you will see my contacts are organized according to how I know the person: "Biking Bob," "London Michelle" or "Electrician Tony." Not sure if it's the best system, but if I can't remember someone's name, I'll still find them by what category in my life they fall into.

"Hi, Susan," I answer. "I just finished teaching aquafit; let me just walk to a quieter spot. The ladies are still gabbing away." Once outside, I listen intently as Susan explains about a connection she has for an available position as assistant manager at Tim Horton's corporate gym.

"I really think you should apply," she tells me. "It's part-time and most of it is admin work. You'd only be teaching four or five classes. It might be better for you if...you know..."

People are hesitant to bring up the miscarriage, thinking they will make me sad. But it's the opposite: I *want* to talk about it. I actually feel more sad when people don't acknowledge it, ignoring my grief and my emotions. "I have the qualifications?" I ask, feeling immediately unsure.

"Yup. You've got the fitness certifications they require. And I think you have the personality for corporate fitness. I already told her you'd be emailing her."

A few days later I'm frantically rummaging in my closet, close to tears. "You don't understand!" I whine to Tim. "I need a corporate outfit for the interview. I don't have anything but jeans and workout clothes. I hate everything I have!"

My maternity clothes are crumpled on the top shelf of my closet. Out of my reach, out of my view. Tim begins to pull items off the hangers, one by one. "How about this?"

"No, I hate the way I look in that!" "This one?" he says, pulling out a red long-sleeved top. "No, that's too fancy. Ugh! I shouldn't even go to the interview! I'll never get it anyways. Or what if I do get it, then get too stressed?

Or what if they hire me, but then they realize I'm not good enough for the job?" Whatever I ended up wearing must have been good enough, and I must have been good enough, because by the following week I am the assistant manager of Tim Horton's corporate fitness centre. Four days a week, six hours a day. The perfect magical 24-hour number. In the past year I had figured out this is my ideal. Go up to 26 hours and I become overwhelmed and stressed; 24 is my max. This is another thing I am fortunate with: the financial ability to work part-time to help my mental health.

One month after starting the job, I'm again sitting on a toilet waiting for two lines to appear on a pregnancy test.

As soon as I see those two lines, I call my family doctor to make an appointment. I call her even before I call Tim. She had suggested we make the prenatal appointments more frequent this time, to ensure the baby's health and to keep my anxiety levels low. Like many women after a miscarriage, I am terrified it will happen again.

I start fretting about telling work. I only just started there. I also want to keep it to myself as long as possible in case I miscarry again. With my slim build, at 13 weeks I need to start wearing looser clothing to hide my expanding tummy. It's time to tell them.

"Rachel?" I say as I knock quietly on my manager's half-open door. I sit down, letting her know I have some news. "You're pregnant," she blurts out. "Yeah, how did you know?" I say with shock.

"Mom's intuition, I guess. Congratulations!

I'm happy for you."

"I'm sorry, I know I just started here. We had started trying, but I didn't expect it to happen so quickly."

She cuts me off. "Probably because you are so healthy," she says, unaware of my bipolar. "Anyways, let me know if you need to adjust any of your classes as you get further along."

That was so much easier than I had thought. I had lain awake at night worrying for nothing. As usual. I wish I had known about the Thought Journal back then (see Chapter 7). How likely is this worry to actually happen? If it does, what is the result, both positive and negative?

I feel great the entire pregnancy, teaching until my last day at work. With two weeks to go until my due date, I begin my maternity leave, hoping to have a little break before Baby Ethan comes.

The day after my 38-week ultrasound, I'm out for a walk in the chilly March air. With headphones playing my favourite artist, Alanis Morissette, I hear my cellphone ringing just in time. It's my obstetrician, Dr. N. "Sandra, we need you to come in today.

We need to induce you."

"Today? But he's not due for two more weeks." She says more, but the only words I hear are, "He's stopped growing.

He is the same size as the ultrasound two weeks ago. We need to induce you today."

"Stopped growing." The last time I heard those words, I lost my baby. Dr. N. assures me that the baby is fine, but that at this point he will grow more quickly in the outside world than in my womb. Babies should gain about a half-pound a week in the last few weeks. He hasn't gained anything in two weeks.

I call Tim, and he leaves work immediately. We weren't expecting this, and we both look at each other. We are not sure if we are excited, anxious or scared. Or all three.

Whichever it is, Baby Ethan is coming into the world now! At the hospital, I'm immediately given Pitocin to induce labour. The cramps come and go in waves of pain. When it becomes too much, I ask for an epidural. Eight hours later, I'm still not dilating.

They begin to talk about a C-section. I plead to hold off. I want a natural birth. I want him to slide out into the world, crying and red-faced, and into my arms. The night is long. The obstetrician goes home, returning in the morning. After 26 hours of labour, Ethan goes into distress. He has been stuck in the birth canal for too long. Immediately, my hopes of a natural birth crash, and I'm whisked away for a C-section. When I hold my sweet, tiny, 5-lb 10-oz baby in my arms, none of that matters.

He is here, and he is perfect...except for the long, alien-shaped head from being in the birth canal for 26 hours. But it makes me laugh, and I know it will change shortly.

Nursing him, I feel oxytocin, the "love hormone," flood my body with a sense of peace. Because of my mental health risk, I'm in a special pre-

and postnatal program at the hospital. I've already met with a mental health nurse twice during my pregnancy.

I made the choice after my miscarriage to discontinue my meds. But I'm well aware that things could spiral up or down into a sparkling pregnant tornado at any point. Lack of sleep is a major trigger in bipolar, so I stay at the hospital for five nights.

At 9 p.m., Ethan is taken to the nursery, where the nurses look after him, giving me the opportunity for sleep. Whenever he is hungry, they bring him to me and help me set up to nurse him. I immediately drift back to sleep, knowing he is in safe hands back in the nursery – hands much more confident and knowledgeable than mine. In my mind, I imagine this is what it was like in the 1960s when moms would stay in the hospital for days, reading magazines and smoking cigarettes while the babies were bundled into the nursery.

I'm also given a private room, for a calmer and quieter atmosphere. When my obstetrician first suggested this whole support program, my first reaction was to say no. I didn't want anything to do with the psychiatric system again. I didn't want to be singled out or have a label put on me. However, over the next few visits, she convinced me. (Or maybe the words "private room" did.)

These supports are meant to lower the risk of postpartum depression. Statistics show that 15 percent of mentally healthy women experience postpartum depression; women with bipolar have a risk of approximately double that. And of those, anywhere from 22 to 54 percent will develop postpartum psychosis.

Unfortunately, even with these supports in place, I will become one of those statistics.

Reflections and Resources

Think of a challenging incident in your life – something you thought might break you, but where you made it through. What were the things you did to get to the other side of it?

Radical Acceptance

This is a DBT tool where you acknowledge and embrace a situation that is beyond your control. You accept its challenges and difficulties, without trying to control it. You recognize that fighting what has already happened only leads to further anguish. When you can accept the situation as is, you can then make more logical decisions and make progress in a healthy way. Accepting a miscarriage is an example of radical acceptance.

Online resource:
1. What was the event?
2. What factually caused the event?
3. Accept the emotions. What are they?
4. Proactive plan/How can I improve the situation?
5. What coping statements can I make to practice radical acceptance of this situation?

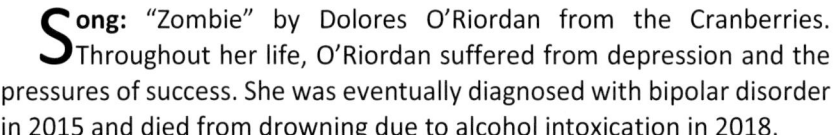

Song: "Zombie" by Dolores O'Riordan from the Cranberries. Throughout her life, O'Riordan suffered from depression and the pressures of success. She was eventually diagnosed with bipolar disorder in 2015 and died from drowning due to alcohol intoxication in 2018.

My parents and I with baby Ethan

A CHICKEN IN THE OVEN

Two days after the slow, careful drive back from the hospital with our precious new cargo in the back seat, we are watching *Survivor*. Ethan is finally asleep, still in my arms. Tim receives an email telling him that he needs to attend an out-of-town business meeting. I'm devastated because I am scared to be alone with the baby. He has taken on the Superdad role, helping with everything short of breastfeeding. How will I manage with a one-week-old baby?

My mom and my mother-in-law are thrilled to be grandmothers and take turns coming over to help. I'm grateful. I know nothing about caring for this tiny baby, so small that he doesn't even fit in newborn clothing or diapers. My C-section is sore, and bending to pick him up pulls on my stitches. Even though I know how important it is to nap, I can't sleep, aware of every sound from downstairs. I also feel a ridiculous need to entertain them, to be a hostess. To show that I have everything under control.

But even grandmothers don't know everything. A few days later, I'm changing Ethan's diaper, alone in a quiet house. His belly button cord stump is dry and hard. The hospital told me not to pick it off, but they didn't tell me when it would fall off. I call my mom – she raised two kids; she'll know.

"Mom, when will his belly button thing fall off? I know it's supposed to happen on its own, but it hasn't yet."

With a casual voice, she says, "I don't remember.... It was definitely off when you started school."

"Seriously, Mom? How can you forget something so important?!" She may have thought it was funny, but my temper is short with lack of sleep. I hang up and dial Telehealth, a new free service in Ontario that you can call to ask minor health questions. The nurse who picks up the phone either answers the question or refers you to a clinic or ER if necessary. As she chuckles about the story of my mom's answer, she assures me it will fall off any day now. She also gives me the name of a local Public Health moms' group.

Nursing Ethan gives me peace. Moments of quiet. Science shows that breastfeeding stimulates the release of calming oxytocin (also known as the love hormone) and decreases the level of cortisol (the stress hormone). It's not just good for Ethan; it's good for me too. I love looking down at his sweet face and feeling his tiny hand waving in the air, trying to grab my shirt, my hair, my face. Swaying back and forth in the rocking chair, I inhale the sweet milky smell, and feel the tension leave my body. Sometimes we even both fall asleep together, and I awake with his head wet from sweat from the combined heat of our bodies.

I miss my other release, though. Exercise. The birth was not easy, and my body still feels the toll of 26 hours of labour. Because of the C-section, I'm supposed to wait six weeks before doing any intense exercise. Walking and pushing the stroller is not cutting it for me. I need to sweat, to struggle, to "feel the burn." The April weather is often rainy and gloomy, but I head out anyway. It takes effort to bundle him up, bundle myself up, and get the stroller cover on to protect him from the rain and blustery wind. Every day I try to add a few jogging steps, thinking, "What's the worst that can happen?"

Even though I no longer cut or self-harm, causing myself a bit of pain still makes me feel better. And if I work out hard enough, it is painful. Exercise produces endorphins, a "feel-good" hormone. Dopamine, our happy hormone, is also released. Consuming food that is 50 percent fat and 50 percent sugar, like that found in a typical doughnut, releases the same amount of dopamine as 30 minutes of exercise. I like doughnuts. I like exercise. Maybe I should try eating a doughnut after exercise and see what happens. Exercise also produces enkephalins, a hormone that blocks pain. In caveman days, this blockage of pain would have allowed you to run at high speed away from a sabre-toothed tiger. Nowadays, many people take advantage of these exercise-induced hormones to lower mental pain. As I recover from the C-section, one of my main stress releases and mental health boosters has been taken away from me.

But I have other advantages that many new moms don't. The pre/postnatal program for at-risk moms doesn't stop once I am home. A lovely nurse, Andrea, has come to the house twice in the last two weeks to check in on me. She has a bubby personality and seems completely confident as she rocks Ethan on her lap while chatting with me. She has a casual way of putting me at ease. Maybe it's her young age, or maybe it's her side-shaved hairstyle and nose ring.

"How are you managing? How is your mood? Do you have thoughts of suicide? Do you hear voices?" She asks these questions as if she is asking me what I am having for dinner, even though they are designed to determine the status of my mental health.

My answers are truthful. "Doing great. No thoughts of self-harm. I'm not hearing voices or seeing intrusive images."

Since all is well, we move to a weekly phone call. When Ethan is four weeks old, Andrea suggests we put the calls on hold and check in again at three months. But three months later, when I see her number on call display, I don't pick it up.

Instead, I listen to her voice message asking to set up a date next week for a phone call, and I hit the delete button. I just don't feel like talking.

My mood has become low, and I'm exhausted by putting out a happy

"Being a mom is the greatest thing ever! Aren't I so lucky?!"image.

I don't know anyone in my neighbourhood or any other new moms. My days are solitary: just Ethan and me. I count the hours until Tim comes home so that I can hand Ethan over.

I'm often in tears by that point, worn down from the day. My nipples are cracked and sore, my C-section scar is healing and it's intensely itchy. I scratch it until it's bright red, focusing my thoughts on the stinging feeling.

On the outside, I'm the perfect picture of what a good stay-at-home mom should be. To Tim, it looks like I have everything under control – full meals on the table every night, a clean house and a freshly bathed, calm baby. I even put on makeup at the end of the day, like a 1960s housewife, you know, to look pretty for my husband.

Our relationship has been under strain the past year. A feeling of drifting apart. Somewhere, the love has withered from an intense flame to slowly dying embers. My thoughts that a baby would bring life to our marriage seem almost hilarious now.

A baby does the complete opposite of that. Our bedsheets don't smell of passionate sex; instead, there is a faint odour of sour milk, dribbled from nighttime feedings. My belly is soft and my breasts are a "no touch" zone to anyone but Ethan. And the worst part is that I feel my mind growing heavy again. As if it is swelling in my skull, filling with thick liquid. I have a sense that depression is knocking, or clawing, at the door.

One evening I'm preparing chicken breasts, ready to put them in the oven. I want everything to seem perfect when Tim comes home. I'm still wearing my bathrobe and notice that its fuzzy fleece has matted. When is the last time I washed it? I had planned to change clothes at some point in the day, but it's suddenly 5:00 and I'm still in my pyjamas. Ethan is wailing in his bassinet. The rocking function is on high, but he hasn't stopped all afternoon.

It's all I can hear, high-pitched and piercing. I've changed him, nursed him, burped him – nothing stops the crying vibrating in my ears. Earlier I had even shut myself in the bathroom with the fan on so I wouldn't go insane hearing his screams.

Then I felt like a shit mother, so I rushed to his bassinet and gathered him into my arms. Rocking him tightly, I apologized over and over. "I'm so sorry, I'm so sorry, I'm so sorry." Minutes later, his screaming changes to whimpering. The house is finally quiet. I return to preparing dinner. I lay two chicken breasts, wet with store-bought teriyaki marinade, into a glass roasting pan.

My eyes get stuck, staring, but not seeing. The pan blurs, then clears up again. I see Ethan, curled tightly in the pan, in his green onesie, his tiny legs tucked up to his chest, his thin dark hair wet with sweat.

I blink several times to pull myself back to reality. "No," I think. "This isn't real." I inhale deeply, close my eyes and count to eight with a long exhale. I'm scared to open my eyes. When I finally do, the pan has only two chicken breasts in it. I whip my head around behind me, and Ethan is still in his bassinet. He's sniffling with tiny quiet sobs, his face scrunched and bright red, snot all over his face.

I grab him into my arms and sink down onto the cold kitchen tile, bawling, my tears mixing with his. I press my back against the cupboard and focus on my breathing by inhaling his sweet baby smell. I'm terrified. What did I see? I don't know how long I sit there, but when I finally get up, I'm stiff and cold, and Ethan is fast asleep. I frantically begin to look for the Distress Line phone number I had been given when I left the hospital.

As I search through my night table, kitchen drawers and bathroom drawers, I feel sweat beading on my forehead. I'm still holding Ethan tucked football style, safely in one arm. I don't want to let him go. I suddenly remember that I never unpacked the bag I brought home with me from the hospital.

I rummage through it, pulling out pyjamas, grandma-style underwear and a never-opened mystery novel. At the bottom of the bag, I find the pamphlet I hadn't thought I would need. I'm embarrassed to call anyone I know, so I dial the Distress Line number.

When I hear a woman answer, I quickly hang up, afraid of being judged. What kind of a mother imagines putting her baby in the oven? Instead, I dial my family doctor and make an appointment "for my baby." I don't want to explain to the receptionist what happened. I feel more in control now, having blocked away the image. It must have been lack of sleep, exhaustion, stress—something, anything, but not a hallucination.

Through the hospital program, I'd learned a DBT technique called **S.T.O.P.**: 1. Stop and don't judge the thought/image. 2. Take a step back and a deep breath. 3. Observe what is going on around you. 4. Proceed mindfully with your goals in mind.

I was in a stressful situation. I did not act on what I saw. I took a breath and a break by hugging him on the floor. I saw the situation becoming more intense and I proceeded to ask for help. I defused my thoughts and did not allow them to ruminate and continue.

I S.T.O.P.ped. I hear the unlocking of the front door, and Tim walks in. "Mmm, smells great. What are you cooking?" "Chicken," I say, my eyes looking away, worrying my face might betray my words.

He picks up Ethan, wiggles him close at eye level. "And how was your day, big guy?" Then he turns to me. "What did you guys get up to today? Did you get out?" "Just for a walk," I reply. He must sense something is wrong, but only asks me when I'm going to check out that Public Health Mommies and Babies group. My mind twists that innocent comment around. "He thinks I'm not a good mom. He thinks I'm lazy. He hates my flabby stomach." But my mouth says, "Yah, maybe tomorrow. I'm not sure what the schedule is."

Truthfully, I'm not sure why I haven't gone yet. I'm an extrovert and usually love being around people. But right now, I want to be alone. It will be quite a few more years until I learn that I am an extroverted introvert – or an ambivert. I do love being around people. I pick up their energy, I laugh, I delight in telling stories. But only for short periods of time. Entire weekends away, in-laws staying over, or guests at our cottage; that kind of thing completely wears me out. I need a few quiet days afterward to recuperate. It's taken me a lot of years to find this balance. Even though it's now 2024, I actually still use a paper "Month at a Glance" calendar, in addition to my phone calendar, so I can count the number of events I have scheduled – whether it's teaching a class, meeting a friend, doing a lengthy errand or going to bike club. I have a limit of what I can do in a week. And it's not always easy to have others respect the balance I have carefully created. Going to a two-hour group with other moms experiencing the same trials, tribulations and joy of parenting a new baby should be great for me. I get to be outgoing, bubbly Sandra, then come back to the comfort and familiarity of my home two hours later. I just need to force myself to go. During dinner, I say nothing to Tim about what I saw in the baking pan. I'm scared that if he knew, he would take Ethan away or bring me to the hospital.

The time I spend hospitalized is not that long ago, and the fear is still always there. It will take me quite a few more years to trust the medical system again, as well as to trust myself. To trust myself that I can recognize what I need and when. That I am a person, not a patient. To not be afraid to question a doctor's advice. Two days later, my mom comes over. She usually comes once or twice a week, excited to hang out with her first grandchild. I still say nothing about what I saw or how I'm feeling. Instead, I put on an extra-huge smile, and we head out for a walk. I'm happy to let her push the stroller. I listen to her coo and laugh at Ethan's little gurgles and his toothless smile. With all the turmoil she has gone through over the years with me, I don't want to take away the joy I see on her face.

The May flowers are beginning to show. Tulips are popping up, and daffodils. The trees have tiny green buds, and the air feels fresh. I have a healthy, generally easy baby. I should be happy. My logical brain understands that this may be postpartum depression. My logical brain knows that seeing my baby in a roasting pan means I may be sliding toward trouble. I remember the statistic of bipolar and postpartum depression, and bipolar and postpartum psychosis.

I'm off my meds, lacking sleep and a hormonal mess. Pretty much every trigger for an episode. But my emotional brain feels like a toddler, stomping my foot in protest. I don't want this! It isn't fair! The move, the job, the baby – this is supposed to be my new, bipolar-free life. I'm determined to make it that. I cancel the doctor's appointment. I don't want to go back on my meds and stop breastfeeding. It has as many benefits for me as it does for Ethan. I know the meds are available if I need them, and tell myself I will get them prescribed at the first sign I can't do this on my own. But I want to hold off for now. Instead, I pull out every trick in my mental health toolbox. I like to picture it as an old-school red metal toolbox, dented and with spots of rust.

It's a cluttered mess inside. CBT and DBT tools mixed up with each other, mindfulness tools burrowed on the bottom and my W.R.A.P. (Wellness Recovery Action Plan, from Chapter 5) folded and slightly ripped on top.

In addition to practicing the CBT and DBT tools of paying more attention to my thoughts and actions, I go back to the lifestyle habits that have helped me before. Change of routine, lack of sleep, and stress are my big triggers.

Here's what's in my toolbox:

Sleep – It's obvious I need more sleep – what new mom doesn't need more sleep? Tim and I come up with a system. I nurse Ethan around 9 p.m. and head upstairs. Sometimes I fall into an exhausted deep sleep; other times I lie there, my mind spinning, tired but wired at the same time. Tim is a natural night owl and doesn't mind staying up with Ethan. He is happy for some solo bonding time with him. Around midnight, he gives him a bottle of expressed milk or formula. It's their private time. Ethan falls asleep in his arms and Tim slowly transfers him to his crib, hoping he doesn't wake. It may be 3 or 4 a.m. before the sound of his hungry cries rouses me out of bed. By then I've already gotten in six hours of sleep, even if it is sometimes restless – better than three hours of restless sleep.

Exercise – I begin to work out more intensely, taking advantage of his nap time or my mom's offers to give me a break. I do a workout DVD in the basement, or Pilates beside his crib. A common CBT exercise is to plan an activity and rate your mood out of 10 both before and after the activity. For me, it's always a 9 or 10 after exercise, even if I started at a 4.

Socialization – I finally make the call to the Public Health Mommies and Babies group. I'm so nervous the morning of my first group that I almost don't go. But I push myself out the door, buckle Ethan into his car seat and drive to the centre, noticing for the first time that it is summer. I hear the room before even finding its door. Moms and babies are everywhere. Some babies are crawling on the floor, others are crying in their moms' arms. It's easy to chat with the other moms, as we all have something in common. The easiest conversation starter is, "How old is your baby?" I leave feeling excited and looking forward to the next one. Again, mood 4 out of 10 before, 9 out of 10 after. Each week we get a bit of parenting education – babyproofing your home, moving to solid foods, teething, etc. I begin to build confidence that maybe I've got this parenting thing down after all. Not only do I attend the group twice a week, but I develop a friendship with several of the women and we meet up on other days. Turns out there is even a weekly afternoon showing at the local cinema reserved just for parents with babies! If your baby cries, no problem; he's not the only one. If your baby poops, no problem; they have a changing table right in the aisle.

Nature – The days are now warm and sunny, so I spend more time outdoors, taking advantage of the freedom of my paid maternity leave. Nature always brings me peace. PubMed Central has studies crediting the negative ions (which ironically are the good ones) in outdoor air with increased psychological health and overall well-being. Factual or not, I feel immediately better when I step outside. Warm sunshine on my face, the sound of trees lightly blowing in the wind, and the clear blue of the sky – it doesn't get better than that. Lying down on a blanket with Ethan, we both stare at the puffy white clouds. I try to imagine objects from their shapes, while he thinks whatever babies think of moving objects they can't identify. I haven't stared at clouds since I was a child, and this brings a peaceful sense of nostalgia.

My toolbox of tricks has helped again. Sleep, exercise, socialization and nature. I had accepted that if this didn't work, and my mood began to go up and down, I would need to reach out for help and medication. Postpartum depression is real and it is serious. Postpartum psychosis even more so. Tragically, 10 percent of postpartum psychosis cases result in suicide or infanticide.

A few years ago, a psychotherapist in Toronto (the city next door to my bedroom community) jumped in front of a train, killing herself and her six-month-old baby. The news reports said her colleagues and family were shocked. They had no idea anything was wrong; she had kept every symptom to herself. And as a psychotherapist, she had the knowledge and resources to recognize this. At that time, there was a lot more stigma than now, especially for someone whose job it is to help people with their mental health.

The night before she died, she had been seen standing on the train platform holding her baby "for extended periods of time." Police were called. They asked her to leave, and she did so willingly. This breaks my heart. This tragedy might have been prevented if someone had recognized her distress.

Many women suffering with postpartum depression still carry a shame. We are told, "What a beautiful baby!" "You are so fortunate to have a healthy son!" "Enjoy every moment; it's so precious." What if you don't feel that way?

Does that make you a bad mom? In Canada, we are fortunate to have paid maternity leave: 12 months for me in 2002. (Now, in 2024, it is 18 months.) I am enjoying every one of those months, watching my baby smile, crawl and walk. As my return to work nears, I have mixed feelings. Do I want to miss these moments? Do I even earn enough money working part-time to justify daycare costs? Tim and I begin to talk about baby number two. If you had asked me five years earlier if I would have children, let alone two, I would have laughed.

How can I have children when I'm barely surviving myself? What if the genetic risk of bipolar is passed on to them?

But when I look at Ethan toddling about, I know a second child is just what I want. To receive paid maternity leave again, I need to return to work for a year. That seems like a fair trade. We start trying a couple of months after I return to work.

My hours have changed slightly. Instead of four six-hour days, I do three eight-hour days, which allows us to find a mix of child care: my mom, my mother-in-law and a nearby home daycare. And I'm still within my magical 24-hours-a-week rule, the amount of hours I can work before my mental health is affected. Six months later, I'm once again in the bathroom, standing over the sink, staring at a little white stick. Counting down the time, waiting for two lines to appear. I see the positive, then look up, catching my face in the mirror. I see a woman with a silly grin. I see the beginning of laugh lines around my eyes. I see happiness.

This time I ask for and gratefully accept the pre/postnatal risk program. I have seen its benefits and recognize the risk is real. I've chosen not to go back on my meds but feel I'm doing ok. Ethan is still breastfeeding, just once a day before bedtime. I love that time. The way he falls asleep still attached. The warmth of his body, heavy on my lap. I feel sad when I realize this special time will have to end soon, as another baby is on the way. Like last time, my pregnancy is easy.

I actually enjoy being pregnant. I feel good. I don't have nausea, or many aches and pains. I continue to teach my fitness classes. Connor, the baby boy in my womb, is an active participant in my workouts. I move, he moves. He does his own kick-boxing classes in there, with strong jabs and kicks to my ribs. This time the birth is easier.

I have an 80 percent chance of needing a C-section again, so the doctor suggests pre-planning it. I'm a bit torn. There is always that wish to have a vaginal birth. You see the woman in movies, sweating, panting, then suddenly a bloody baby slides out, and directly is placed into the mom's loving arms. I wish I could have that.

Last time, I was barely conscious by the time Ethan was cut out of my uterus. But the 80 percent chance is too high to go through the agony of 26 hours of labour again.

The day before I'm scheduled to go into hospital, I get my toes painted a bright pink, shave my legs, wash my hair, and arrive at the hospital at 8:30 a.m.

Fifty-two minutes later, I'm holding Connor in my arms while the doctors work away at closing my abdomen. His birth has been much easier for me. I mentally knew what to expect, so I have no anxiety about what may happen. I physically knew what to expect, so brought loose clothing with no waistband, and I carry no assumptions of a quick recovery.

I have no hesitancy this time to take advantage of the program for women at risk of mental health problems. Having the five days in hospital with nurses to help throughout the night is even more important this time.

I will have a much busier house to come home to. When a psychologist comes to my hospital room to talk with me before my discharge, I debate telling him about seeing Ethan in the roasting pan. I'm scared it may happen again.

How will I handle two kids? But the words never come out of my mouth. I don't want to be targeted or labeled. I'm still wanting to put out the persona of a perfect mom, who has overcome bipolar. Having a two-year-old and a newborn feels like chaos at first. But we also have experience this time. Tim and I immediately begin "Sandra's Sanity System." Tim does a nightly bottle feed while I head to bed early. I happily let my mom and mother-in-law take Ethan to the park or the pool, while I stay with Connor.

It's not easy to get one-on-one time when you have two kids, so I enjoy being able to massage Connor's tiny back and legs, or to let him fall asleep on my chest after nursing while I doze with him. I return to the Mommies and Babies group as soon as I'm able to get organized enough to get out of the house.

And when you have a toddler with energy to burn, you make that happen pretty quickly. After all, just because you are tired and sore doesn't mean your toddler is. But it's not all altruistic. It's easier for me to make the short daily walk to the nearby playground, than it is to have a revved-up toddler in the house needing to play and jump and dig. Ethan runs up and down the slide or makes tunnels in the sand, while I sit on the park bench and wiggle Connor's stroller just enough to keep him happy. I feel content.

I still crave more sleep, so I sneak in a daily nap by tricking Ethan. It's too easy. I use the same trick every day. When Connor drifts off to sleep, still in my arms after nursing, I carefully lay him in his crib. Inch by inch I slowly pull my arm from under his warm body, hoping he won't wake up. And that's the moment Ethan protests having to have a nap of his own.

"That's fine," I tell him.

"But you need quiet time. Just stay in your room until your *Thomas the Tank Engine* CD is done. Then you can come out." Every single time, he falls asleep. And then so can I.

Fitness is a small world, and many of us instructors either know each other or have heard of each other. When Connor is three months old, the local community centre calls me. They are running a Mommies and Babies fitness class – would I be interested in teaching it twice a week? I can bring Connor into the class with me, and they'll have free babysitting there for Ethan. Uhh? Yah!

So again, I use exercise, nature, sleep and socialization. This keeps me sane.

I wonder: if I had known this formula in my 20s, would things have been different? Had I learned CBT and DBT then, could I have prevented episodes from building?

When my maternity leave comes to an end, I don't return to work to the corporate Tim Horton's fitness centre. I really want to stay home with the boys. Tim and I discuss if we can make the financials work. I didn't earn a lot of money there, and by the time we've figured out costs of driving, daycare and lunches out, we see it doesn't make sense.

Instead, I pick up a few more classes at the community centre. Now both boys go to the babysitting while I teach, and afterwards we visit the library attached to the centre. A couple of times a week, we go to a play group or meet up with other moms I've met. Our life has a routine. Even though I'm home, this time I don't feel that I need to have full meals ready at the end of the day or a perfectly clean house. I'm a mom. That's my job. And I love it.

I nurse Connor as long as I can, well over a year. It is still the calm in my day. He is a more finicky baby than Ethan was. Cries more easily, doesn't sleep as well. He also has more energy. Just like he moved more in my womb, he moves more in life as well.

Even with their nap time, I need other breaks in my day, so I find ways to sneak them in. Playing doctor is a good one. They are the doctors and I am the patient. Nothing they do can revive me. They try their stethoscope, their bandages, their thermometer. I lie down with my eyes closed while they try to heal me, to no avail. That gets me a good 10-minute nap.

Being a "stay-at-home mom" alleviates another stressor for me – the guilt of not working full-time and bringing in the bucks. When I discovered the magical 24-hour-week sanity saver, I felt guilty at not contributing more financially, but I didn't have a choice mentally. Tim never once said anything to imply I should feel guilty. It was my own Unhelpful Thinking Style (from Chapter 3) of 'Shoulding and Musting.' "Everyone else my age works full-time, so I should too." "I should be able to handle more stressors." "I must not be as smart as that well-put-together banker I met last week at the gym." I'd like to say that I eventually got over this, but I still Should and Must about things all the time.

Before kids, there was also the awkward small talk at dinner parties.

"Oh, you work part-time? Are you doing something else on the side?"

"You don't have kids? What do you do with the extra hours?" I never had the courage to answer,

"I have bipolar, and it's a part-time job on its own just staying healthy." Now that I'm a mom, no one questions why I'm not working. I'm raising two human beings.

I'm happy. I have two funny little kids who make me laugh. Instead of waking up to the blare of an alarm and driving through traffic to work, I get to wake up to the sound of their voices, or their warm bodies creeping into bed with me.

They have a great dad who supports me to be a good mom. Even if our "couple time" has disappeared,

I hear the same from other moms while we push our little ones in the swings at the park.

It's Easter weekend, just before Ethan's fourth birthday. The past two years have been a blur of play dates, diapers, and the general chaos and hilarity of toddlerhood. Our marriage has become less of a relationship and more of a partnership of parenting.

There is no time for romance. No time for conversations about life outside of the two tiny humans occupying our every moment. We have somewhat forgotten each other in our desire to give our kids our best selves.

We spend the Saturday before Easter at a nearby hobby farm with another family.

I met Chandra at the community centre a couple of years back. She was attending my Mommies and Babies fitness class with her four-month-old son.

I was trying to teach with Connor strapped to my chest in his baby carrier. I had to turn off the microphone I was wearing because he wouldn't stop crying, his face close to the mic. Chandra's son was deep asleep on the mat besides her.

The moms all recognized my building frustration and despair. I was supposed to be teaching!

Whoever thought it was a good idea for me to teach with my baby?! Chandra approached me. "Do you want me to try?" she said, reaching out her arms. "Please," I responded gratefully. Connor looked up at the stranger, his little chin wiggling from crying. The shock made him stop crying.

After class, when I picked Ethan up from the babysitting, he was deep in play with a blonde girl his age. They were stacking colourful blocks, building a train bridge. For some reason the playroom always smells like playdough, even though I have never seen playdough there. From behind me

Chandra's voice said, "That's your son?"

Yah, Ethan. He's almost three. Thanks so much for helping today. It was getting really distracting to keep teaching."

"No problem. We've all been there, right? That's my daughter. Looks like they are having too much fun to even notice us." She laughed. We instantly hit it off and spent many days together, the kids having a great time, and us as well.

So now, with the kids almost two and four, we meet up for an Easter event at a local farm.

As it's the weekend, we even invite our neglected husbands along. Her husband is in finance in Toronto, and Tim is still in pharmaceutical sales. It feels like a perfect day.

The spring air is warm. The kids jump from hay bale to hay bale, sweet-smelling dust floating into the air with each jump. The sound of kids laughing, screaming and playing is all around.

The excitement of baby bunnies and chocolate eggs burns off the kids' energy, leaving them more cranky and tired than they will admit. Putting them to bed is a routine Tim enjoys doing when he is home.

By 7:30, he walks into the kitchen. My back is turned, my eyes focused on the plastic sippy cups I am washing.

"Ok, they're both in bed. Ethan is passed out, but Connor is still awake. I'll turn on the baby monitor," Tim says. His voice sounds strange, stressed. "Thanks. I guess we should figure out our dinner

"I've moved on to loading the dishwasher. Tim pauses, then mumbles, "Actually, I'm going." "To get a movie?" I ask. We've fallen into the habit of collapsing on the couch with a DVD once the kids are asleep.

"No. Going." I turn around, a plate still in my hand. "Where?"

"To my mom's. Can we sit down?"

We sit on the loveseat and I listen with shock, dumbfounded. Apparently, he feels we have grown apart.

We were young when we got married. We went through a lot when I was sick. He was by my side every step of the way, but now our paths are going in different directions.

He says he isn't just going to his mom's tonight. He wants a separation. I had no idea this was coming. Am I an idiot? How could I not have seen this? I didn't see he was unhappy.

I begin to turn everything around in my head, wondering what I did wrong. This is the most stable I have ever been. This is me at my best. How am I not enough?

I've worked really hard to get here, and now apparently my life is going in a different direction from his. My life is going to fall apart. I envision a thermometer breaking, the tiny beads of mercury splitting and rolling on the floor.

Suddenly, anger floods my body. I feel a prickly heat. I can't catch my breath. I'm completely out of control. I don't understand this emotion. Anger. I've never really felt angry. I don't even know how to process it. My red, dented toolbox has no tools for anger.

I lash out at Tim, hitting him on the chest, yelling and crying at the same time. He just lets me do it. His face looks sad and ashamed. Five minutes later, I've exhausted myself.

An ironic thought floats through my head that I am no different than my toddlers, bursting out with emotion, only to give up. He holds me tight, tighter than he has in four years.

He says he still loves me, will always love me, but is no longer in love with me. This confuses me more than ever.

I sit on the bed watching him pack a bag, my swollen, red eyes brimming with tears. For the next few days, Tim comes in the evening to see the kids and tuck them into bed. It feels awkward.

I stay downstairs, pretending to tidy up, but keeping one ear open to hear him reading *Thomas the Tank Engine* to them. They love it when he reads that book. I feel tears begin to slide down my cheeks. My kids are going to grow up in a broken home. Whose home will *Thomas the Tank Engine* be at?

When he walks into the kitchen once they are asleep, I want to beg him to stay. Tell him that we can work this out. That the kids need us together. But I don't.

I'm only 33, and not as strong as I am now. I don't like rocking the boat, even when that boat is my marriage. So, with my silence, each night he returns to his mom's. The kids don't even notice that he is not sleeping there.

For three days I tell no one, not even my parents. I think this is just a "blip." An early mid-life crisis for Tim. I don't want them to hate him for doing this.

I'm sure it will pass. When I finally call my parents, their response is

"How can we help?"

No judgment, just support and hugs. A few weeks is all it takes for me to start to accept this new reality.

I've never been a person who fights and perseveres until the end. I tend to give up when the going gets tough. I want things to be stress-free. I *need* things to be stress-free. I don't want to fight for a marriage where one person isn't happy. I'm even starting to ask myself: was I happy, or just complacent?

We didn't argue. We spent time together. We didn't say negative things to each other. But that was it. We no longer laughed at silly things together.

We no longer had much physical intimacy. Two weeks later, Tim plans to have the kids with him at his mom's for the weekend.

The kids are excited for a sleepover at Granny's. Being so young, they don't understand what has happened.

Tim and I are extra civilized around the kids, careful not to argue, wanting them to see only happiness.

I stand at the front door, watching Tim buckle the kids into their car seats. As he drives away in the silver Audi A4 he was so proud to have bought just a couple of months ago.

It makes me recall last year when he needed a rental car. It was drizzling slightly, so I was out on our long, covered wraparound porch, watching the kids play with dinosaurs.

It felt wonderful to be in the fresh air, yet sheltered from the rain. A brilliant yellow sports car pulled up. I'm not really into cars, so I didn't even know what the model was, but it looked fancy. The door opened and Tim struggled to slide his tall frame out from the low seats.

I saw pride as he told me he had upgraded the rental car for a few days. Maybe that should have been a clue for me that he was seeking some kind of external happiness – maybe experiencing an early mid-life crisis.

But I only shook my head, thinking it a silly waste of money. I bring my thoughts back to the present as I watch him and the kids drive out of sight, on their way to their sleepover at Granny's. I sit on the front steps for a few minutes, unsure what to do.

I realize this is the first time I have been alone in the house in the four years since Ethan was born.

"I should be productive,"

I think. I start picking up toys, putting away clothes and cleaning the kitchen. That takes an hour. I have a whole weekend of unfilled time to kill. I send an email to several of the moms from my group and my neighbourhood.

I'm raw and honest, telling them what happened a couple of weeks ago. Within an hour, the responses flood in. That evening they show up at my house, bottles of wine in hand.

For the first time, we are together without children. We are not moms struggling to get in an uninterrupted conversation between doling out Cheerios and wiping baby bums.

We are a strong group of women, banding together to support the first one of us to get divorced. In everyone's mind is the same thought: "Can it happen to me?"

Or the more shocking thought, "I almost envy you. I want out of my marriage but don't have the courage."

In the upcoming months this will be a secret whispered to me by several people.

Two hours later, the bottles of wine have been enjoyed and emptied. All of us are slightly tipsy.

The women become angry for me. "Well, fuck him. He's an asshole!" "What the hell does he want? You're gorgeous!"

I'd already started to leave my anger behind. I'm just sad. I don't consider him an asshole. He's a great dad.

And he stood by me through some very hard years. But they don't know that. I've never told any of them. The wine has fuelled their bravado. Two blocks away is a pond where we often go to let the kids stomp around in rubber boots, tossing lettuce, carrots and bread to the ducks and Canada geese.

Tim has a collection of hand-painted wooden decoy ducks. Dozens of them. A couple of times a year he would visit the artist to get a new one. We even commissioned a pair of baby crows painted with the boys' names painted on them.

Natasha, the feistiest among us, pauses mid-conversation, her eyes lighting upon the ducks.

"We should take his ducks to the pond and set them free!" "Yeah, his precious ducks should join the real ducks," shouts Marie.

"Ducks! Ducks! Ducks!" the women start chanting. I suddenly feel like I am amid a coven of witches. I seem to be the only sane one. Me, the one secretly hiding my bipolar life – I'm the only one with the sense to say,

"No, we can't do that." But the next day I do sneak a couple of the ducks into my closet, deciding that these are mine. In fact, I actually still have them.

The next morning, I wake up hung over. I'm not used to drinking. My mouth feels like something has died in it.

My head pounds as I grope around in the medicine cabinet for Advil. As I look at myself in the bathroom mirror, I see a 32-year-old woman, with bags under her eyes, and hair recently cut short to chin length.

I realize that I am looking at a 32-year-old single mom with a two-year-old and a four-year-old and no real job. I have no idea what is ahead of me. What will my future look like?

How will my kids handle growing up in two homes? How will I handle going through the divorce process? But I know one thing. I don't want to be angry.

I don't even know how to be angry. I've only ever turned anger inward. Hating myself. Hurting myself. If I become angry about this situation, I don't know how to make myself feel better from that anger, and that can be a slippery slope for me.

My toolbox has specialized tools. But these tools just help me with bipolar – that's it. Imagine that all my screwdrivers are flat heads, and now I need a Phillips screwdriver for anger. I don't have one.

How do I stay stable without that specific screwdriver? In my mind, I think of women I have met over the years. Women in their 40s with frown lines, downturned lips and cold eyes. You can feel anger seeping from their pores, and you hope you don't catch it. They are angry at their ex. They are angry at men.

They are angry at the world that left them single and alone. They can't move on from that anger. I don't want to become one of those resentful women. I need to move on. While I might be stable right now,

I never know what is around the corner. People fight for feminism, and I'm slightly ashamed to admit that I don't want to be alone, that I don't want to live without a man. I need support. I need help. I will need to quickly move ahead to another relationship. My mom loves to tell a story of a ski trip we took in Switzerland. I was maybe five years old, but

I'd been skiing since I was two. She and I accidentally ended up on a black diamond run, the most challenging. I was crying, saying I couldn't do it.

Of course, we had no choice but to ski down, but I was glued to the spot, my skis in a snowplough, my poles digging in tight to the steep pitch. She offered to take me between her legs, so we could ski together as we had done when I was learning. "No," I sob. "I need a man!" And that is exactly how I feel right now.

Reflections and Resources

Reflect on a situation where you weren't open with someone about your mental health, even though you were struggling.

What held you back from sharing?

What would have been the worst-case scenario with discussing this openly?

What would have been the best-case scenario with discussing it openly?

Problem-Solving Worksheet

In a marital separation, there are a lot of problems to be solved and decisions to be made. I mentioned earlier that I have a difficult time making decisions. Writing everything out – the pros and cons, the steps to take and the desired outcome – really helps me.

This is a great worksheet for making your way through all that:

Song: "Girl Anachronism" by The Dresden Dolls. Their video of this song does a great job of showing the manic nature of the words, and is quite fun to watch.

I'm now a single mom to these two sweet boys. Can I be the mom they deserve?

DIVORCE, DATING AND DISEQUILIBRIUM

Three months after Tim's bombshell announcement, I'm sitting in the waiting room of a divorce mediator. I'm wearing one of the few "nice" outfits I own, most of my clothes being more suited for playing with trains on the floor with the boys. In a sparkly black, off-the-shoulder top and dark boot-cut jeans, I look more like I'm going to a dance club than to divorce mediation. I still have an odd, lingering desire to look nice when I see Tim. To show him what he's lost. To show him that I have it all put together.

I'm early, as per usual. I pull out my phone and scroll through my contacts. Not for any particular reason, just a habit I've developed since getting my new flip phone.

The sound of size 13 feet making their way down the hallway pulls me away from my swiping.

Tim is in his work clothes, squeezing this into his day. His style over the last couple of years really picked up. He looks good in a sporty blazer and open-neck dress shirt.

This new hip style maybe should have been another clue to me that he was growing away from the 22-year-old guy I first met.

The last few months were easier than what most people experience during divorce. I'm not a fighter. I don't like confrontation, especially with someone who I know still cares for me, even if it is no longer as a wife. He'd used the classic "It's not you, it's me" line. "It's just different paths."

Which seems like one of those things people say to let you down gently. But it doesn't make it sting any less to be suddenly single.

We've each already consulted our own lawyers, and we both agree that we don't want to drag this out. Lawyers are expensive. Tim is being fair financially, and I'm being passive, wanting the least stressful route possible. Neither of us wants to make this any harder than divorce already is. We agree that the kids are the most important aspect, and our relationship shouldn't affect theirs. I'm not claiming that we were somehow righteous and superior to others going through divorce. I understand that amicable separations aren't possible for a lot of couples. Sometimes one partner is bitter and spiteful. Sometimes the kids are used as pawns. Fighting over money can often drag things on so long that the lawyers end up the only winners. We don't want that to happen. We both acknowledge that for us, the relationship just kind of ran its course.

A good friend of mine, Kim, a gynecologist who might also be the wisest person I know, is in the process of writing a book, *Everything Sex Ed Never Taught You*. It also contains relationship advice. In her chapter about monogamy she ponders her thoughts on how relationships should be a seven-year contract. At the end of seven years, you either renew the contract or say, "That was good, but I'm going to move on." Kind of like a job. No hard feelings, just a realization that the contract isn't serving its purpose anymore. I wish I'd had her wisdom to see it like that back in 2006. Basically, our contract had run its course. There will be a new relationship, a new contract, waiting for us down the road.

Tim gives me a hug when he sees me. The kind of hug guys give their friends – brief, one arm over shoulder, a little pat on the back.

As he opens the door to the lawyer's office, I take in the three bookshelves. Rows of titles with long legal words I don't understand. She looks like what I expect a lawyer to look like. Red (power colour) skirt suit. Overweight, as if her long workdays give her little time for healthy cooking or exercise. Even her pale skin implies she can't get out to enjoy the late spring sunshine. I begin to feel sorry for her, until I remember her expensive hourly rate of $350, which was a lot in 2006. Nah, she's doing fine.

Ninety minutes later, she says, "You guys should give a course on how to separate amicably. I've never seen a couple so civil."

That's all the time it takes to determine my child and spousal support, how to split the 50/50 schedule with the kids, vacations, Christmas holiday time, and even who handles the medical appointments and passports. It's almost too easy. A few years down the road, though, I will regret agreeing to the clause of living within 40 kilometres of each other. That single line will become the most challenging piece of our co-parenting.

Three weeks later, we sign our separation agreement. I'm now officially a single mom.

I'm still living in our "matrimonial" home. Connor is almost two years old, still in a crib, just out of diapers, and dragging his "chi chi" (blankie) everywhere he goes. Ethan has just turned four. Our life hasn't changed yet. Three mornings a week, we walk 10 minutes to his Junior Kindergarten. I push Connor in his stroller, and trailing 20 feet behind is "Blue," the black cat we got one year earlier. She follows us to the school, a discreet distance back, kind of like I used to do as a teenager when I was at the mall with my parents. When we cross to the schoolyard, Blue stops. She has no desire to be among the running, excited kids. After handing Ethan over to the JK teacher, I push Connor's stroller back over the bumpy grass. When we reach the sidewalk, Blue slinks out from a bush. Once we pass her, she again begins her discreet trail. I think she believes we don't know she is there.

Part of what makes the split so simple is that the kids are too young to realize that having Mom and Dad live in two different houses is not usual. I'm thankful the kids are so young. Their emotion is excitement about having two houses, rather than anger or confusion. I'm holding it together, going back to the CBT and DBT techniques I learned six years earlier at Credit Valley Hospital. The two techniques I find most helpful in this major life change are Radical Acceptance and Thought Journals.

- **Radical Acceptance** – This situation is not changing. I'm divorced. My life is not taking the path I thought it would. How can I change my thoughts and feelings about it? How can I come up with a plan to move ahead? Radical Acceptance is not about passive behaviour or giving up. It is about creating a positive out of a negative situation you cannot control.

- **Thought Journals** – I can't stop ruminating or wondering what is wrong with me. Why am I not good enough to be his wife? Will I be alone forever? With my Thought Journal, I can break down those thoughts step by step and figure out a more helpful way to view the situation. I am good enough as I am. It is highly unlikely I will be alone forever. In fact, it will soon turn out that I will not be alone for long.

Even with these, I can't always keep my feelings as controlled as I'd like. The kids sometimes see my tears, when I can't stop them from spilling out of my eyes when I think they are distracted by watching *The Wiggles* dancing on TV. They both climb on my lap and ask me if I have a boo-boo. "No" I say, "sometimes Mommy is just a bit sad." They cuddle deeper into me and say nothing at all. Kids understand that sometimes we are just sad. Kids can't give solutions. But they can give big hugs with their tiny arms.

Even with child and spousal support, I need to sort out my finances. My housing, groceries and budget needs don't balance with teaching a few classes a week.

If I want to stay in our house, I need to give Tim half the equity...which of course I don't have. At night after the kids have gone to bed, I delve into the internet rabbit hole of real estate sites, private sales and rentals. I even briefly consider being caretaker to an elderly gentleman living in a large house on Lake Ontario – cooking, basic care and companionship in exchange for room and board. But the kids are a deal breaker. As cute as they are, I am aware of the decibels of their play. And, somehow, living with an old man on a lakeside estate seems a little creepy as well.

My parents have a proposition: they become half owners of my house. Just as in London, they view it as an investment financially for them, and a way of helping me out. And, though they don't say it, they probably think that otherwise, this situation might be the thing that breaks me. If I don't have to pack up and find a place to rent, it saves me a lot of stress. If the kids retain the stability of their living situation, their bedroom and their play buddies, it's better for them as well.

However, there is a hitch in this plan. It's something I had never realized before, and I hope my realization comes as a public service announcement to everyone reading this. It's important to build credit in your own name! I had never had a credit card in my own name; they were all joint cards. I had never had a car payment or mortgage in my own name. Again, they were all joint. So now the bank looks at my fitness income, which is piddly and unpredictable. And so far, Tim and I only have a separation agreement, not a signed divorce agreement, so the promise of spousal and child support doesn't count toward my income.

My dad comes with me to the bank so I can sign for my half of the mortgage – which he has to co-sign for. As I sign page after page, I begin to worry if I am taking on too much. Financially and emotionally. When I hand the thick stack of papers back to the bank employee, I muster the courage to ask about a credit card.

He assures me I can qualify for a Visa card, starting with a low limit: $1,500. I feel a surge of pride – I'm on my way. Now that I can give Tim his half of the house equity, we can finalize our agreement. And he can get his own place, a townhouse just 10 minutes away.

Next step, I need a job. I suck up my pride, and start being open with people. The response when I explain the situation warms my heart. Hugs come first. Then, "How can I help?" My supervisor at the community centre offers me a couple more classes, which is ideal, as I can bring Connor along to the gym babysitting, while Ethan is at kindergarten. I need exercise more than ever to maintain my mental health, so this ticks three boxes – sanity, child care and income.

My work network builds. A neighbourhood mom who is also a personal trainer is moving to another city, and refers me to her clients. Then an instructor I have never met before, Melanie, calls me one day. She needs someone to cover her Pilates class.

Would I be available? Our conversation continues for another hour, and I learn she divorced last year and has two little boys as well. I am the first of my friend group to go through this (although several more will in the upcoming years).

Talking with someone who has experienced the legal and financial process and understands the emotions is amazing. That one-hour conversation turns into outings and playdates on weekends, our four boys running around, wrestling on the grass and having fun. And those outings turn into a lifelong friendship for Melanie and me. All around me, people want to help.

One neighbour mows my lawn, my ex-mother-in-law drops off food, my parents come to play with the kids.

I won't learn this for many more years, but apparently my superpower is that people will help me. Around my 50th birthday, Tony, my "adventure buddy" (meaning our friendship has formed over biking, hiking, skiing and anything else active and adventurous), will ask me an interesting question.

"You are half a century old. What is your superpower?"

I'm in the middle of hiking a root-entangled climb on the Bruce Trail, so my eyes are focused on the path ahead. I stop and look backwards at him. "Superpower?

What do you mean? I don't do anything powerful."

"Sure you do," he says. "Everyone does. Everyone has one thing that they do really well, even if they don't know it. Mine is that I can convince people to do almost anything."

(I should mention that since I've met him, he has convinced me to take my bike on a chairlift and ride down a mountain, jump off a cliff into a lake and steer a sailboat with one injured arm in a sling.)

I resume hiking, silently mulling it over. I can't think of anything. "I don't know. I like to be adventurous."

"That's a good trait, but it's not a superpower. What would help you in an apocalypse? How would you survive?"

When I don't answer, Tony says, "I have an idea." "What is it?" "People help you!" He says triumphantly.

"Oh, my God," I say, my eyes opening wide. "You're right. They do! I could totally survive an apocalypse because people would give me food and shelter." He chuckles.

"Yup, I've seen people help you more than once." In 2006, though, as I was rebuilding my life after the separation, I didn't know about this supposed superpower.

Even though it was happening all around me, I never realized that I always receive a little extra support. My 20s may have had a lot of hardships, but all of it was made a bit easier by those around me. This support has given me an advantage many people with mental illness don't have.

The first weekend Tim has the kids, I wander the house aimlessly. I don't know what to do with my time. Everyone I know has little kids and is busy with family things during the day.

If I try to organize an evening get-together, it requires massive planning. "Let me check with my husband." Or "Oh, we have Emma's birthday party. I'm going to need to collapse on the couch with a Pinot Grigio afterwards."

Even if we can organize something, suddenly someone's kid has a runny nose and they need to cancel.

A couple months of this and I begin to consider online dating. Remember last chapter? "I need a man!"

There were no dating apps back then. No swiping left or right, or notification that a potential date is somewhere in the same bar as you. Just a few basic websites such as eHarmony, Plenty of Fish and OkCupid. I'd heard horror stories about bad dates and fake profiles on Plenty of Fish.

To my mind, free websites mean drunken Saturday night hookups or cheating partners.

But now I'm thinking about it. I can't pay a lot, but Date.ca is a site with a $20 monthly fee. Just enough that people are sufficiently invested in looking for love to fork over their credit card.

My first step is finding profile pictures. And that's when I realize I don't have any pictures of me alone! In every photo, I'm with Tim or the kids. iPhones hadn't launched yet (they would come out the next year, 2007), so any photo I have has been taken with a grainy five-megapixel digital camera. Unlike today, where you take a selfie, airbrush it, add a filter and look like a model. I go to my bookshelf of photo albums, ranging from when I was a kid to just last month. I peel a couple of recent photos out of the album and go to work with scissors. A few snips and I'm alone in my photos.

There's one of me sitting on my porch reclining on an Adirondack chair. Another of me skiing, no helmet, in the style of 1999. And the attention grabber – a slinky black dress and high heels from a party last year. I scan them from our large printer onto a USB and upload them to the site. Now I need to think of a profile name. I want to attract someone with an active lifestyle, so my profile needs to express that right away. And "Yoginifit" goes live on the web!

My criteria for a man: -Skis, or is willing to learn -Non-smoker -Active lifestyle -Open to kids -Ambitious (the polite way of saying I don't want him to be broke) -Lives within 50 kilometres After I click "upload," I sit at the computer for a few minutes. I'm not sure what to expect. It's a Saturday afternoon. Do people check the site frequently?

My large desktop computer is in the chilly basement that used to be Tim's office. I'm shivering, so go upstairs and start to put away laundry. I'm too curious to wait. Remember earlier when I mentioned that I experience all human emotions at a larger level? Nothing to do with bipolar, just a large breadth of emotions. And that includes excitement. The computer has gone to sleep. I touch the enter key to wake it up, and my profile page is still open. I have eight messages. In 10 minutes!

Then disappointment kicks in. I look at each of their profiles. Nothing I listed as my criteria is in theirs. Did they even read my profile? Several of them are smokers, one is morbidly obese and looks like he wouldn't be able to bend over to tie his shoes, never mind get up on skis. One lives in Chicago, 10 hours away.

Another has spelling and grammatical errors throughout his profile. Did he put in no effort at all? If this is how online dating is, I won't have the time for this. Or the heart. I don't open it up again until Sunday morning. I wake up to 50 responses. I'm assuming I'm a new fish in the pond, meaning fresh bait. The boys won't be back until 7:00 tonight and I have nothing else to do, so I scroll through the replies.

I head upstairs and pour some coffee grinds into my French press. As I wait for the water to boil, I look around my kitchen and family room and think how much things could change if I date. If I find someone I want to be with. I like my house. I like my life.

Do I really want it to change? Pouring the water into the press, I slowly lower the plunger, lost in thought. As it reaches the bottom, I make a decision. I'll date. Why not? I'll just go on coffee dates, which means I'm not committing to anything besides coffee.

If it's not going well, I can be out of there in 10 minutes. Still in my pyjamas, I head back downstairs to my computer, wishing I had a laptop and could sit cross-legged on my comfy reclining couch.

Another five messages have come in while I made coffee! I need a system to filter through these – I can't read each one. I know my friend Melanie had tried online dating, but she gave up after just a couple of months. Now I think I understand why. It could be a full-time job! This time, I don't read their whole profile. I scan for hobbies and smoking first. Then location, job and kids.

I spend less than a minute on each one. Either save or delete. Once I've done that, I read more in-depth. This may sound a bit snobby but, forgive me, I am a writer after all. Spelling mistakes or typos? You're out. (I mean, dude, take some time or ask for help.) No mention of skiing – you're out. I'm not even open to my "or willing to learn" statement anymore. And more than 10 years older or five years younger than me – you're out.

That leaves me with about 10 responses. I respond to their messages with a "wink." I want to leave the ball in their court. So I've narrowed down the pool of messages from the weekend...but now it's Wednesday, and there are more. They have slowed down, though – partly because

I've already burned though 200 guys and partly because I am no longer the new girl on the site. Throughout the next two weeks, I sort and wean. Then, if I'm interested, a few message exchanges. Then to phone calls. Those are the most uncomfortable. Talking to someone you have never met, when you are both trying to show the best of yourself. Awkward. Phone calls to people I don't know, restaurants, making appointments, etc. – it all still makes my heart beat a little faster even all these years later. I'm still worried about saying the wrong thing – something like, "Hello, you're Sandra. I'd like to make an appointment for a giraffe order."

I currently attend a bipolar support group, and when this topic was brought up recently, I was surprised at how many people felt the same way. A technique I learned is to write down what I want to accomplish and what questions to ask. Had I known that technique then, I could have applied it to dating calls as well! The next time the kids are with their dad, I have a full weekend of coffee dates lined up. Tea dates, actually. More than one cup of coffee and I'm bouncing, which wouldn't be a great first impression. Some studies suggest that people with bipolar should limit their caffeine intake.

Caffeine boosts dopamine levels, which is why people feel a pick-me-up. This uptick can be problematic for some people. It may also affect some medications (for example, coffee's diuretic effect lowers lithium levels). I have a full schedule that weekend:

Friday 4 p.m. – Starbucks: Brian. A cop five years younger than me. I'm a bit worried about his age, but he turns into a second date the following week at a golf driving range.

Saturday 10 a.m. – Second Cup: Paul. Very nice guy, but everything on his profile is off. He actually lives in Boston, even though he listed Toronto as his home. He says he travels to Toronto a lot on business and may move here. He also admits he is five years older than he indicated, making him 15 years older than me. Too bad about those lies, because otherwise he's cool.

Saturday 12 p.m. – Starbucks: Andrew. Within minutes, we realize we have nothing in common. No hard feelings as we say goodbye and let's keep in touch...though neither of us means it. Home for a quick rest and change.

Saturday 4 p.m. – Independent coffee shop in neighbouring city: Armeen. This guy is weird. He downs his coffee in five minutes and says, "Let's get a real drink." I should probably say, "No, I'm good," but I don't feel I got to know anything about him in those five minutes. I want to at least give him a chance. We agree to each drive ourselves to a nearby restaurant. Just for a drink, not a meal – a safeguard to keep my easy getaway strategy. We can't resist ordering bruschetta, however. And that raises a red flag. Armeen looks at me picking off pieces of bread and setting them aside.

"You're not going to eat that?" One of my weight management strategies involves leaving behind as much of the starch as I can on the plate while still enjoying the good stuff. I try to think about whether the calories are worth it. I love the tomato topping of the bruschetta; the bread is a mere vessel to get more tomatoes into my mouth. I understand everyone is raised differently, and I was raised that I didn't need to eat everything on my plate. I can save it and eat it later, or not at all. When I tell him my thoughts on picking and choosing what I want to eat, he looks upset. My jaw drops when he tells me I need to eat the pieces. He watches me eat them one by one while he drones on about his business, his boat, his house in the Middle East. While my profile does indicate I want an "ambitious" man, I'm realizing I should add "humble" as well. I finish the last crumb on my plate and thank him for the drink, telling him I don't think we are a fit, as I make a quick exit.

Thankful to be home, I put on my PJs and settle in to watch a movie in my quiet house. And to screen more potential matches. Obviously, I need to improve my screening skills. How did a liar and the clean-your-plate police sneak in? I'm hoping my two dates tomorrow go better.

Sunday 10 a.m. – Starbucks: Don. Avid skier, but our conversation doesn't have much depth other than skiing. At least he seems quite normal, but no connection.

Sunday 1 p.m. – Second Cup: Mario. Once again, nice guy, no red flags, but also no connection. There is a bullet to dodge in dating that I hadn't thought about: my scars. In a few years I will laser them off, but for now the multiple scars on my tanned left arm are quite visible. (My wrist scars are lightly faded on my pale forearms, so they're not as noticeable, and the scar on my leg is quite high, so it's hidden under shorts.) Some of the guys are too polite to ask, but I see them glance at them, then quickly away. Others are curious, I'm sure wondering if this is a red flag. When they ask, my answer is always the same – with a coy smile, I say, "Oh, that's a story that needs to be told after a few glasses of wine." I've also returned to therapy, desperate to stay on top of this mental balance I am somehow maintaining. Between the kids, fitness classes, PT clients and now weekly therapy, my schedule is pretty full. But not too full for another weekend of coffee dates.

Saturday 9 a.m. – Therapist's office: Lorena. Finding a therapist is kind of the same as online dating. Do we have a connection? Can we talk about things? Do I like her vibe? Can she give me what I need?

Saturday 10:30 a.m. – Starbucks: Al. When I walk in, I recognize him immediately from his bald head on his profile photos. He is waiting at a table at the far end. He sees me and rises, pulling out a chair as I approach. A good sign. I like chivalry.

I don't think it's dead. I've already had a cup of coffee in the car on the way to therapy, so another would make me too jittery. When he asks what I would like, I give him my favourite order: tall, 1% chai latte, steamed to 140 degrees. He pulls out his Palm Pilot and a tiny stylus. (Palm Pilots were the precursor to smartphones.) I see him scribble my order into his phone. He looks at me and says, "I'll save it for next time." Hmmm, I like his confidence. He assumes there will be a second date.

Our conversation flows easily. Al is Austrian and an avid skier. He seems to know a little about a lot – meaning he can talk about anything and have some knowledge of it. I feel like I can't quite read him, though. I'm not going to pretend that I'm a very good judge of character of people. I often can't pick up on negative aspects. I have a trusting instinct. But I'm very good at feeling people's "energy."

When someone has a positive, light-filled energy, it fills me up as well. A negative energy surrounds me in a dark cloud of doom, bringing down my mood. According to Neurolaunch.com, people with bipolar tend to be empaths, extra sensitive to the energy of those around them.

"Research into the relationship between bipolar disorder and empathy has yielded fascinating insights. Studies have shown that individuals with bipolar disorder often experience heightened empathy, particularly during manic or hypomanic episodes. This increased sensitivity to others' emotions can be both a blessing and a curse. On one hand, heightened empathy can lead to deeper, more meaningful connections with others. Individuals with bipolar disorder may find themselves particularly attuned to the emotional states of those around them, allowing for profound understanding and compassion. This heightened empathy can contribute to the creative and charismatic qualities often associated with bipolar individuals. "On the other hand, this increased sensitivity can also lead to emotional overwhelm and difficulty in maintaining healthy boundaries."

Yet, I can't read Al's energy. My tea is drained, and he looks at me.

"Would you like to go to lunch?" "Lunch?"

I question. I'm thinking, "Does this go with my plans? Just coffee, remember. In and out. No commitment." However, his interesting profile handle of "Black Tie and Blue Jeans" makes me want to know more about him. He sees me mulling it over and offers to drive me. At some point in our conversation, I had brought up my aversion to driving. Living in the suburbs, it's a necessity, but always a little anxiety-provoking for me. My brain goes into overdrive. The restaurant he suggests is on Lake Ontario with a view of the water. Twenty minutes away. I don't want to drive for 20 minutes with a stranger. But he intrigues me. Who is this man whose vibe I can't figure out?

What if I can't figure him out because he is a psychopath hiding his personality disorder? What if he is an axe murderer who takes women in his car and rapes and kills them? Do I drive myself or risk getting murdered? Going with my gut, I choose the chance of getting chopped into pieces and hidden in a suitcase. As I slide into his white Mercedes, I think, "He wouldn't risk getting this nice car full of blood."

We get there safely after all, and sit on the patio, with a beautiful view of the water stretched out before us, seeming to reach to the edge of the earth. Unlike Armeen, he doesn't make me finish the leftover pieces of my appetizer. He doesn't ask me about my scars. Both good signs. This is only the second time I have gone on a second date. Although, is it really a second date if it is the continuation of a first date?

After our entrée arrives, he gets up to head to the restroom, walks a few steps away, then returns. I look up as he approaches the table. "You just look so beautiful," he says. I decide to test him. As I dip my spoon into my gooey chocolate lava cake, I say, "It was tight for me to meet you today because I had a therapy appointment before." I watch his eyes to see how they react. His face betrays no emotion, stoic as always.

"I did a few sessions after my divorce, too," he says casually, as he reaches across the table to sneak a spoonful of my dessert. Lunch has to end, because I have a 3:00 p.m. coffee date with someone else and it's already 1:30. Darn. And tomorrow I have two more dates.

As he drives me back to my car, I realize I don't want it to end. I know I will say yes to a second (third?) date. Sunday's dates are easy. Nothing wrong with the guys, just no connection. I'm a little distracted because I can't get Al out of my mind. I had given him my cell number, and Sunday night he calls, on his way back from his parents' cottage. Would I like to meet for lunch on Tuesday?

I have a space in between my PT clients, so say, "Sure, I'd love to." He suggests a restaurant close to where I will be working, so I don't need to drive too far. Another point for him. I show up in workout clothes; he shows up looking handsome in a suit, coming directly from his office. As the server approaches the table, I feel self-conscious in my casual attire.

When Al tells me how amazing I look, I relax a little. Somehow, he makes me feel comfortable, like I have known him for longer than two dates. He tells me he is leaving for Austria the next day but will be back on Saturday. He is going for only four days to pick up his kids from an international camp they are attending there. I realize his profile age of 44 must be accurate, as his kids are 12 and 14. Seems about right.

Ten years older than my kids. Which makes him 12 years older than me. Two years past the criteria I had set. How did I miss that on my sort and wean?

Even though he will be jet lagged, he wants to see me Sunday, which works out because I have two coffee dates on Saturday, leaving Sunday free.

As Al has treated me to two lunches, I want to treat him. When he suggests we go to Niagara, Ontario's wine country, I feel myself gulp. I know I can't afford a restaurant there.

I don't want to admit that, and instead say I'll bring a picnic. I imagine a romantic scene, like in the movies. We'll sit on a blanket, watch people strolling through the park, and feed each other grapes while sipping wine from our wicker basket.

When Sunday arrives, the sky is dark. The smell of rain is in the air. Even though it is early August, the temperature feels like October. It's not picnic weather. Tucked into the soft leather of his passenger seat, I start to see the green vineyards appearing through our wet windows. I begin to fret about the cost of a restaurant in prime tourist season. I'm thinking that if I order an appetizer as my main, and no wine, I can lower the bill. But we are in wine country. And I've learned Al likes wine...good wine.

As the rain beats harder against the windows, the windshield wipers pick up speed until we can barely hear each other talking. I spot a casual-looking restaurant and suggest it, thinking the prices will be lower. Al says he knows a good restaurant, the best in Niagara.

"This is my treat," he says, eyes focused ahead on the wet roads.

"You packed a nice picnic, but the weather has other ideas."

I try to protest but am grateful when he insists. In the next two weeks, we meet up a couple more times. I also have a few coffee dates with other guys, but no connection to make me want to see them again.

On our fifth date, Al takes me back to his house. His kids are at their mom's. His situation is different from most. His son lives with him full-time, and his daughter with her mom full-time. On weekends, the kids are together at one house or the other. Unconventional, but it seems to work for them. I'm impressed that Al manages his own financial planning business plus a son in rep hockey with multiple games a week. And plays hockey himself in the beer league.

When I walk in his door, I smell scented candles. The glow of candlelight is emanating from the kitchen ahead. My first thought is, "Did he leave burning candles unattended?" Then I get distracted by the size of the house. It's huge.

And it has that odd post-divorce look, as if some main pieces of furniture had been taken and never replaced. The front living room is full of boxes labelled with his ex-wife's name. The paint on the walls has faded marks where you can tell a painting had hung for many years. His divorce had only been a year ago and, like me, he stayed in the matrimonial home. I also smell garlic.

It draws me toward the kitchen. Steaks are marinating on the counter, drizzled with olive oil, pepper and garlic. I see a decanter filled with red wine, and two large wineglasses besides it. Brie is softly melting on a cheese plate. Ok, now I am hooked! I've never been spoiled like this. After we finish the wine, we move to the couch. After the couch, we move to the bedroom. Not being a big drinker, I'm a little tipsy but enjoying the passion. This is something new for me. For so much of my relationship with Tim, I had been unwell or in hospital. Sex wasn't at the top of our to-do list. Forty percent of psychiatric medications cause libido problems.

On the other end of the spectrum, hyper-sexuality often accompanies mania. How is a partner supposed to know from day to day what your response will be?

But Al isn't aware of any of that. We are just two bodies exploring each other, trying to give and receive pleasure. The next morning, I wake up after him. I wonder how I looked sleeping when he got up. Was I drooling on his pillow? I hadn't brought anything to stay overnight, and my mouth has the stale taste of garlic and wine.

I look at my watch and realize it is 9 a.m. And I have a 10:00 coffee date! I gather my clothes strewn on the floor. In his bathroom, I find toothpaste and use my finger to brush my teeth.

I realize I won't have time to go back to my house for fresh clothes and makeup. I don't want to cancel the date, as I would feel terrible standing someone up. Not canceling is one of the things that has carried me through some bad, dark moments. Guilt of canceling means I drag myself there no matter how low I feel. And my mood always ticks up a few notches afterward. I apologize to Al, explaining regretfully that I need to leave. I'd rather stay there, though. I show up at Starbucks in yesterday's clothes, no makeup and bad breath. Not my best effort. I gratefully take the latte my poor date hands me.

I'm trying to be polite, but my heart isn't in it. When I talk to Al the next day, I tell him about my date. He encourages me to keep seeing others.

And to keep seeing him. To explore what is out there. It's both refreshing and unsettling to have a guy so comfortable with me seeing other guys at the same time.

So, I continue scrolling, deleting and answering messages. I go on several more coffee dates over the next month.

On my "no kids" weekends, I plan two or three morning dates, leaving my evenings for Al. Finally, on a Sunday morning, I'm grabbing my clothes once again from the floor of Al's bedroom, rushing off to my next date. I look at him unhappily.

"I don't want to go. I want to stay here."

"I think you should go," he says. "You committed. Then come back here if you want. And if you don't want to, that's your choice too. You have choices."

"I'll go because I don't like to cancel plans. But I don't want to do this anymore. I choose you. I want to date you, and just you." "If that's what you choose," he says. What I want him to say is, "I choose you too." To hug me and whisper, "I've been waiting to hear you say that." But he doesn't. He just walks me to my car and asks if I know the directions. That evening, Tim stops by my house. Lately our conversations have been mostly by email, organizing the kids' schedule or sorting out finances. When exchanging the kids, we have brief, superficial conversations. Both being polite, recognizing the years together, but also aware of our different paths now. When he starts with "I need to talk to you about something," I become more alert.

"I just want you to know that I am dating someone," he says. "I knew that. The kids told me a lady is sometimes there, and that they like her."

I hadn't yet introduced Al to my kids, as I'm still seeing where our relationship is going, so was surprised that Tim's girlfriend seems to be there whenever the kids are.

"Well, she's moving in with me," he says slowly. "Actually, you know her. Christina, from work."

I'm shocked, for two reasons. One, it's only been a few months since we separated. Two, she is someone he's known for a few years.

And that makes me wonder if something was going on before. His voice grows quiet.

"I didn't want you to hear it from the kids. I know it seems soon, but she is going through a divorce too, and living together just makes financial sense for us both." I'm trying to think of what to say.

Definitely not "Congratulations." "I'm happy for you" is wrong, too. At this point I don't want to ask if anything had been going on before. Whatever answer I get would upset me. We've both moved on and things are looking bright.

I don't want to derail my stability with thoughts of what may or may not have been. I think of the S.T.O.P. technique I mentioned in Chapter 6. I take two deep breaths.

"Thanks for letting me know." He gives me a hug, which I accept but don't return. When I close the door behind him, I sink to the floor and let the tears spill from my eyes.

After a few minutes, I pick myself up. I can't succumb to this. I mentally work through a Thought Diary. Our thoughts affect our feelings, our feelings affect our mood.

I play devil's advocate to my thoughts. My thoughts are lying to me. The truth is, I'm finding happiness in my present moment.

I'm finding my strength and my confidence.

I've survived the worst that bipolar can throw at me. I can survive anything.

Reflections and Resources

What is a positive way bipolar has affected your relationships (family, friends, intimate partner)?

What is a negative way bipolar has affected your relationships?

Dialectical Behaviour Therapy (DBT)

The DEARMAN technique is intended to help us develop effective interpersonal communication. Used regularly, it can help us get our needs met while maintaining a healthy relationship. Definitely useful when going through a divorce!

D: Describe the situation, using only facts.

E: Express to the other person how the situation made you feel, and how it has affected you personally or professionally.

A: Assert exactly what you want to happen in the future.

R: Reinforce your message to ensure that they understand.

M: Be Mindful of what you are saying. Think before speaking.

A: Act confident.

N: Negotiate. Be open to other possibilities.

Song: "I'm Not Okay" by Jelly Roll. A wonderful country song that contains my favourite line, "So if I say I'm fine, just know I learned to hold it well."

> *2006*
>
> **3 Thursday** N. Nat.
> 7³⁰ Andy
> 8³⁰ Nancy
> 10⁰⁰ - Lindsay
>
> **4 Friday**
> 9:30 - Chiro
> 11:00 - Step Class
>
> Darrin 8⁰⁰
>
> **5 Saturday**
> 9:00 - Loring
> ~~11⁰⁰ Lindsay~~ ★ 10³⁰ - AL Starbucks ★
> 3:00 Mike - TH
>
> **6 Sunday**
> Lori?
> 10:30 Phillip - Starbucks
> Chandra - ?

Yes - I actually saved the calendar page of our first date! And yes, I have extremely poor handwriting. You should see it during hypomania - fast and furious!

WHAT'S ONE MORE?

"Are you ok? I've already called 911. I was behind you and saw it happen." An elderly woman is walking toward us.

"I think we're all right," I say, shaking, but I really have no idea. I could be missing one leg and not feel it. Adrenalin is pumping through me as I stand at the side of the road looking at my car in the ditch.

The kids are crying, my mom and I holding them tight. I touch their arms, their legs, their heads, feeling for broken bones, looking for blood.

There are sirens in the distance. I see a cloud of dust plumes on the gravel road as a fire truck makes its way toward us.

Four firefighters in full gear get out. Another siren grows louder, and an ambulance pulls in.

Two ambulance attendants approach and ask if we have any injuries. I have no idea. Isn't it their job to find out?

She instructs us to sit in the ambulance so we can have our vitals done. Stress tears start pooling in the corners of my eyes. I shakily explain how my wheels slid on the freshly poured gravel, as slippery as marbles under my tires. I couldn't get control as we veered into the ditch and onto our side, our roof hitting the hydro pole and bouncing us back onto all four wheels. Miraculously, we are all ok. My car, however, is not.

When she asks us, "Is there someone you would like to call? Your husbands?" I start crying.

"I don't have a husband," I say, acting more composed than I am. I feel like wailing, but want to be strong for the kids.

Once the car is towed away and we make it to my parents' chalet in Collingwood, I pour myself a large gin and tonic. I feel muscles that had tightened in impact release as the alcohol hits my system.

I call Al, but the phone rings to voicemail. I need to hear his voice. He is always calm, always confident. He is a problem solver. While I sometimes wish he was more emotional and empathetic, right now I need problem solving. I have no car. No child seats. I need to call the insurance company, get a police report, call the tow yard. It's overwhelming to think of the million things that need to be done.

After another call to Al goes to voicemail, I send him a text. He always has his phone with him. Why isn't he answering?

Hours later, I still haven't heard back from him. I worry that he's gotten into an accident too and has died. Dramatic thinking, but I'm utterly exhausted from the events of the day.

It's not every day you total your car and all four people walk away completely unscathed. I try to sleep, but the sound of gravel crunching under my tires keeps replaying in my ears. Lying in bed, reliving the accident over and over, I finally drift off at 3 a.m.

The sound of my phone ringing wakes me up at 8 a.m. "Al" pops up on the screen and I answer with, "I've been trying to reach you. Didn't you get my voicemail?"

"I was with clients all day and didn't see it until 10:30, and didn't want to wake you. Anyways, I'm in the car, on my way there now. I'll see you in an hour."

An hour later, the doorbell rings. I'm still in my pyjamas, sipping a coffee on the couch. My dad arrived late last night and is making pancakes in the shape of elephants and reindeers for the boys, their favourite animals. I see Al's outline through the door glass. When I open it, he is holding two bouquets of flowers, one for me and one for my mom. And a bottle of champagne. I guess celebrating we are still alive.

That afternoon, Al and I go to see my car at the garage. The mechanic says it can't be repaired. It will be a complete write-off. The realization that I will need a new car hits me. I can't afford a new car. The replacement value the insurance company will give me for my five-year-old Saturn won't cover a new one.

All around me, guys are trying to give me advice. My neighbour, my ex-husband, Al, my friends' husbands. "Toyotas are the best." or "You should get a minivan." or "AutoTrader has the best deals."

I don't know what I am looking for, and I don't want to haggle over a second-hand car that may need repairs in the next month.

There is a Mazda dealer near my house. I wander in, feeling a little nervous. This was always Tim's job. I see a CX-7 that checks all the boxes: lease payment in my price range; two-year warranty; good on gas. It's the first car I've looked at, but I don't care what make I buy. I need a car and I need it now.

The sales guy opens the door with a flourish and says, "Try it out." I sit there for two minutes, not sure what I should be doing. I hop out and tell him I'll take it. No negotiation of price, no questions about the engine or the features.

That night, I'm excitedly telling Al all about it – it's black, it's an SUV, it's a Mazda CX-7 and it still has that new-car smell.

"How did it feel when you took it for a test drive?" he asks.

"A test drive?" I ask, feeling foolish. Of course I should have taken it for a test drive! I'm an idiot! "Well, I sat in it. It felt good. But I didn't drive it." He looks at me incredulously. "You never took it for a drive??"

It had never occurred to me. The sales guy probably thought it was his lucky day. No bargaining, no test drive, no questions. A complete sale in less than 15 minutes.

The next day, I return to do a test drive before filling out the paperwork for the lease payments. The finance guy is sitting across from me, flipping through my application form. "I'm sorry, but you don't qualify for financing. Do you have someone who could co-sign for you?"

I leave the dealer and cry in my rental car. How can I be 32 years old and not qualify to lease a car on my own, or get a credit card, or get a mortgage? I call Al. He always has a way to fix things. But his response is something I never expected, as I've only known him six months.

"I'll co-sign for you."

I return the next day, feeling a little smug, kind of like that scene with Julia Roberts in *Pretty Woman*. The clothing store won't serve her character, Vivian, a sex worker. The next day she returns to the store with Richard Gere. "Do you work on commission?" she asks, displaying her multiple shopping bags from other stores. "Big mistake. Huge."

Would I have felt better if I had qualified on my own merit? Of course. But I'm still leaving with a car, and a feeling that my relationship with Al is moving to the next level.

What's missing is good steady employment with a stable income. With fitness, if I have an injury, I can't work. No workers' comp or disability. Just no income. No groceries, or extra money for books from the monthly Scholastic catalogue Ethan loves so much.

My Pilates friend Melanie recommends me for an office job she is resigning from. It's simple administrative work, 20 hours a week. Plus my classes, plus my clients, plus being a parent 50 per cent of the week. I feel nervous, wondering how I will balance it all. I get the job, not realizing that this would be another macho male hiring based more on appearance than on skills. One day when I had no work assigned, I asked the manager of the office what he would like me to do. His response? "Just sit there and look pretty."

Where was the Me Too movement back then? Where was it when Ken would grab my 19-year-old ass at the work counter of that mailbox business?

Bipolar is an illness with times of depression, mania, euthymia and periods of remission. Triggers can disrupt that remission at any point. I am now at my maximum stress level. Stress and sleep are still my biggest triggers to this day, and something I protect myself against as if I'm guarding the Queen of England.

The pressure from two months of juggling the new office job, personal training, fitness classes and the kids is building. I feel the tornado start swirling up and down, around and around.

One night, three months into my new job, I'm up late, well past my usual bedtime. I haven't been able to sleep properly for days. I think obsessively about my schedule. I look at the schedule on my phone. I transfer it to a monthly paper planner. I print out weekly schedules so I can confirm it a third time. I use different coloured pens: bright green for fitness classes, black for the office, purple for PT clients and red for kid stuff. The calendar looks like kindergarten artwork with its multicoloured, chicken-scratch printing. Just looking at it stresses me out.

My mind begins to whisper menacingly, reminding me of my main stress-relief technique from years ago. "Cut, cut, cut." I have not self-harmed in 10 years. I'm so proud of myself for that.

At this point I have no family doctor, no psychiatrist and no medication. I've been in denial that I even have bipolar. I haven't had an episode for years. I try to block out the images that are stuck on repeat in my head. I stare at my pale forearm and imagine the layers of thin skin, bubbly yellow fat and red muscle under the surface. I push away the thoughts. They return. My mind and I play this game for two hours. Who is stronger? Who will win?

The kids are at Tim's for the night, excited about their newly painted bedroom. Al is off at his 13-year-old son Bretten's hockey game. I'm alone, desperately trying to pull tools from my imaginary toolbox of CBT and DBT, but the tools are too old. I haven't needed them in a few years. They are rusted, broken and misplaced. It's as if I am in a dim basement, with only a solitary bulb swaying overhead. I feel like I'm rummaging through someone else's toolbox, but none of them are right. I throw each one away in frustration. None of them will stop the building tornado.

I urgently want to cut. I want to feel the sting, see the blood and feel relief flood through my body. But I can't. I am a mom. I am a victim of an incorrect diagnosis. I am not bipolar. I am not mentally ill. I am a survivor. I rewrite my schedule several more times. I tell myself how fortunate I am to have three jobs, each with their own perks. I look at photos of the boys' smiling faces. I watch videos of them playing in the yard, tiny plastic golf clubs in their hands, laughing as they try to land balls into the sandbox only two feet away.

I can't cut. I don't want another scar. Instead, I kick the hard wooden coffee table a few times. It feels terrible. It makes me hunch over, clutching my foot to stop the throbbing. This is only pain, not relief.

It's one of those rare October nights that trick you into thinking it is still summer. I'm wearing shorts and look at the scar on my left leg from years ago. Really, what difference is another one? I'm planning to laser my scars to reduce their appearance as soon as I have the money. So, whether it's eight scars or nine, does it really matter?

My first cuts are hesitant. Just scratches. Then, the fourth time, I press the knife deep and drag it. I see the flesh open. A one-inch gap in my thigh – small by past standards, but enough to distract me. Relief floods my body as the endorphins release. For a few minutes I feel better. Then guilt, disgust and disappointment raise their heads. "You've ruined everything!" the voice in my head tells me. "Tim will see it and say you are an unstable mother." "Al will realize you are mentally ill and leave you."

I press a cloth on the still-bleeding cut, then tie a dishtowel as a tourniquet to keep the cloth in place. I'm so angry at myself. I remember how I had to lie when I was asked about my scars on dates. Now I'll have another one and will have to tell another lie. I still haven't told Al how I got the scars, though he once told me that he had a pretty good idea what had happened. But we left it at that, neither one of us wanting to talk about it. I guess we'll have to talk about it now.

A startling sound brings me out of my thoughts. It's the ringtone I had set for Al, the theme song from *Mission: Impossible*. Should I answer it? What would I say? The cut isn't deep, but it's still bleeding and may need a couple of stitches.

"Hi," I answer, trying to sound casual but knowing my voice sounds creaky. Suddenly tears flow, dripping to the corners of my mouth. I taste their saltiness.

"What's wrong?" he immediately asks.

"I've been so stressed. I can't balance three jobs, I can't sleep, I'm having bad thoughts."

"What do you mean?"

"You know how I told you I'd had problems with depression and anxiety in the past, but that it's not a problem anymore? My scars... I did them, I..."

He cuts me off. "Yah, I figured that. But what's going on now?"

"I did it again."

"Fuck!" His response shocks me, the opposite of Tim's empathetic reactions. "Do you need stitches? You know what? That doesn't matter. I'm walking to my car right now. I'll be there in 40 minutes."

He makes the drive in 30 minutes, first aid kit in hand. Within five minutes he's cleaned the cut and puts Steri-Strips on it, pulling the sides of the cut together. I give Al credit. He is not the most emotional man, but he is a very practical guy who gets things done.

He wants to take me to the hospital, but I refuse. I'm experienced enough to know that Steri-Strips will do the job. He can't stay overnight with me, as Bretten is only 13 and needs a ride to school in the morning. If I won't go to the hospital, he insists on taking me to my parents, but I insist more vehemently that I don't want that. They don't deserve to go through this again; they have gone through enough already. As usual, I'm trying to portray myself as the perfect daughter. I want them to be proud of what I have come through, not worry that it is starting again. Instead, we head up to bed, spooning under the warmth of the feather duvet. I feel ashamed, and don't want to talk about it. I don't want to know what he is thinking of me. When I wake up a couple of hours later, his side of the bed is empty. He has gone back to his house. My mind ruminates, assuming he will break up with me tomorrow. I don't know if we are even a couple. We have never formally committed to each other and we're open about occasionally seeing other people.

When I hear his Mission Impossible ringtone in the morning, I pick it up, ready to hear him say that he can't deal with this, that he is not able to take on a girlfriend who is obviously crazy. Instead, he gets to the practical. "How do you feel?" "Do you have any classes today?" "I suggest you go to a clinic and get it checked."

Though the cut is not deep, I cancel my classes and clients for the day. I don't want it to start bleeding again. With my day now open, I feel almost happy. I have a free day. I delete every item on my phone calendar, take whiteout to my multicoloured paper calendar and feel like a bird floating in the sky, able to drift wherever I want. But what I want to do and what I need to do are two different things.

I go to a walk-in clinic near my house to see if I need a stitch or two. I debate lying about how it happened. I've been out of the psychiatric system for years, and desperately want to avoid going back into it. But there is also a part of me that wants help. Maybe I should go back on my meds. I haven't liked the way I have been feeling – unpredictable mood swings, holding it together during the day, then burying my face into our cat Blue's fur as soon as the boys are in bed, my tears wetting her black fur.

The doctor at the clinic is young. I wonder when he finished med school. Or does it just mean that I am getting old? He tells me the cut should have had two stitches, but after that many hours there is a risk of infection if he closes it up. The Steri-Strips should stay on. I begin to slide off the exam table, the crinkly paper sticking to my paper gown.

"Can you tell me more about what was going on when you did this?" he asks.

I hesitate, but then give him the Coles Notes version of my story. I admit I need help. I'm a mom and can't slide into depression or mania. When he tells me that the wait time for a psychiatrist is six months to a year, I feel a pit of despair in my stomach. I assume I will need a psychiatrist to prescribe my meds.

Unlike many family doctors in our overcrowded healthcare system in Canada, this clinic doctor is accepting new patients. He is also willing to prescribe lithium, which is the last medication that my psychiatrist at Credit Valley Hospital prescribed for me and has always been the quickest and most effective med for me. That prescription will cover me until I can get an appointment with a new psychiatrist. While many family doctors are comfortable managing depression, anxiety or insomnia, they often refer patients to psychiatrists for long-term mental illnesses like bipolar or schizophrenia, at least for the initial medication decisions.

I'm still on Tim's medical plan, so the cost of the drugs could be covered.

But I don't want him to know. However, I also know that I am on the edge of a precipice, with a slippery slope on either side. Being a generic medication, lithium is not expensive compared to some other meds, so I take the prescription the doctor hands me and stuff it into my purse. I don't realize it, but my kids are saving me. They make me want to be the best person I can be, even if that means putting myself back into the medical system. Actress Selma Blair, who has battled depression, anxiety and alcoholism, credits her kids with saving her life as well. "Being a mother has been everything to me. I don't know if I would've had the energy to bother otherwise. It's too hard. I'm upside down."

As I get back into my Mazda (still with that new-car smell), I look back at the two empty car seats. Yes, I think firmly, I am making the right decision. I still haven't really talked to Al about my full past.

I've used the words "depression" and "anxiety," but never "bipolar." It's 2007 and people are beginning to talk about mental health.

The word "self-care" is thrown around a lot. But people still don't like to talk about mental illness – and bipolar is a lifelong mental illness. I've somehow convinced myself that I was misdiagnosed. A few years earlier, my thyroid began cycling between overactive and underactive. Each fluctuation brought with it a change in energy.

I tell myself that maybe my bipolar was actually an undiagnosed thyroid problem, even though I know that the years of taking lithium are what damaged my thyroid. And even though the endocrinologist – who has more years of medical school than hours I spent on Google – tells me thyroid symptoms do not mimic bipolar symptoms. Then again, that same endocrinologist gave me a breast exam, which felt wrong at the time, but I was too intimidated to say anything. There was no need for him to examine below where the thyroid sits, at the base of the neck and collarbone. So why should I trust his words?

Al plans to come over that evening, telling me he is still worried about me. Ethan and Connor go to bed at 7:30, so we will have the evening to ourselves.

Only last week Al helped me take apart Connor's crib so I could move him to a "big boy" bed, which means he is leaving his bed and coming downstairs every 10 minutes for any multitude of imaginary reasons.

Tonight, though, I need undisturbed time with Al. I need to talk to him honestly. If he accepts my past, I also want to talk to him about being in a committed relationship with each other.

With the kids fed and off to bed, I prepare an adult dinner. I've learned to barbecue, something I had never done before, as it was Tim's domain. (I had always thought barbecuing meant you had to stay outdoors the entire time. I now realize that is just an excuse guys use to hang out in the backyard.)

I wait until the grill reaches 500 degrees and lay two steaks on it, hearing the sizzle. I drop the temperature and go inside to finish making the salad.

I'm not much of a wine drinker, but Al is, so I've opened one of the bottles of Cabernet Sauvignon from a case he left. I'm outside pulling the steaks off the grill when he walks in through my unlocked door.

I limp to him, my leg feeling a little tender as my jeans rub against the wound.

"How are you feeling?" he asks.

"Everything is ready. Let's eat. Connor will probably come down a couple of times."

We talk about what triggered me. My workload. We talk about options. Al is a financial advisor and offers to help me come up with a budget. He encourages me to expand my personal training business, but this only stresses me more. He always thinks bigger is better. Smaller is better for me. What we don't talk about is my mental health.

What I don't bring up is that I picked up a prescription for lithium today. I've even shoved the prescription bottle into a tampon box so he won't see it. I want to bring up that I haven't gone on any dates with anyone else in a few weeks. It's him I want to be with. He is so different than Tim, but he makes me feel safe in a different way. Secure. Looked after. I know that whatever I need, he will be there to help. He may not have the empathetic words or the understanding of mental health, but he will look after me in ways that I need. Unfortunately, I'm still working on looking after myself.

Al and I talk about our relationship. I've done enough exploring. He is the man who makes me feel happy. He is the man I love. I still haven't mentioned the word "bipolar" to him, but I tell him about the hospital stays, the ECT, the suicide attempts.

He tells me, "When we had our first date and I saw your scars, I knew you were messed up somehow. But I couldn't resist. This is something I still remind him of to this day whenever "Bipolar Sandra" makes her appearance."

"You saw the scars, I told you I was coming from my therapist; that was your chance to run. And you didn't." The next week, I resign from the office job.

I pretend that my expanding fitness business has to be prioritized. Instead of viewing my decision as a sign that I am succeeding as a personal trainer, I view it as one more job I couldn't handle. One more thing I've messed up.

Reflections and Resources

What is in your mental health toolbox?

What strategies have you tried that worked for you?

What strategies have not worked for you?

DBT Mindfulness

Mindfulness means being in the present. It can be simply described as observing, describing and participating in a moment. For me, it helps to distract me from anxious or intrusive thoughts.

My favourite exercise is to take a moment to observe what I'm gathering in from my five senses. It doesn't have to be anything dramatic. For example, tonight after dinner:

What can I see? – The leaves on the big oak tree in my backyard.

What can I taste? – The meat sauce from the pasta dinner.

What can I smell? – The faint aroma of onions, tomatoes and beef.

What can I feel? – The cold kitchen tile beneath my feet.

What can I hear? – The whooshing of the dishwasher.

It's great to practice mindfulness even in moments of stability. Last week I realized I was rushing through a hike, thinking of all the other things I needed to be doing. Meanwhile, all around me, nature was in her glory, begging me to stop and enjoy what she had created. I paused and saw the sun creating dappled light on the trail. I tasted the cleanliness of the water I had just sipped. The earth smelled rich and woodsy. I could feel the breeze on my skin and hear the birds in the sky. I was present. I was mindful.

Song: "Diagnosis" by Alanis Morissette. She has been open about her early struggles with bulimia, and later, after the birth of her third child, she announced that she had experienced postpartum depression with every pregnancy. Another great song from this album is "The Reasons I Drink."

My dating profile had said "Must ski". I found my skiing partner.

A Wedding in a Blizzard

They say the five biggest stressors in life are divorce, moving, illness, death of a loved one and job loss. I've crossed three off my list, and a fourth is right ahead of me.

It's March 2009, and outside my window the gusts of wind are blowing the shutters on the plastic playhouse in the yard, each slam as familiar to this house as is the creak on the third stair. In a few months, I'll be leaving the only home that has been mine and truly mine. After three years of dating, I am readying to move into a house that is still cluttered with Al's past and his life with his ex-wife. There are boxes with her name written in fat, black marker tucked into corners of the basement. Half-used face creams and old makeup abandoned in the bottom drawer. How is this a fresh start when I am the one cleaning out another woman's stuff to make room for my own?

I'd been at a crossroads in my relationship with Al. He was content with our arrangement, enjoying each other's company but living our own lives. I wanted more commitment and stability, and if that wasn't going to happen, I wanted to explore whatever or whomever else might be waiting for me. I had told him early in our relationship that I would eventually want to live with and marry whomever I was in love with. I'm an old-fashioned romantic at heart. Or maybe I grasp on to people who can hold me up if I fall down. The words in Elton John's song "Candle in the Wind" resonate with me – "Never knowing who to cling to when the rain set in." Al is very good at holding me up when I need it.

Despite my history of hospitalizations, self-harm, suicide attempts and ECT, he doesn't seem concerned that I might spiral again. We both silently hope the pain and devastation will remain in the past.

I'm joining a family where feelings are not discussed, especially in regards to mental health. As welcoming as my in-laws are, I know that opening up about my struggles is not something that would be comfortable for anyone.

It's 2009 and the understanding of mental health is greatly improving, but the understanding of mental illness is not. They are two different things. I've heard it said that you can have mental illness and good mental health, and you can also have no mental illness and poor mental health. That's both a brilliant statement and a hard concept to grasp. Media portrayals of bipolar are depicted as out-of-control mania, potentially dangerous and debilitating. Until the name was changed to bipolar disorder in 1980, the DSM label was manic depression. Even after the manic depression label was changed, it still took many more years for it to stop being used. Even today, the media rarely highlight the lawyers, businesspeople, entertainers and stay-at-home parents living a successful, well-managed life thanks to proper treatment and support...because that's boring. That's just normal life. But with medication, lifestyle adjustments, therapy and a toolbox of coping techniques, all this is within our grasp. I'm proof it is.

Al sometimes says that as he sat across from me at my kitchen table watching me sign the listing papers for my house, he realized that he was now responsible – for everything. Finances, as I make 10 percent of what he does. Having a live-in girlfriend with past mental health problems who still has ups and downs. Being a step-parent to two little boys. A big weight on his shoulders, but a weight he says he is prepared to carry. Yet, when he sometimes brings this up in moments of frustration, I'm hypersensitive to my perceived faults and read his words as meaning he regrets taking on this responsibility. Having taken on me. My thoughts spiral further to thinking he must not love me. I can't tell you how many Thought Journals and 'Put Your Thoughts on Trial' worksheets I have done on this, at different stages of our relationship. It always turns out to be the same Unhelpful Thinking Styles. I am Making Assumptions, Catastrophizing and Mindreading.

When the school year ends, a small moving truck pulls up to my house, and two guys with biceps bulging out of their sweaty T-shirts begin loading my belongings. I have already sold almost all my furniture, keeping only the kids' bedroom set, hoping to recreate a room that is familiar and cozy to them. The rest of the truck is packed with boxes brimming with photo albums, clothes, toys, fitness equipment, paintings and personal items. When I started lithium again three years ago after the isolated relapse into cutting myself, it was never my intention to stay on it long-term. After a year of taking it, I tapered myself off it. I still find myself wondering, "If I truly had bipolar, wouldn't I be unstable still? Wouldn't I have spiraled into a manic or depressive episode during the stress of parenting young children through a divorce?"

I never returned to the family doctor who had prescribed that lithium, because I knew I would be told that I needed to keep taking it or risk a setback.

Moving in with Al brings several concerns. How will his children adjust to me and my boys living there? How will my children adjust to their new house and school? Ethan and Connor love that they now share a room, with Ethan on the top bunk and Connor on the bottom bunk. They spend their evenings playing long after they should be asleep. Al's daughter, Alexis, makes it clear that she is not happy to have rambunctious, loud boys around. She mostly stays at her mom's, but on the nights she is with us, I try to take the boys to the park the moment they wake up and let them run off their energy outside, playing as loudly as happy, healthy kids do. Like many 16-year-olds, she has been acting out, stretching it to the limit with both her mom and her dad. The house is filled with tension when she is there. She and her brother, Bretten, don't get along. She and her dad don't get along. I feel like I am soon going to be in the same target zone. I don't want my kids picking up this negative energy. At 14 years old, Bretten is quite neutral to the whole situation. His life is about skateboarding, hockey and hanging out with his friends. He's an easygoing kid. He tries to stay out of Alexis's way and seems happy to have some more energy in the house, which Ethan and Connor definitely bring. They are in awe of him, a "real teenager," and scavenge all the toys he has recently abandoned in his teenage-hood.

My stress load has increased with the move. I have 40-minute drives back and forth to Tim's house, dropping off and picking up the kids. I'm also still teaching and training clients in Oakville – 40 minutes away as well – until I can find work here. And a bigger house means more upkeep, and four kids means more cooking and cleaning.

Two months in, Al suggests an adventure weekend getaway to go whitewater rafting. The adventure doesn't last long, however. Navigating a rapid, he gets tossed out of the raft, cutting his leg; he develops a serious infection that leaves him limping with a cane and on an IV for four weeks. I've gone from living with two cuddly boys to living with an injured boyfriend, an active 14-year-old boy and an extremely emotional teenage girl. I have no idea how to parent teenagers. And, besides, I am not their parent. I don't want to replace their mom or dad. According to a book I read titled *Stepmotherhood*, I should be there to offer support, guidance and friendship, not to take control.

Just as soon as Al is mobile, off the IV and back to full functioning, another wrench gets thrown into our lives. There was a fire at Alexis's mom's house – Alexis is coming to live with us.

I find myself looking forward to the days when Ethan and Connor are with their dad. I need a break – not from them, not from my step-kids, but from life in general. Things are harder than I thought they would be. I find myself crying on the floor of my closet, overwhelmed with all the things being thrown at me. I'm scared that I may be slipping into depression, but I don't feel the darkness and the bleakness that usually comes with it. Instead, I feel the racing heart and fast shallow breaths of anxiety. I also feel a burning rash on my left rib cage. It's small but feels like electric bolts shooting into my ribs.

After two days, the pain of the rash is intensifying. I don't have a family doctor here, but I've driven past a walk-in clinic a few times, so when the pain gets really bad, I go in. The moment I meet Dr. G., I like her energy. She is young and speaks efficiently, but also with compassion.

She peers at the rash and asks if I had chicken pox as a child. Of course I did – we all did in the '70s. In fact, our parents had "chicken pox parties" to purposely spread it and get it over with.

"Shingles," she announces, taking off her gloves with a snap.

"But I'm too young to have shingles," I protest, thinking she needs to look at it more closely.

"People can get shingles at any age," she says. "Are you going through any stress right now? That's a common trigger."

While I'm shocked to have "an old person's rash," I also feel validated. The stress isn't just in my head; my body is reacting as well. I don't tell her about my past medical history. I don't want to go down that path. I just want to get rid of these electrical pulses in my ribs. At this visit, I thought she was just a walk-in doctor who would prescribe a cream for me; I'd walk out the door and never see her again. Little did I know that just over 10 years from now, she would make a decision that would send me back to the Psych ward and save my life.

Four weeks later, I finally have an appointment with a different family doctor who is accepting new patients. Connor has started kindergarten and Ethan is in Grade 2. I have taken on some fitness classes at the nearby community centre, with the plan of slowly shifting my workload closer. The uncomfortable jumbled race in my head should be calming down, not picking up speed. But Instead of slowing down, my anxiety intensifies.

My senses are on high alert, my shoulders and neck stiff with tension. My heart seems to be beating faster and louder. I look down at my chest, half-expecting to see it visibly beating in my chest, but it is safely inside my rib cage. I know that I am not depressed and I know that I am not manic. I'm just stressed, like many people in these modern times. I don't have bipolar, remember?

There are seven other people in the family doctor's small waiting room. I'm a few minutes early for my appointment, and the receptionist tells me the doctor is running a bit behind. No problem, I think, pulling out my phone to pass time with Angry Birds. Thirty minutes later, only one person has gone into the doctor's office. At 7 p.m., the receptionist starts gathering her papers. "He will come out and call you when he is ready," she says to the six of us watching her go.

An hour later I'm still waiting, becoming more anxious. I'm texting Al, looking for some kind of reassurance. With three people still ahead of me, I have fidgety energy pulsating through my muscles. I need to get up. I need to move. I need to leave. I need to see the doctor. I call Al, stress tears brimming in my eyes.

"Give me the address; I'll come and wait with you," he says. That is one of the things that I love about him. He takes action. Fifteen minutes later, he calls me from the parking lot.

"The building is locked. I can't get in."

"I can't leave. What if that's when he calls me in?"

I swallow some hiccups. "I don't want to stay any longer, though."

"Can you look out the window and see the parking lot?" he asks.

I get up and go to the window. At first, I don't see him, but then I crank my head all the way to the left and see him standing outside his car, looking in my direction. A sigh escapes my lips and my shoulders drop down.

"I'll be waiting here," he tells me. "When you come out, I'll still be here." Just knowing he is there makes me feel better. As I sit back down in my chair, still warm from 90 minutes of me sitting in it, the doctor emerges and tells me to go to room number four. I assume he will be following me, but after a few minutes alone, I realize he must be with another patient. It's not just about waiting – it's about everything. Meeting a new doctor, revealing my complicated mental health history, the stress of work and home life – I'm feeling everything at once. This is compounded by bipolar. My body feels like a live wire, every nerve buzzing with unease. A few more minutes go by, and every inch of my body is filled with anxiety: anxiety about meeting a new doctor, anxiety about revealing my past mental health history, anxiety about having waited two hours, anxiety about work, home, kids, my relationship with Al.

When the doctor enters, I see that he is older than I first thought. He apologizes for the lateness and explains that his elderly mother is quite ill, and it backed up his day. It's obvious to him that my emotional state is not good at this moment. He leans back in his chair and crosses his ankle on his thigh as if we are having a social chat. I'm sitting upright, fidgeting with my hands and feet. He doesn't ask why I am there but instead asks me what I do for work, do I have children, do I have pets? I don't realize it at the time, but he is trying to put me at ease, to lower my visible frenetic energy. I explain that I have had problems with depression and anxiety in the past (still not bipolar!) and that I am here because the anxiety is affecting my life. After a few more questions, he prescribes 90 Ativan tablets. That is a huge amount: benzodiazepines like Ativan are an addictive medication. For example, my current doctor only prescribes 10 at a time, to use as a "Plan B" when I can't regulate myself back with my usual toolbox of coping techniques. It's actually irresponsible of this doctor to write such a large prescription for someone whose history he knows so little of. Though I am grateful to have a little chemical help for the moment, I decide that he isn't the right doctor for me.

As the hot days of summer become cooler, things begin to stabilize at home. We become used to the routine, the kids are happy, Bretten and

Alexis are back at school, and I begin to feel more confident in my living situation.

Al helps me build my personal training business by transforming the unused formal living room into a personal training studio. I begin training clients at home, taking away the stress of driving from client to client. It also allows me to work when the kids are home, even if they occasionally peek in through the door, making silly faces at my clients.

It's easy to believe everything bad is behind me. I'm living in a large home, financial worries are gone, and I have a guy who is dependable and generous, both to me and to my kids. We have adventures together – weekend trips on his motorcycle, skiing in Europe and hiking waterfalls in Jamaica. Life is good. I am stable. I've come out the other side from the living hell of my 20s.

After almost three years of living together, I finally get a proposal. It's Christmas morning at my parents; Ethan and Connor are busy playing with their new toys and we adults are enjoying the last sips of our coffee, our traditional Christmas croissants already gobbled down.

"One last gift," Al says, handing me a long, flat box. I open the box and pull out two fuzzy, brown gloves. My mom, who's sitting beside me, takes one. "Ooh, these are soft," she exclaims, beginning to put it on.

"Sandra," Al says hurriedly to me, his voice a bit more intense than usual.

"Try them on."

Confused, I take them...and feel something hard at the bottom of the left glove. I look at him, but his emotions are hard to read, as usual. I pull out a beautiful diamond ring, with a large square centre rock and two smaller ones beside it. It fits perfectly. My life feels perfect. What a change from a decade ago. There will be no more grippy socks in my future.

Fast-forward one year later, to January 2013. I'm struggling to get into my ski boots, trying to stop the tears that are brimming in my eyes from dripping out onto the slushy floor of the ski chalet.

Months of planning have led to this moment: a wedding ceremony atop Whiteface Mountain in Lake Placid, New York, with friends and family taking in the stunning scenery in the background. But instead, the day has begun with chaos. A swift stomach bug has been sweeping through our guests and family. My nephew, niece, brother and sister-in-law, and now...10-year-old Ethan. I silently plead to the universe – please don't let Al and me be next. With only two hours until our ceremony, I look out the window and see the wind picking up, snowflakes twirling faster. Al's phone buzzes in his pocket. It's the ski resort. They need to close the gondola because the blizzard is causing high winds. Our best option is to have our ceremony at the base, just outside the lodge that sells chicken fingers and French fries.

So, instead of a breathtaking view of the surrounding foothills, we have a ski school of five-year-olds practising turns behind us, strangers stopping mid-ski to take photos, and the stomping of ski boots as people try to shake the snow off before heading in for a hot dog or burger. I'm in my white ski suit and helmet veil, which is instead haphazardly pinned to my undone hair and threatening to blow off with each wind gust. Al stands beside me in a black ski suit, his bald head freezing in the cold temperatures.

Our guests are bravely pulling their hoods closer around their heads, taking gloves off only briefly to take photos, then blowing on their hands. And poor Ethan? He never makes it. He's still back at the hotel, trying to keep down banana slices. This is not what I had envisioned. As we read our vows to each other, shaking from the cold, the word we both bring up is "adventure." My mind shifts. This wedding is an adventure, and we will have a great story to tell. The snow is now slowing down and landing softly on my eyelashes. I hear our family and friends clapping, and strangers yelling "Congrats!" as they ski by. The officiant pronounces us officially married and finishes with well-thought-out words to ease my disappointment. "At least your marriage is not going downhill on its first day."

Reflections and Resources

Our body reacts to stress and mood in physical ways. It does not have to be as extreme as shingles, but can manifest as muscle tension and changes in our blood pressure and energy levels.

What are the physical symptoms you feel when depressed? For example, I sigh a lot, because I feel like I can't catch my breath. My body feels heavy and slow.

What are the physical symptoms you feel when hypomanic/manic? I feel like my body is vibrating, and my enthusiasm wants to burst out of my skin.

CBT – Putting Your Thoughts on Trial

When we are depressed, our mind tells us untrue thoughts such as, "You're a burden; they don't love you; you are not smart." For example, I incorrectly believe that because I have never successfully worked full-time, I am not valuable. Let's put those thoughts on trial:

The Thought – Because I don't work full-time, I am not valuable.

Evidence For the Thought – 1. I don't contribute a lot financially to the household. 2. I get stressed when my schedule is too full, and it affects my family.

Evidence Against the Thought – 1. My fitness class participants often tell me how great my class makes them feel. 2. The kids benefit from my being home more and being available for them. 3. I do a lot around the house, which take the load off Al.

The Verdict – 1. I am valuable to society by improving the health and fitness of the community. 2. I am valuable to my kids by having time to help with homework, snuggle on the couch and drive them to activities. 3. I am valuable to Al by taking care of tasks and freeing up his time.

This YouTube video does a great job of explaining the technique simply:

Song: "Hurt Alone" by Witt Lowry. We all need a friend like this, ready to sit by our side during difficult times.

Our blizzard wedding adventure!

THE TORNADO SWIRLS AGAIN

The sun has just risen when I take a break on the baseball bleachers in a Little League park. I've been pedalling hard for over an hour, trying to burn off the excess energy that had kept me tossing and turning all night. When the clock struck 6 a.m., I felt it was a reasonable time to start my day, a stark contrast to my usual preference to sleep in as late as possible.

Sitting on the bleachers, I pull out my phone and call my parents, even though it is only 7:30 a.m. I'm buzzing with excitement about the 80-kilometre race I impulsively signed up for last night at 1 a.m. This is only my third ride on my new road bike and I'm still getting used to the curved drop bars, so different from my mountain bike, but I'm confident that 80 kilometres should be no problem. The charity ride that Al and I did last year in the spring of 2014, 220 kilometres over two days, stirred a passion in me for cycling. Pedalling, one rotation after the other, is now my form of meditation. Sometimes challenging and exhausting, other times exciting and energizing, but it always brings balance to my mood. I'd had rotator cuff surgery six months ago, and I am still emotionally struggling with not being able to do activities to my usual full extent. Losing one of my main coping techniques has been hard. Exercise is the biggest tool in my toolbox, and it's gone. Biking is the first activity I've been able to do to fill that void.

I ramble to my mother about my upcoming race, the trip to France we've just returned from and the kids' summer plans. Words are pouring out of me. I start pacing around the bleachers, unable to sit still, itching to get back on my bike.

Mom interrupts. "You're talking really fast. I haven't heard you talk like this in a while."

This annoys me. I like the way I'm feeling, and I like the speed I'm talking. Maybe she should listen better. I tell her I have to go, and jump back on my bike, pedaling fast, trying to outrun the vibrations filling my body. That night Al tells me I'm "buzzing."

It's only been three days since we returned from France, and my sleep schedule is still out of synch from the six-hour time difference. I haven't experienced a full hypomanic episode in years. Still, this buzzing feeling is as familiar to me as the mole on my upper lip. I like it. I feel like a butterfly dancing from flower to flower, pollinating the world with beautiful colours. I want to share this joy, and feel sorry for those who are not seeing the soft yellow petals and the waxy green stems swaying slightly in the wind as the flowers smile back at me.

Ethan and Connor are happy to have me back from the trip. I'm at my best – a fun mom, an unstressed mom, a mom who has the enthusiasm to bake like I own a bakery. I make brownies, cookies and banana bread. For dinner I plan to make one of the kids' favourites – homemade pizzas. I pick up the ingredients I need – cheese, sauce, the special Italian flour I use to make the dough. I head to the self-checkout. The thought of waiting in line irks me. I don't have time for this. I have food to make.

As I push my cart toward the exit, something catches my eye: a 4x2 foot painting on an easel. It's a vibrant, abstract Indigenous print that immediately draws me in. I see a bear, a bird, a fish; every animal speaks to me. I've always felt that nature is my religion – Mother Earth, Father Sky, the sun, the wind. In my hypomanic state, the animals in the print are almost singing to me.

The price tag states the cost is $200. Oops, that's just the starting bid in a blind charity auction. I do not want to lose to a higher bidder. I quickly scribble $650 on the slip of paper beside the ballot box, along with my contact information. I head to my car and forget all about it.

After dinner, I go for a walk with my neighbour and good friend Kim. She is my walking buddy, my "Hey, want to have a gin and tonic on the porch?" buddy, my tell-it-to-me-like-it-is buddy. She is also a physician, and one of the few people aware of my bipolar diagnosis.

We head toward our favourite path, only a block from our houses. I have so much to tell her. So much to get out of my head, out of my mouth, and into the world. I dominate the conversation, rattling on and on until Kim stops walking and turns to me.

I see she has her "doctor face" on but, keeping a casual voice, she says, "What's going on, babes?" "I registered for nutrition school!" I say excitedly. "You know how I've always talked about it? I'm actually doing it!" "You're spinning. Have you been sleeping?" I admit I haven't, but that it's just jet lag. Lack of sleep is a major trigger in bipolar, so travelling across time zones can be tricky. On this trip there had been no time to recoup the lost sleep, as we were busy every night with Al's conference colleagues, drinking and eating too much, and sleeping too little. Another trigger – overstimulation.

"Maybe go see Dr. G. Get something to help you sleep,"

Kim suggests. Dr. G. is the physician at the walk-in clinic I had seen for my shingles; she has since become my go-to family doctor. Kim is the third person who has commented on my high energy level.

The next day, I suggest to the kids that we go to the park. They grudgingly agree, even though at 13 and 15 years old, they are now too old for the playground. This is more for me. I even take a turn on their scooters and swing on the swings. I'm having more fun than they are. Why not? Who says adults can't enjoy the playground too? What's with that grandmother on the bench staring at me? I've always been the type who prefers to be in the midst of the fun rather than sitting on the sidelines watching.

After another sleepless night, I head to the walk-in clinic, hoping Dr. G. is in. I'm feeling irritable now. The happy, buzzing feeling is dissipating, morphing into something else. We've touched on the topic of my mental health at past appointments, but I have always brushed away her concerns. When she enters the tiny exam room, I'm standing, looking at a picture of the skeleton on the wall. The knee bones fascinate me. "I'm only here because my friend, who is a doctor, told me I should come," I start. "My mom, too – she thinks I'm talking too fast." I don't sit down; instead, I continue to ramble, explaining that even though I'd been diagnosed with bipolar in the past, I don't have it anymore. I'm just excited about biking, and no one seems to understand this. She raises her hand in a "stop" signal. "Can I talk for a moment?" she says, telling me to take a seat.

"I agree that you are talking fast. I'm having a hard time following you. I know that you previously said you don't want to be on medication, but I'd like you to discuss your options with a psychiatrist."

I try to explain that I don't need a psychiatrist, I just need sleep. Dr. G. begins typing on her computer. "I'll prescribe zopiclone for sleep. That should help slow things down. I'm also sending a referral to Brampton Civic Hospital. In the meantime, try to take it easy. Don't make any big decisions." That night, I get the first full night's sleep in days, thanks to the zopiclone.

When I open my eyes at 8 a.m., I notice I don't feel vibrations coursing through me. I feel – normal. Just normal. Nine hours of sleep have put a stop to my growing mania. A few days later, I feel a heaviness building. I'm curled in bed, crying. It's 9:30 a.m. and Al has delayed heading to the office, trying to rouse me. I'm supposed to be teaching two classes at 11 a.m. I don't know why I am crying, which perplexes him. It perplexes me, too. How can I explain that this is just what happens? I've been down this road many times before. He's just never been on this journey with me. "My legs are too heavy," I tell him. "I can't get them off the bed." He takes hold of my legs and swings them over the side of the bed. "You just have two classes today. Two hours. That's it." I bury my face in my hands, sobs heaving my shoulders. I feel ashamed. I'm afraid my legs won't hold me when I stand up. Al goes to the closet and pulls out some leggings and a tank top. "What about this? What else do you need? A gym bag or something?" I feel more shame. How many people have the luxury of only two hours of work, doing something they love? I'm a terrible person for not appreciating my life. I don't deserve what I have.

He's right, though. It's just two hours. If I don't do these classes, the tornado will spiral faster. I think of the CBT tool of rating one's mood both before and after an activity. I know the score never goes up with lying in bed crying, but it always goes up with exercise. Teaching fitness is like acting. People want energetic and bubbly. Half of what makes a great instructor – maybe even more than the actual exercise instruction – is personality. I just need to fake a smile for two hours.

My first class is seniors' fitness, and many of the attendees are regulars, there as much for social connection as exercise. One guy makes me laugh with a corny "dad" joke. "Why did the airplane get sent to his room? Bad altitude!" he says.

When I pick the kids up from the bus after school, I plaster on a smile and ask about their day. I even cut off a few slices of Pillsbury chocolate chip cookie dough and pop them in the oven. I'm acting the role of a good mom.

O ver the next few weeks, I can't shake off what I know is building toward a deep depression.

Now I want help. I don't want to feel this way anymore. I'm still getting the kids to their activities, helping with homework and cooking dinner, but I'm just going through the motions. The moment I'm done, I retreat upstairs and bury my head in my pillow.

Al doesn't understand. "You have no stress right now. What is it you need? Do you want to work less? Is it the nutrition course? You don't need to do it. Is that what it is?" He's desperate to find a reason for my depression, so that he can fix it. But it isn't fixable.

Five weeks earlier, I'd put a $500 deposit on a Registered Holistic Nutritionist course, during what I now recognize was the surging confidence of hypomania. How can I manage it now? I'd signed up for the online version, which is estimated to be 10 to 15 hours a week for two years. What was I thinking? I burrow into bed, distraught at my impulsive decision. I don't want to lose the deposit. I don't want to fail at something again. My muscles and joints ache, stiff from being burrowed under my duvet for two hours. The bipolar roller coaster has swung down again to the deep pit of depression.

My cellphone vibrates on my nightstand. Reluctantly, I roll over and look at the call display. It's an unfamiliar number. The last thing I want is to talk to someone. I let it ring.

The next day, when I muster the energy to check my voicemail, I hear an unfamiliar man's voice saying, "Congratulations! You are the winning bidder of Norval Morrisseau's print 'Circle of Life.' Please call me back."

I don't even remember what the painting looks like. Now I'm committed to paying $650 plus $80 shipping for something that I only vaguely recall. My depressed and anxious brain tells me, *"You'll be in trouble if you don't pay. What kind of person refuses to give money to charity? If you don't call back, he will keep calling every day."* I dial the number and hand over my credit card information.

What will Al say when I tell him? Another impulsive decision made when my mind was in a world full of sparkles.

But Al seems more disappointed than upset...as if he expected this. With a sigh, he says, "When you see those paintings, it's not really an auction. They have multiple copies. It's just a print. You could have had it for $200."

When the painting arrives, my friend Kim comes to see it, slightly amused by the story. Tilting her head right and then left as she studies it, she says with a smile, "You should call it 'Manic.'"

A week later, on a rainy Monday that suits my gloomy mood, I return to Dr. G. for a follow-up appointment. This time when she walks into the office, I'm not standing inspecting the skeleton's knees, but instead sitting with slumped shoulders, my eyes to the floor. Instead of speed talking, tears well up in my eyes. Without a word, I pass her the Depression Rating Score sheet they had me fill out in the waiting room.

She looks at my numbers, noting my high score. "Are you ready to talk about medication?" she asks.

I nod, thinking of my sweet boys, and how they deserve a mom who is present and happy.

When she asks about which medications have helped me in the past, I think back on all the meds I'd been on in my 20s. But I also think of how I made it through my 30s mostly unmedicated and thriving-*ish*. Then my thoughts turn again to my boys.

"Lithium," I respond, knowing I need to be responsible for my own mental health.

When the pharmacist asks if I've been on this medication before, I hesitate. Do I want to pretend to be newly diagnosed, or admit to decades of bipolar? I tell him the truth. I'm no longer in denial. I know I have bipolar and that jet lag and overstimulation triggered a hypomanic episode.

I go home and swallow the familiar orange and yellow pill. 300 mg. The plan is to titrate the dose up to 900 mg until I see the psychiatrist next month.

Two weeks later, I'm on the roller coaster again. Kim tells me she can see I'm on that ride as soon as I walk up her front porch steps. My body language gives me away. Whenever I was depressed, she could tell by my slow walking pace and downcast eyes. "Agony is optional," she once said brightly. "Your brain just happens to be missing a few chemicals. And guess what? The pharmacy has them."

One month later, I'm at 900 mg of lithium and I'm excited, confident and happy. Too happy. I'm hypomanic once again. And today is my appointment at the hospital. I want to cancel it because I feel so good.

"I really don't think that's a good idea," Al says.

"I'm so on track! I don't need to see him! Here's two reasons. One: I feel good. The depression is over. The lithium is working. Two: I don't want to get back in the psychiatric system again. In London, they just made everything worse."

"You may as well go and see what he says. That's all it has to be. If you don't want to go back after, you don't have to."

The lobby directory says the Outpatient Mental Health Services are on the ground floor. The wording is different from 20 years ago. "Mental Health," not "Psychiatry." Does that mean I shouldn't say "Psych ward"? I don't know what the proper politically correct wording is now.

I unknowingly arrive during the drop-in time for patients receiving antipsychotic injections. A half-dozen people are in the waiting room clutching white paper pharmacy bags with their vials of risperidone, olanzapine and aripiprazole. They are administered every two to eight weeks, depending on the medication, which increases compliance and decreases hospitalizations. I wonder if this kind of treatment would have helped me in my 20s. I hear the nurse call each person's name, see them follow her to a cubicle, and exit one brief minute later, empty-handed and bloodstream full. No worries about forgetting doses.

In my revved-up state, I feel superior to them. I don't need injections. I don't even really need medication. In fact, I don't even need to be here. Dr. Y. has a soft South African accent. It's calming, and encourages me to open up.

I'm riding the pleasant edge of hypomania, chatty and energetic.

Our appointment stretches past the 60 minutes I expected. He asks a lot of questions about my history, and a lot of questions about my current state. Some of them are questions I've been asked many times before and some of them are new.

At the end of the session, he ups my lithium to 1200 mg to prevent the hypomania from progressing to full-blown mania. He also suggests the hospital's 10-week outpatient Mood and Anxiety Program.

In my confident state, I don't see any need for hanging out with a bunch of sad and anxious people, especially when I learn it's two three-hour sessions a week. I'm going to be busy becoming a nutritionist! I'm on a new career path!

The increased lithium dose evens me out for a couple of weeks but gives me the dreaded lithium shakes – fine tremors of the hands. This is common: 35 to 50 per cent of people taking lithium get it, and it is a common reason for discontinuing. The lettuce falls off your fork when you eat salad, and lifting a glass for a toast is embarrassing, as the wine tilts back and forth.

But those aren't my biggest concerns. With the tremors, I don't feel in control of the gear shifters while mountain biking. I've fallen in love not just with road cycling, but also mountain biking. The adrenalin rush and excitement I feel with it are addictive – the need to be fully present, focused only on the trail ahead, picking which line to ride, which rock to hit. It's impossible to think of anything else but the path, rocks and roots ahead of you. Like mindfulness, but on a bike, in the woods. And you need your hands to be 100 percent steady.

So, Dr. Y. prescribes one more pill: propranolol, a beta blocker for blood pressure with an off-label use to stop lithium tremors – which it does effectively and quickly, giving me back my confidence on the trails. Biking gives me more than that, though.

Soulmates don't always come in the form of romantic partners. They also come in the form of friends with a similar "love at first sight" feeling. When I meet Andrea on a ride with the bike club, it feels like I've known her my whole life. She comes into my life just as it's swinging like a pendulum, moods cycling back and forth. Yet she accepts these shifts, taking me for who I am now, and for who I will become when I get to the other side. The increased dose of lithium has stopped my hypomania from building, but now I'm on the other side – the black dog of depression. I can't believe I'm in this cycle of ups and downs again. I don't want to go back to the chaos of my 20s. I have kids.

I have a husband. I have great part-time work in fitness, maybe even a nutrition career ahead of me. That is, if I can get back to feeling normal again and actually complete the program.

On my third appointment with Dr. Y., I arrive in tears. I'm depressed and experiencing suicidal ideation. It's been years since my brain has whispered to me, "You could just kill yourself. You could just kill yourself. You could just kill yourself." Yet rather than admit how much trouble I'm in, I instead question him about my diagnosis. "I'm wondering if it could be peri-menopause? I hear that causes a lot of mood changes."

"Yes, absolutely menopause causes mood changes in women. But it doesn't cause suicidal thoughts. It doesn't cause hypomania. Tell me – how many psychiatrists have diagnosed you with bipolar?" "Including you?" I ask.

"Three out of the four I've seen. Just not the one in high school. I thought maybe you used that diagnosis because I told you that's what I'd been diagnosed with, instead of re-evaluating." He shakes his head gently. "Certainly, I took your history into consideration, but all your past symptoms, and your current signs and symptoms, meet the DSM-5 criteria for bipolar 2.

The assessment tool you completed strongly supports the bipolar diagnosis. The noticeable shift in energy and mood from your last appointment supports it, as does the fact that you have responded well to lithium in the past."

This time, I agree to the Mood and Anxiety Program. A new session starts in three weeks. Al doesn't understand why I'm up one week, then down the next, but he helps in the ways he knows how. And that's the practical stuff. He's a fixer, and frustrated that he can't fix how I'm feeling. But he can cook dinner. He can help me organize my schedule. He can push me to get to work. We are both starting to see the roller coaster slowing down, and that's encouraging.

I feel comfortable enough with Andrea to be open about what's going on. One winter's day, we are in the car together, on our way to a ride with our bike club. Metal studs on our tires; fresh, cold air in our lungs; and a couple of dozen energetic people who don't let snow stop them from enjoying the outdoors.

I should be happy, yet I don't feel the beauty of the winter day.

I really had to force myself to keep my commitment. In the car, I start crying, not wanting to be around all the cheerful people. I test the water with, "I'm a little extra emotional right now.

I'm going through some medication changes." With every nod of support from Andrea, I open up more and more. It feels like such a relief: a secret I have been keeping has been let out. A tight band has been loosened from my chest. Sharing my diagnosis with her means that if I am having a bad day, it's ok not be ok with her. That's such a relief from forcing a smile, faking a laugh. If I need to cancel, she tries to encourage me to come, but if I don't, she's not offended. Why had I not been vulnerable with people before? Slowly, one by one, I start talking to carefully chosen friends. The memory of losing all my friends in my 20s as my bipolar raged is a painful one, but this time every response is positive, empathetic, encouraging. Every response lifts a bit more weight off my chest. I also become more open with healthcare providers. My dentist doesn't know my medications, because telling them my medications would mean revealing my illness, yet lithium decreases saliva production, increasing the risk of cavities and gingivitis.

Seeing my physiotherapist for tendinitis, I say, "You can add as many exercises as you like, but you can't take anything away. I probably won't stop my activities. I have bipolar disorder, and exercise is as important to me as medication."

"I'm glad you told me that," he responds. "We can work around that for sure." At my osteopath, tears begin flowing down my face as his hands work around my head and neck. I had come to the appointment feeling quite down. I'm mortified by these tears, which seem to come from nowhere, but I can't control them. I apologize, explaining that I have bipolar and have been feeling down.

He quietly says, "No problem. It happens. I know you came for your shoulder, but your body needs a lot of cranial work today."

I can't explain it, but my body feels lighter, my head clearer.

It's suggested that osteopathy can activate the parasympathetic nervous system, reducing stress. It may also balance the autonomic nervous system, helping with fatigue, anxiety, and restlessness - all the things I was feeling before my appointment. The change wasn't visible just to me though. I had dropped Connor off at his gym on my way to see my osteopath.

When I pick him up afterward, we haven't even pulled out of the parking lot when he turns to me and says "You must have had a really good appointment."

Feelings of shame and embarrassment, or worries of stigma, make some people with bipolar hesitant to talk about their condition.

Fear of how others may respond is another potential barrier. Things have greatly improved with mental health awareness, but we still have a way to go with decreasing the stigma. Everyone has mental health. Not everyone has a mental illness. In a 2019 Harris Poll, 87 percent of Americans said, "Having a mental health disorder is nothing to be ashamed of." Yet in that same poll, 55 percent said they feel "mental illnesses are different than serious physical illnesses." I wonder, is "mental health disorder" not as scary sounding as "mental illness"?

There is also "self-stigma." This is something that is a huge struggle for me. Self-stigma is described as "having the diagnosis, or having experienced public stigma, which can lead us to feel negatively about ourselves." I subscribe to the International Bipolar Foundation e-newsletter. They often have requests from universities worldwide for participants for research studies. I'm currently in an eight-week study on self-stigma and bipolar. Not only will I be learning how to help myself, but I'll also be improving research that may help hundreds of other people. I highly suggest checking out International Bipolar Foundation ibpf.org

For a couple of years now, I've been working off and on with an amazing therapist, Shelly. We spent our last session working through how to tell the people close to me about my bipolar, so I can get rid of this secret that's weighing me down. Shame and guilt are a frequent topic during our sessions.

I've opened up to a few friends and healthcare providers. Now the ones I try most to shield my diagnosis from are all the kids. By this point, Alexis has moved out on her own. Bretten is away at university and home only on some weekends.

I decide to open up to Ethan first. At 16, he's more emotionally aware and empathetic than a lot of teenagers. He recently had a friend, Aiden, drink bleach in an attempt to end his life, so mental health is probably on his mind.

We are walking to Pizza Pizza to grab a slice. It gives me 10 minutes to get up the courage, with the eventual reward of biting into cheesy goodness.

I open the conversation with, "So, how's Aiden doing?"

"He's back at school. He's not great, but at least doing better."

"Good to hear. Actually, there's something I need to talk to you about. You know how I told you guys I got my scars from falling out of a tree? I'm sure by now you know that's not true. I have bipolar. Since about your age."

The first thing he does is give me a hug. A good, long hug.

A 30-second hug. "Thank you for telling me. I'm so glad you are still here. You are the best mom ever."

I sigh with relief, my shoulders dropping as the secret is released. "I was so worried about telling you. I'd hoped I'd never need to."

Ethan is curious, wanting to learn more. "Why were you worried to tell us?" "What does it feel like?" "Do Mimi and Opa know?" "Does Al's family know?" "Is this why you only work part-time?"

I don't want to wait too long before telling Connor and Bretten, so that nobody feels they were last to know.

The next afternoon, I'm behind the wheel of our blue pickup truck, bikes loaded on the back ready to get to the trailhead that will be the start of today's adventure. Connor and I have a 30-minute drive ahead of us – a good time to talk. Mountain biking is one of my special activities that I do with Connor. It's a pastime we don't share with the other kids.

I decide I'll get right to it and break my building nervousness. "You know last week when I was filling out the medical forms for you at the clinic? There was a section about family history. Because you are 14, You can technically ask to see those forms, and I don't want you to be surprised. Under 'Family history,' I checked off bipolar disorder. I have bipolar."

He pauses for a moment. "Oh, that makes sense."

It's one of the traits we share. We say whatever is in our head before filtering it to see if it's a good idea or not. It's also one of the reasons he often makes me laugh.

I smile, my worry lifting. "I had hoped it wasn't noticeable!"

"I didn't mean it like that," he backtracks. "But now I know why you sometimes get so stressed."

"Do you know what it is?" I ask, taking my eyes off the road briefly to read his face.

"Kind of. Well, just from a show I'm watching. *Shameless*."

"I know of that show," I respond. "I haven't watched it, though. I've heard mixed reviews on how it portrays bipolar. Often media wants to make it more dramatic than it really is." I give a brief explanation, then offer to send him some website addresses.

"Yah, that would be good. Are we still going biking?" I laugh again, his response breaking the tension that only I am feeling. "Of course! It's one of my main coping tools! After you look at what I send you, feel free to ask me any questions."

A couple of days later, he approaches me as I'm watching TV. "Is bipolar genetic?" "When did you know you have it?" "Could I have it?" Understandable questions from a teenager still figuring out their identity. I answer as honestly as I can. "Yes, there is a genetic component." "I'd say symptoms started in my teens."

"No, I don't think you have it, but it's important to pay attention to how you are feeling and to recognize you have an increased risk." That night, I approach my 26-year-old stepson, Bretten, as he's at our kitchen table, eating a late dinner. "Do you have a minute?" I ask. "Sure, what's up?" I pull out the chair beside him, take a deep breath and begin the story once more. He puts down his knife and fork and stops eating, turning his body and his full attention to me. "I wish you had told me earlier. It would have helped me understand things."

A huge weight has been lifted off me. I have received love, respect and curiosity from all three boys. I decide to hold off on telling my stepdaughter, Alexis. She's living on her own now, so there is really no need. She's having a hard time with depression and anxiety, and I don't want to add to her emotional burdens. My next hurdle looms larger in my mind – Al's brother and sister-in-law.

Al and I purchased a cottage last year, and they are helping us tackle the gazillion projects that need to be done, for which I am so thankful. They are ideal cottage guests – helpful, pleasant and enjoyable to be around. Yet when they're there with us, I'm completely drained by the end of the weekend, needing two days to mentally and socially recuperate.

During times when I'm more up and down, it requires tremendous energy to don a mask. Al's family handles emotions differently than I'm used to. More of a "sweep it under the rug" and avoid deep discussions about feelings. This makes it harder to find the courage to tell them, but I need to. There have already been a few weekends when I didn't go to the cottage, not because I didn't want to but because I didn't have the energy to fake it. Finally, one weekend, it is just the four of us, no kids. A better opportunity will never come up.

Through dinner I'm nervously taking extra sips of wine, trying to build liquid courage. When I eventually bring it up, the response is neutral. Not great, not bad. While I don't feel shame, I don't feel the same interest and support as from my friends. A few questions from Frances, then the guys shift the topic away, as if we had only been talking about something as light as what to eat for breakfast. In some ways, that makes it easier, but in other ways it makes me feel more shame. I've seen the family rally around physical illness, helping in any way possible. But this seems like an uncomfortable discussion for them.

The topic won't be brought up for six more years, until I'm frantically scribbling down as many phone numbers as I can before the hospital staff take away my phone before admission. And my sister-in-law Frances will be the one who picks up my calls from the Psych ward the most often. At this point, I'm in the midway point of the 10-week outpatient Mood and Anxiety Program at the hospital. Opening up is something they've suggested: being vulnerable with people is encouraged, to break the shame and receive help from those close to us when we need it. With each person I tell, the elephant of shame sitting on my chest grows lighter and lighter.

The program itself is excellent. Each session has us learn and practice a new CBT or DBT exercise. Of the dozen participants in the program, though, I don't really relate to any.

One woman is suffering extreme grief for a daughter who died in a car accident 10 years ago, in the passenger seat beside her. Another has so much anxiety she had to quit her job. A woman in her 70s has been in depression for five years, and her family is considering transferring her to long-term care.

One young man has just been diagnosed with schizoaffective bipolar, a form of bipolar that also includes symptoms of schizophrenia. I don't feel like anybody is like me. Eight weeks in, one of the facilitators, Emily, asks me to stay behind afterward. She is the younger of the two facilitators and seems to really love her job and to care about us.

"The hospital is running a new group program, specifically for bipolar," she tells me. "I think it would be a better fit for you. What do you think?" "When does it start?" I ask, eager to be done with spending two afternoons a week in a windowless room on the Outpatient Mental Health Ward.

"Next week, actually. I know the abrupt change might not be easy, but this group is only for people diagnosed with bipolar. We've never run it before, so you'd be one of the first ones." I like the thought of being a pioneer, and agree. I jokingly tell Al I've been kicked out of the Mood and Anxiety Program for being too crazy and promoted up a level. The next week, six of us sit in the same room – different facilitators, different patients.

I had expected Sophie, a 22-year-old girl from the Mood and Anxiety Program to be there. The psychiatrists are still trying to confirm a diagnosis, but she sure sounds bipolar in my non-medical opinion. Two hours later, I return home with a smile.

I have found my tribe. These are my people. Every sentence someone said, every experience, every emotion – I could relate. In discussing triggers, everyone lists sleep, stress and disruption of routine.

I look at my worksheet, and see I've written these as well. Under positive qualities we have received from bipolar, creativity comes up. Many creative people are in our tribe – Selena Gomez, Ernest Hemingway, Carrie Fisher, Vincent Van Gogh and, whether we want to admit it or not, Kanye West. And, of course, your favourite author, Sandra Steiner.

I was really happy to learn a new term – hyperthymic temperament. In a healthy balanced state, there is a link between bipolar and hyperthymic temperament, which Wikipedia defines as "increased energy, vividness and enthusiasm for life activities." It's not hypomania, but basically means we are bubbly, energetic people, which is the way I like to view myself – 80 percent of the time. I start this program in February 2020 – which means Covid is just around the corner, and the program will be cancelled after only four sessions. The pandemic opened up crucial conversations about mental health – isolation, lack of resources, job loss, anxiety and fear of the virus itself. I had a different outlook, as did many of the people I know with mental illness. Stress is a significant trigger for those of us with bipolar and, for me, Covid is actually a respite from that. I can cozy up at home, because I know we are supposed to. I'm doing my part to stop the spread.

Many people with mental illness have difficulty explaining that while they look fine, they can't work or, like me, can only manage part-time hours. Now, with Covid, everyone is home! Family time is relaxed, the kids are home from school watching me learn how to bake sourdough bread, like the TikTok cliché. I have a pause from driving them to school bus stops, activities and friends' houses. I can relax without self-stigmatizing myself for not doing more, not *being* more.

Yet even without Covid entering our home, health concerns arise. My recent blood work shows I have raised creatinine levels, indicating my kidney function could be affected by the lithium. When I was in my 20s, I would passively let the doctors make the decisions.

Now I research before my appointments. Of course, it helps that the internet has given us a world of information at our fingertips. I advocate for myself, which takes courage to do. Doctors can be intimidating with their multiple degrees and white coats. To educate myself, I post on a Women's Bipolar Facebook group, looking for advice from others.

According to a 2021 study published by the National Library of Medicine, 10 percent of patients who had been taking lithium for five years met the criteria for chronic kidney disease. The responses to my query on the women's Facebook group vary. Some people have decided to continue with lithium, prioritizing their mental stability over their kidney health. Others try different medication options, but I don't want to play medication roulette at this point.

My interest is piqued by those who say their doctor decreased their lithium dosage and added Lamictal (which is usually prescribed as an anti-epileptic and anticonvulsive drug, but is also used to treat bipolar), and that they loved this combination. The combination has no side effects, as each medication is low dose, but together they work effectively. When I explain to my psychiatrist, Dr. Y., that in an online forum I follow some people who had high creatinine levels decreased their lithium dose and added Lamictal with success, his response is positive. "Firstly, I'm glad you found online support,

" Dr. Y. says. "Sometimes patients have the best suggestions. And, yes, that is an option we should explore. I know lithium has been your most effective med, so I'd prefer to just decrease the dose, rather than stop it. We'll titrate down the lithium and increase the Lamictal over the next month."

The next month is challenging, even with the low stress Covid has brought. My mood swirls up for five days, calms for two, then spins down for five.

What's helpful is that I can now be open with the kids that I'm doing a medication adjustment, and it might take a couple of weeks to level out. After a month of this combination, I can say that I love it. At the lower dose, the lithium tremors are gone, which means I no longer need to take the beta blocker. I feel stable and happy. Both medications are bipolar mood stabilizers, but each manages the opposite end of the spectrum. Lithium has the most positive effect on mania, and Lamictal on bipolar depression.

I feel able to take on a huge responsibility – property management. Al has just made a major investment, acquiring a commercial property with 22 tenants. With the debt of buying the building, there is no money left to hire someone to manage the leases, rent, renovations and tenants.

I offer to do it. I am confident I am making this decision in a rational state, not in hypomania. I hadn't realized how my past decisions in hypomania had affected Al, because he always supports my new enthusiastic interest. He is a man of few words, so just like on our first date, it's hard to read his thoughts. Summer is now making way for autumn, which means tuition is due for Ethan's second year of university. Al is often multi-tasking while listening, but usually seems to absorb what I'm saying. If I doubt he's hearing me, I use my neighbour Lauralyn's trick to pull him away from the computer – talk to him topless. A sure way to get a man to look up. But today my shirt is on. "I need to withdraw money from the RESP to pay Ethan's tuition by next week." Al turns from his computer, looks me straight in the eye, and sighs. "What course did you sign up for now?"

He's assuming I'm hypomanic and taking on a new course, career or hobby. It makes me realize I've never thought how my sudden, excited projects affect him, because he's always encouraged and financially supported me. Over the course of our relationship my brilliant ideas have included:

1. Transforming our living room into a personal training studio, which lasted a solid three years.

2. Getting accreditation to certify other fitness instructors, for which I hosted only one course.

3. Renting space for couples' yoga classes, of which I did one session.

4. Taking online classes to become a Registered Holistic Nutritionist (I finished this program!).Renovating our living room once again as a consultation office for nutrition clients (lasted about six months).

5. Doing corporate wellness presentations. (I was quite successful but quit after a year. The self-doubt and stress overwhelmed me. One night, I canceled my website in frustration and threw out all my promotional material.

My headshot from my business cards stared up at me from the garbage, taunting me, so I threw leftover Caesar salad on top of it. I could not look into my own eyes.) The new combination of meds has made me feel stable and secure about my future. The tools I learned in the hospital programs have enabled me to tolerate stress more effectively and manage my work schedule.

I recognize that low-stress jobs keep me mentally healthy. When I'm in front of a fitness class, I get a boost of confidence and a transfer of energy from them to me. The kudos and thanks from participants lift my spirits and self-esteem. On days when I'm not feeling my best, I remind myself that it is only one hour, and I can maintain that mask for that time.

And like any exercise, be it hiking, biking or weights, the fitness classes are a dopamine boost.

Exercise always leaves me feeling better than before. And the best part? I'd be going to the gym anyway – might as well get paid for it! My impulsive decision to enroll in the Holistic Nutritionist program has brought me to a career path I never expected. While I quickly learned that managing my own nutrition business was too stressful for me, I discovered that I'm pretty good at chatting with customers to educate them on how they can improve their health naturally.

I work with CanPrev, a Canadian supplement company, part-time on my own schedule, with a roster of stores I visit once a month. I chat with the staff about our products, educate customers on what supplements can help them, and get to work with amazing people who are passionate about health.

Through the work training with naturopaths, I've learned to care for myself in other ways. While medication will always be a part of my life, I've discovered that diet, lifestyle and natural supplements also play a vital role in mental health. GABA, a neurotransmitter that we produce but can also buy as a supplement, calms me when I'm stressed. Magnesium relaxes my muscles to help with sleep.

Omegas supports my mood and brain health. Even probiotics help mental health. A 2018 study from Harvard University showed the connection between gut health and mental health. Upon discharge from hospital for a manic episode, 33 patients were given probiotics and 33 were given a placebo, while both groups continued with their regular medication. The probiotic group had a 77 percent lower readmission rate than the placebo group. Among the patients on probiotics who were readmitted, their average stay was 2.8 days, compared to 8.6 days for the placebo group. Pretty incredible for a supplement with no side effects and a host of other benefits.

But even with all these supports, bipolar is a treatable, but not curable, illness. It's always there on the horizon, waiting for us to slip up – forget some pills, a stressful event, a disruption in our routine or sleep schedule. It's lurking in the background, managed but dangerous, like a well-trained circus lion.

And I won't be able to keep the lion at bay forever.

Reflections and Resources

What resources are available for you to improve how you manage your mental health?

What professionals can you reach out to if you are in crisis? (Look back to the Plan of Action you developed in Chapter 2.)

Online Resources

CAMH – The Centre for Addiction and Mental Health in Toronto offers both in-person and online programs with no fees. The is a free, collaborative learning college available via Zoom that offers initiatives such as peer support groups and resumé writing. CAMH is also an in-patient hospital and mental health emergency department.

www.camh.ca

CMHA – The Canadian Mental Health Association organizes several groups, with various focuses – self-esteem, mindfulness, anxiety and, of course, bipolar (I've attended several). They are available both online and in person, all at no cost, are self-referred and have short to no wait times. I can't say enough good things about CMHA, which has locations throughout Canada. The weekly bipolar peer support group gives me grounding and support, and I always leave with a helpful "tidbit" of information.

www.cmha.ca

IBPF – This organization is excellent at providing education and resources. They have a newsletter, webinars and videos.

www.ibpf.org

BPHope - Bipolar Hope has a free quarterly magazine, in addition to other educational resources.

www.bphope.com

Song: "Everybody Hurts" by R.E.M. A wonderful reminder to "hold on."

A cycling fundraiser for youth mental health.

2023 – GRIPPY SOCKS

I'm staring at his gun, only a few feet away from me, within arm's reach. It looks heavy, and I am so tired. I would need two hands to hold it, I think, noticing the strap encasing the gun handle. There are six police officers in the room. Reaching for it would cause them to react, to draw their guns on me. It could all end right here, right now.

These are the kinds of illogical thoughts you have in crisis. It's just part of the chaos in the ER I'm in. If a patient is brought into hospital by police, two officers stay with them until they are either admitted to ward or discharged from hospital. I was forced here by my doctor, not the police, but he is standing within arms reach, guarding another patient. My world has shrunk to the mental health emergency room I have been forced to go to. The nurses in the station in the middle of the square room keep a sharp eye on all the waiting room patients. Occasionally I hear the psychotic, rowdy or angry patients, but I can't see them. They are in locked rooms for the safety of both themselves and the staff. I sit in this square room with people who are staring blankly at their laps and others who are crying uncontrollably, like me. Being a large hospital, there is a separate mental health emergency department, but there is still no privacy. The unit is overcrowded, with chairs squeezed into the small spaces between the beds, trying to fill the growing need for mental health care. While the busy staff are doing their best, this is a scary place for people who have never seen this side of humanity. People like Al, who is trying to offer me comfort but doesn't really know what to say.

I never expected to be back here. In fact, when my family physician, Dr. G., called Al and asked him to meet me at the hospital, I thought I was going there to be prescribed the meds I had stopped taking months ago. When her clinic's pharmacy filled a prescription for Ativan, a sedative, which she wanted me to swallow right in her office, I thought it was to quiet the suicidal thoughts that were incessantly yelling in my head. When she called a taxi for me because she said I wasn't in a state to drive, I agreed, knowing I wasn't in a state to drive. When her clinic's nurse handed me a piece of paper and closed the taxi door, I still thought I would be going home that night. When I read the paper in my hand, I began to clue in. How did I get here? It started eight months before this, and it was by my own carelessness.

It's 2022 – October, my favourite time of year. The leaves are glowing with reds, yellows and oranges. I'm enjoying a mountain bike trip with friends in Vermont. Nine days of riding in the crisp fall air with stunning views and challenging trails. All my best riding buddies are with me, but only two know about my bipolar: Andrea, my closest friend, and Tony, who jokes that my "superpower" is having people always step in to help me.

Vacations always make it difficult for me to remember my meds, but especially this one. Early-morning rides don't leave me enough time for the one-hour gap between my thyroid pill and my bipolar meds. By the time we return from rides, exhausted and exhilarated, I often just forget.

Riding with people brings you close. You literally shed blood, sweat and tears. On the sixth afternoon, halfway through the ride, I feel a tear slip down my cheek. Then another, and another. I'm behind the other riders, struggling to keep up, the tears affecting my vision. I'm mentally and physically drained – not just from the riding, but also from the constant social contact.

All afternoon, I think about how to explain my tears. My stomach dances with butterflies. I've known these fellow cyclists for at least two years. Why do I think I'm revealing a shameful secret? My mind always goes back in time, remembering how I lost all my friends as they blossomed in their 20s and I spiraled in and out of the hospital. Logically, I recognize that mental health understanding has come a long way in the past 25 years. Logically, I know that from the small circle of friends I have already told, I've received nothing but love and support.

As we finish the last bites of dinner, I take a deep breath. I begin with, "I'm sure you've seen the scars on my arm." I reveal my past and my present and highlight my successes, and it's received with love and understanding. A weight is lifted off my shoulders.

Like most people with bipolar, the thought of going off my meds often crosses my mind. As in several times a month. Just to see what would happen. Maybe I don't need them anymore. How will I know if I don't try?

I'd already been taking them only sporadically in Vermont, and when I get back home, I wonder what will happen if I don't take them at all. This year, Ethan and Connor are both away at university. If I go off the rails a bit, so what? My kids won't be there to see it.

The next morning, I put my three pills in my hand: two lithium, one Lamictal. I pause, my hand hovering below my mouth, glass of water in my hand. Then, without a rational reason, I put the water down, and I put the pills in the garbage. I just don't want to take them anymore.

Over the next two weeks I taper down, skipping days. Playing doctor.

I tell Al I am lowering my "chemicals," as he calls them. He doesn't think it's a bad idea. Cut it down a bit and see how it goes. Even though he deals with my pharmaceutically controlled roller coaster, he is a type A who doesn't quite understand mental illness. His personality is controlled, stoic and focused, and it's hard for him to imagine others can't have the same control.

I've also told Andrea that I am reducing my dosage, but subtly imply it is under my doctor's supervision. And then, two weeks later, I stop completely – without telling anyone.

A month later, I need my thyroid medication renewed. Dr. G.'s first question at every appointment is, "How can I help you today?"

I'm feeling a bit nervous, wondering if I should take the lithium and Lamictal prescription and just not fill it, or be honest with her.

"I need my Synthroid renewed." That's for my thyroid.

"Sure, let me just check your blood work from last time," she says, typing into her computer. "Looks good. I'll fax it to your pharmacy."

"Great," I say, getting up from the chair.

"What about your other meds? You should be due for a renewal on them now as well."

"Oh," I say casually, "I'm not taking them anymore."

"Did your psychiatrist change this?" she asks, lifting her fingers off the keyboard, looking directly at me.

"No, I haven't seen the psychiatrist for a couple of years. I've just been getting the repeats from you." It's not uncommon for family doctors to take over prescription refills, as specialists are overloaded with patients. "I can't advise this," she says. "I'll send a referral back to your psychiatrist. This is something you need to discuss with them."

"I'm going to give it a go without meds," I interrupt. "I've been feeling really good."

"Exactly," she says. "Don't you think the medication might be why you've been feeling good?"

"I had quite a few years without meds in my 30s."

"I really do hope things go ok for you, but come back any time you need to. I mean it. Don't wait until things get bad."

I'm touched by her concern and promise her I will.

When I pick up my Synthroid, the pharmacist asks, "What about your others? They're due now too."

"Oh, I'm not taking them anymore," I say, my fingers brushing over the display of cough syrup in my effort to look casual.

"Dr. G. removed them, or your specialist?"

"I only see Dr. G., but she knows."

I'm starting to feel frustrated. Would they ask these questions if I had stopped my thyroid medication?

"It's a trial," I say hurriedly. "If anything changes, you'll see me back; don't worry." I take my white paper bag and rush out the door.

Thanksgiving comes and goes, Christmas comes and goes. I feel good. Maybe I never needed these meds after all.

My parents are fortunate enough to trade the cold Canadian winter for the warm sunshine of Puerto Vallarta every year. With both kids away at university, I have a new freedom that allows me to visit them for an entire month. My fitness classes are covered by other instructors, my CanPrev store visits are delayed until March and the building management tasks can be done remotely from Mexico.

I bring my bike with me, having met a group of Canadian cyclists down there last year. We explore parts of Puerto Vallarta I could never see by car. Children running barefoot on dirt roads in small, poor villages smile and wave as we pass. We eat corn tortillas made by hand in cafés tucked into the back corners of the countryside.

My days are routine and stress free. Remember, bipolar stability thrives on routine, low stress and consistent sleep. Each night I sleep deeply, lulled by the sound of the Pacific Ocean waves crashing on shore and the smell of sea salt in the air.

I never mention to my parents that I'm off my medications. Why would I? Everything is going so well.

Until it isn't.

Returning to Canada is a jarring change. I struggle to catch up with work; I have no routine and an overwhelming schedule.

Items I thought had been looked after have snowballed. The building I'm managing occupies my mind all the time. I don't have the education, training or skills as a "property manager" to deal with the crises that constantly arise, and my confidence in my ability is shattered.

I have extra fitness classes on my schedule and try to catch up on my CanPrev demos.

Everything is piling up at once. I feel overwhelmed all the time. I feel guilty that I took a month off and am now flailing in the storm beginning to fill my mind.

When mid-March becomes warm, and spring is in the air, I meet my neighbour Kim, a physician, for a walk to catch up.

She's on her porch, watching me walk up her driveway. Her first words are, "Did you stop your meds?"

Startled, I ask, "Why?"

"Your face, your posture. I can see it." "Uh, yah, I did. A few months ago," I stammer. "I was doing fine." My chin starts to quiver. "But now it's as if coming back from Mexico changed my brain. It's heavy and slow. Kim, I'm really depressed."

"You need to call Dr. G."

"She knows I stopped my meds in the fall." I feel my eyes begin to fill with tears and try not to blink so they won't fall down my face. "She referred me back to the psychiatrist, but I never returned the call. I was doing fine. Everything is stressing me out now. I hate life."

Any time my phone rings and it's about the building, my stomach twists into knots. I don't want to pick up. Al's aware that this is eating away at me, but we don't have the budget to hire a property manager. So for now, it's me.

Things keep getting worse. I feel myself slipping every single day.

Al and I have planned a trip to Banff. Al has a two-day work conference there, and then we're going skiing for a few days. I'm crying all the time now. I should be excited about this trip, but I'm dreading it. I don't know how I will manage. How I will smile, talk, pretend everything is ok?

We have a dinner with his team on the first night. I debate not going. I feel terrible. But I hate cancelling plans. It makes me feel worse – like I've failed. I'm pretty good at putting on the fake smile. I've had lots of practice. I tell myself I can do this.

Masked depression, also known as "smiling depression," is the term used to describe when a person's depressive symptoms are concealed behind an illusion of normalcy or even happiness. We've been primed socially to put on this happy face. When someone asks, "How are you?" do they really want to know? Do we really want to tell them?

Another woman at dinner has been open about her bipolar. Turns out, I'm not the only one. I've always admired that, wishing I could be more like her. I pull her aside and tell her I am not doing well. I'm struggling. She understands that there isn't anything she can say or do to change that, but a "So sorry to hear that. That really sucks. Let me know how I can help" goes a long way toward helping me feel supported.

I have a few extra drinks with dinner, hoping to calm my nighttime thoughts. My mind has been playing games with me at night all week. Intrusive, violent images keep me awake. I see my hand stabbing myself in the stomach. I see blood, the knife protruding from my belly. It's terrifying.

The next morning I pop an Ativan, which calms me enough to make it through a full-day bus tour. I make sure I have my own seat on the bus by sitting right behind the driver and putting my backpack beside me. I don't want to talk more than I have to. Slowly, with each kilometre, the beautiful view of the Rockies, the emerald green of Lake Louise and the brilliant white snow perk me up, reminding me that the world can be beautiful. Still, what should have been a day enjoying the glorious nature of the Canadian Rockies was a day of trying to "fake it till I make it," being relieved when the bus pulls up outside our beautiful hotel. I skip dinner, instead ordering room service and wrapping myself in a fluffy feather duvet. I watch Chevy Chase's *Vacation*, attempting to laugh at an old favourite.

"You are so lucky," I repeat to myself like a mantra.

"Enjoy this, appreciate it."

Then the positivity fails and the darkness in my mind whispers, "Don't you know what you have? Look at you. Look at this. What kind of a terrible person doesn't appreciate this?" There is a term called "toxic positivity."

It is the belief that people should always maintain a positive mindset. Of course, gratitude journalling is a common thing, and the benefits of positive thinking are well recognized. But ask any person who has gone through a clinical depression how they felt when someone said,

"You have so much going for you. What can you possibly feel sad about?" or "Just think positive, and positive things will come." They will probably answer, "Exactly. I felt like a shitty person because I couldn't make those positive thoughts come." Or "I want to feel positive; I want to appreciate my life. But I just feel dead inside."

A few weeks earlier, Isabel, one of the other wives at the conference, had messaged me: "Are you coming to Banff?

Do you want to play in the snow?" I was still in Mexico and with enthusiasm responded "Yes!" at the thought of a winter activity. Now, I look out my fourth-floor window at the green pines swaying in the wind, brown pinecones hanging like Christmas tree ornaments.

I desperately try to think of a reason to cancel our hike. I see my hiking clothes I had laid out the night before, hoping it would push me to commit. Beside them are my "spikes" or crampons, which strap to my boots to grip to the snow and ice.

When I say "my" spikes, it's not accurate. They are my friend Doreen's spikes. She passed away from cancer the year before. Her family wanted her friends to have her cycling and hiking gear so we could take a part of her with us on our adventures. Doreen hiked and biked through chemo, surgeries and Covid until the cancer took away her life. She would have wanted to explore the mountains. She wouldn't let cancer or depression stop her. I need to go.

When I meet Isabel in the lobby, I see her husband, Dominic, is with her, too. They are both super fit, and I have a moment of self-doubt at my ability to keep up – and to keep up my happy mask. "Go; you'll feel better after," my logical mind tells me. "Go back to bed," my depressed mind counters. "The world is a terrible place."

I look at Dominic and Isabel, and paste a smile on my face.

As we walk, we chat about cycling, as they are both avid cyclists as well. We chat about skiing. Every topic reminds me of the good things in life. As we approach the bridge that signals the end of town and the beginning of the climb, I realize I'm not faking the smile. It's naturally there. Later that night, Isabel and I meet up for dinner.

My mood has lifted. Maybe the wine over dinner has loosened my tongue. Maybe I think telling her about my past will keep it in my past. Or maybe my fears that I am heading into depression make me want to talk about it. Regardless, I open up about my past mental health problems…although not my current ones.

Feeling better after the hike, I'm thinking that maybe I've managed to dodge the "Black Dog," as Winston Churchill called his lifelong depressions.

And once again, being vulnerable and truthful was met with kindness and curiosity from Isabel. I like when people ask questions. It means they want to learn, they want to understand, they want to know how to help people. I'm never offended.

"Please, ask me," I want to say to them. Al's conference concludes, and now it's time for fun. Skiing is one of our favourite activities. But the terrifying intrusive images are still keeping me awake all night. Even sleeping medication can't keep away the dreams…or are they hallucinations?

Our first run is on smooth groomed snow, glistening in the sun as if it's filled with diamonds. I want to appreciate this. I snap pictures for social media. Me, smiling with the Rocky Mountains towering behind me. Al and me on the chairlift. On Facebook, I look like I'm having the time of my life. In reality, though, thoughts of suicide are beginning to brew. Intrusive thoughts whisper and repeat. "You could just kill yourself." Intrusive images replay violently when I close my eyes at night. Again I see a knife protruding from my belly. Al is a fast skier, but as an ex-racer I can usually keep up. Now he is waiting for me every few minutes. My body is heavy and tired. We play this cat-and-mouse game all morning. Al knows I'm depressed, but he thinks nature and exercise, my usual coping tools, will change this. It usually does. This time, though, it's not working.

After lunch, I pull up my neck warmer, covering my face up until my goggles. Not an inch of skin is exposed – not because it's cold but because my mouth is quivering. Tears are starting to form. With my mirrored goggles and full-face mask, my emotions are invisible to anyone else.

I slow down even more because I need to keep lifting the goggles and wipe away tears. I hate myself for crying when I am in the best spot in the world. I'm an ungrateful asshole. My goggles fog with moisture. And then that moisture freezes. I can't see. My tears have literally frozen to my goggles.

When I finally ski up to the chairlift, Al says, "Did something happen?" "My tears froze to my goggles," I respond. "What?" I repeat myself. "My tears froze to my goggles. I couldn't see." He takes my face in his hands, lifts my goggles and wipes my wet cheeks with his ski glove. "Let's go inside and have a drink." "No. I don't want to go inside. I'm embarrassed. I can't stop crying." "So what?" he says. Al never cares what anyone thinks – the opposite of me.

I keep my hood up in the restaurant, trying to remain invisible. When the waiter comes, I let Al place the order. "Two glasses of your California Cab. And a chocolate lava cake," he adds as an afterthought, knowing it's my favourite dessert. We never go back out skiing. My tears can't stop flowing. I want to go back to the safety of the fluffy duvet at the hotel. My preference is for room service, but Al insists we go out. I still have tears occasionally starting up for no reason. We walk to an Asian restaurant. I look at the menu, but there are too many choices. I can't decide. I don't really want anything. Al looks at me. "What do you want?" "To die" is my blunt answer.

"What?" This seems to be his response to a lot of my statements now. Perhaps he can't think what he hears is correct. "To die. I want to die." Just at that moment, the server arrives. I'm still wearing my ski coat, hood up, and I shrink my head in further like a turtle. I always feel cold when I'm depressed, as if a damp darkness has filled my body. Al takes charge and places both our orders. His patience has worn thin. He doesn't know how to respond. "Look, you wanted to go skiing. We're skiing. So many people don't get to do this."

You don't "And that's exactly what makes me a shitty person who doesn't deserve a place on this planet."

The restaurant is loud. I don't want to continue the conversation, and neither does he Lying in bed that night, the intrusive thoughts won't stop. I see me stabbing myself over and over in the stomach, this time with the hotel corkscrew. My tossing and turning wakes Al.

"You need to get some sleep," he says with a groggy voice.

"Why don't you take a sleeping pill?"

"I can't. I can't sleep. I'm scared."

He rolls over to spoon me, wrapping me in his arms. "Baby, it's going to be ok. I've got you."

"You don't understand," I cry. For the first time, I tell him about the images and how, if I sleep, I'm scared I might do it.

"You won't. I've got you," he repeats, holding me tighter as he drifts back to sleep. I'm dropping off the deep end fast, images of a corkscrew and blood repeating on a gruesome loop.

The next day, I feel worse. I rally myself for a couple of runs, then stop at the top. My goggles are fogged once again with my tears.

"I want to die," I say again to Al. I'm hoping for a solution, for help. Al whisks out his phone. "Ok, then. I want you to make a video to your kids. Tell them why you did this. I can't explain it to them. Tell your parents. Justify why you killed yourself."

His frustration is making things worse. He doesn't know how to deal with me. I can't blame him. I don't know how to deal with me. We call it a day and go back to the hotel, where I sleep the afternoon away. Al's son, Bretten, is driving in from Calgary the next day to join us. How will I make it through the day?

How will I put on a happy face?

"Fake it till you make it" sometimes works. Research shows that forcing a smile spurs a chemical reaction in the brain, releasing the hormones dopamine and serotonin.

These hormones increase happiness and reduce stress. Nature and exercise release the same feel-good hormones. Today I have the trifecta - forcing a smile, being in nature, and skiing, and I do feel a boost of happiness, for that day at least. Once the trip is done, things don't get any better though.

Thoughts of suicide play on a constant rerun. I ask my pharmacist if I have an old prescription for lithium and Lamictal on file. I desperately want back on my meds. He can't help me – my doctor will need to write a new prescription. I don't make an appointment with Dr. G. I debate giving in to my thoughts.

Why live? Why burden everyone? Al will be better off without having to deal with my emotions. The kids will get an inheritance to buy a house. I struggle, though, to think of how my parents would be better off. A plan begins to form. I don't want anyone to find my body. That would be unfair; too traumatic. I decide on drowning, so my body is hidden under the water. It's early April, and the ice at our cottage is melting. To walk on it would mean falling through. But I've read that the body does everything it can to survive. I will probably instinctively try to climb out. I go deep into the internet and come across a website that gives steps to a "successful" suicide. My plan solidifies. An empty stomach, two gin and tonics, 12 sleeping pills and 12 steps on the ice. I even write my plan down, so I won't forget. But some small part of my brain still wants to live – I half-heartedly reach out for help.

I call Kate, a friend who worked in mental health before her retirement. I don't reveal the plan I've made; instead, I just tell her how low I am. When I tell her I went off my meds months ago, she encourages me to call my doctor. I text Kim, telling her I'm really struggling – but again, I don't disclose my plan. She immediately calls me and encourages me to go to the clinic. I text Andrea, even though she is in Mexico. She insists I call the doctor to book an appointment. I get one for nine days from now. The ice is melting. I can't wait that long. My parents are abroad, eight time zones away. I want to protect them from what I'm thinking of doing, keep them in the dark of the cliff I've dropped off since seeing them last.

Al knows I am doing badly, but he has never experienced this before, and he lacks the knowledge or tools to help me. Sunday morning he suggests a bike ride, assuming it will give me the usual pick-me-up. He loads the bikes onto the car, selects my bike clothes and practically pushes me into the car. I'm crying. We start pedalling, an easy flat trail. I beg to go back. I want my bed. He keeps pushing me on. I can't keep up, even though we are slower than our usual pace.

Not just my mind, but now my body has lost interest in life as well. I stop and get off my bike. Snot and tears are running down my face. Al recognizes the battle is lost. We go home.

I retreat to my duvet, obsessing about my plan. I realize I can't drown myself at our cottage lake. It's Al's happy place. If my body is buried in the lake, how can he ever enjoy it again? Instead, I pick a closer lake, only one hour away. My mind believes I am making a rational, logical decision. Then my phone rings. It's a call that will save my life. Dr. G.'s receptionist tells me they've had a cancellation, and brightly asks if I can come in tomorrow for my appointment. Looking back, I think this was a guardian angel looking out for me. In the waiting room next day, I fill out a Depression Rating Scale sheet. I answer every question with the top score. Instead of my name, I scrawl in large letters: "I want to die."

When I get into the examination room, I immediately tell Dr. G. I need my meds. I'm crying and talking about ice and zopiclone. "Time is running out," I say. "The ice is melting."

My disorganized sentences are not making logical sense.

"I don't understand," she says. "What ice are you talking about?"

"The lake won't work anymore," I try explaining to her.

After it becomes clear that I am urgently talking of suicide, she asks if she can call my husband. I can't remember Al's number and need to look it up on my phone. I hand it to her.

The numbers don't make sense to me. I only hear her side of the conversation. "I'm sending her to the hospital. Can you meet her there?"

She prints off a note for me to give at the hospital, and a prescription for Ativan to take immediately while waiting for the taxi the office receptionist ordered. In the taxi, I read the paper. "Patient is at extreme risk of self-harm. Patient has stopped all medication."

For the next part of the story, I've asked Al and my friends for details. I remember only fractured bits and pieces – some vividly, some not at all.

At our large city hospital, Brampton Civic, I hand the Triage nurse the note and am immediately moved to the Mental Health Emergency Department. (This is where I started this chapter, staring at the police officers with guns hanging at their side.) I have my "Life Chart" (see Chapter 1: Reflections and Resources) that I had completed in my bipolar group in 2017 saved on OneDrive on my phone. This spares me the agony of repeating my history to every medical staff person who interviews me, while teetering on the edge of psychosis.

I keep insisting that the ice is melting, and I don't have much time. "I've already changed my lake," I tell them frantically. Everything happens quickly. When Al arrives an hour later, I'm now quiet, my urgent energy drained. Two hours later I hear the words "Form 1. Seventy-two-hour hold". Al doesn't know the weight of these words, but I do. Everything is being taken from me. My clothes, my shoes, my phone – my freedom. I let out an animal-like sound, having no control, no awareness of social norms. Al rubs my back, trying to calm me down, telling me I'll only make things worse.

It's 10:30 p.m. and I've been here nine hours, but there is no bed on the ward for me. I will be spending the night in the ER, identified as Form 1 by my patient scrubs and the grippy socks flopping on my small feet. There is no privacy, the lights are bright; it's busy, it's loud. People brought in by police remain in handcuffs, watched over until they are either deemed fit to be released, or admitted.

Al says he will wait with me throughout the night until I get a bed in the morning. That's when it hits me – today is his birthday. I hadn't even wished him happy birthday. I'm a terrible person. Guilt crashes over me. "Go home," I beg him, "Please, go home." No one should spend their birthday like this. As he reluctantly leaves, a sense of resignation washes over me. I'm exactly where terrible people belong, I think.

The next morning Al returns in his suit, on his way to work. I'm shivering, huddled under three thin hospital blankets. Even with medication, I haven't slept. Seeing my untouched breakfast tray, he goes to the cafeteria and returns with a sandwich, which I devour. I can't remember if I ate yesterday – did they even give me food?

Later, my friend Kim, a surgeon at this hospital, swings by between cases, just as Al leaves. I'm in a wheelchair, waiting for a second porter, as per hospital protocol, to take me to the ward. Kim steps in, whisking me off to the Psych ward, off to safety. From myself.

My room is meant for two beds, but an extra cot has been squeezed in. It's not just the Emerg that's overcrowded, but the ward itself. A young girl walks in, smiling brightly with manic energy, the complete opposite to my depression. Two bipolars sharing a room: what a combination. I barely listen to her enthusiastic chatter as she gives me a tour of the small room, explains the schedule of the groups and meals, where the shower is and how to ask for toothpaste. She smiles as she tells me her name is Lovepreet, but that everyone calls her Love.

Even though it's 2023 and masks are required in most medical settings, mental health patients aren't required to wear medical masks. They assume we can't follow protocol anyway, so don't bother with the masks; instead, we are given a Covid test before admission.

A nurse suggests I might feel better after a shower. The shower room is large, and the door doesn't lock. I see black hair clogging the drain. Someone has left a pair of disposable underwear on the floor – not everyone has family to bring them essentials. I try to be as quick as possible, nervous someone will open the door. When I look in the plastic mirror, I see my curly hair has dried to a frizzy mess, but my appearance is the last thing on my mind. The nurse was right. I do feel better, like a bit of the clog in my brain went down the drain.

The suicidal thoughts are still haunting my mind, blocking out the staff, the doctors, the patients. I need to talk to Al. He has to take me home. I wait at the patient phone beside the nursing station. Even our phone calls are not private. A man in his 50s is currently on the phone. I try to avoid looking at the large angry scar running up the length of his left arm. It looks fresh, as if the stitches have just been taken out. Later, I'll learn that not only did he cut his wrist, but he also survived a massive fentanyl overdose.

When Al answers, I break down, begging him to take me home. He calmly tells me it's not an option, reminding me it's out of his control. Seventy-two hours is my minimum required stay. I give up startlingly quickly, instead asking for a notebook and pen. I need to record notes. Love sees me hang up the phone and rushes over. "Did you look at the board? Come, I'll show you," she says, pulling my arm, oblivious to the tears streaming down my face.

"Look," she says, pointing. "They write the day, and who your nurse is. You have Linda. She's great. I have Bhavna." My mind is numb, and she's speaking too fast. Her words slip by me.

She taps the board, explaining the schedule. Four group programs a day: two in the morning, two in the afternoon. This afternoon is "Self-Esteem" and "Yoga." Yoga should interest me, but it doesn't. My mind is consumed with other thoughts. When I get out of here, the ice will have melted. I'll need a new plan.

"You should go to every group," Love says. "They're great. And if the weather is nice tomorrow, we can go outside." It's as if she actually likes this place. She's obviously crazy.

"Thanks," I mumble and walk away.

I glance at the clock above the nurses' station. Visiting hours start at 4:30. When dinner arrives at 5:00, it's as unappetizing as lunch was. Because of the space crunch, the dining room has been converted for group programs, so instead we eat wherever we want: in our rooms, in the TV room or on a chair in the hallway. I carry my tray to my room, worrying why Al isn't here yet. Is he relieved to have me gone? I poke the meatloaf with the plastic fork, and it crumbles apart. I can't eat this. Al finally arrives at 5:30, and I rush into his arms, pleading for him to take me home. Instead, like distracting a child, he pulls a notebook from a bag. He discreetly stuffs the plastic bag into his pocket as per the nurse's instructions (it's a suffocation risk). The notebook is a green softcover, left over from my kids' elementary school days. For a brief moment, I see myself filling page after page with details for alternative plans if the ice is melted by the time I get out.

During visiting hours, the nurses open up the small consultation rooms to allow us privacy. The rooms are empty except for a desk and two heavy chairs. Nothing we can destroy, throw or hurt ourselves with.

Al tries to make small talk, but I'm not listening. Everything outside of these walls seems unimportant. When a nurse taps on the door to tell me I have two more visitors, I panic. Who could it be? Who knows I'm here? I don't want anyone to see my like this.

Before they took my phone yesterday, I'd called and texted several people. Some made sense – my parents and my close friends who knew I'd been sliding. Others didn't make sense – acquaintances whom I wouldn't normally reach out to. I'm sure that's one of several reasons why phones are not allowed.

Joan and Blair, my close biking friends, are being buzzed through the locked ward doors. I don't remember texting them, but then again, I don't remember a lot from yesterday. I see a takeout container in Joan's hands and greedily take it, even before giving her a hug. The visit doesn't last long. After five minutes of trying to be social, I'm drained. I don't want to talk. I don't want visitors. I want to be alone.

Nothing to do now but wait until 10 p.m., for a deep, medicated sleep, hopefully ending the thoughts swirling in my head. Love is still flitting about the ward. I take my green notebook and begin writing in green ink, jotting notes on her appearance, her actions, her voice, eventually falling asleep with my pen in my hand.

I wake up to a nurse's loud call into our room. "Breakfast is here."

My third roommate, who hasn't spoken a word to me yet, shuffles toward the door with arthritic knees. "Come on, get up and get your breakfast tray."

I reluctantly roll over, searching for the grippy socks I'd kicked off in the night. My plastic mattress is bare, the sheet having slid to the floor during my nighttime tussling.

I find a tray with my name, but back in my room realize there's nowhere to set it on. How did I eat last night? I don't remember. There is only a chair beside my bed, so I balance it carefully on the seat and sit cross-legged on the bed, hunching over the chair. I'm desperate for coffee but find just a package of decaf instant powder. The lukewarm water doesn't dissolve the crystals no matter how much I stir. I drink it anyway.

At 8:30, any leftover breakfast trays are free for the taking, so I dash over to grab another "coffee," desperately hoping to get even a tiny boost from the decaf. A nurse directs me to consultation room three to meet with the psychiatrist,

Dr. P. After we talk, he calls Al (on speakerphone) to discuss my treatment plan, more with Al than with me. Dr. P explains I was close to a psychotic episode and anticipates I'll need at least a week as an in-patient to get the medication on track.

He asks Al about any stressors I've had. "She's mentioned a building a few times," Dr. P. says. "What is that?" The building....

In my mind, it has become the heaviest strain in my life.

At group therapy time, we all pass through a locked door, then a small cubicle, then another locked door. I wonder if this two-door system became standard practice after my failed escape attempt in 1996. I half-heartedly listen to the occupational therapist's teachings on positive affirmations. Nothing she says makes sense to me.

Why would I tell myself I am good enough, kind or intelligent? I am none of those things. I'm crappy. I'm a burden. I put my head down and drip tears onto the table.

The first full day on the ward is always the busiest. A medical doctor gives me a quick physical check. I ask for pain cream for my shoulder and when she examines it, she finds bruising. I don't know what happened. I don't remember. It was in another world.

Pilates?

Skiing?

Overuse like my other shoulder?

She schedules an MRI for the next day. Later, a pharmacist explains my medications, but his words sound like a complicated science class. How can they expect someone to understand all that when their mind is so broken that two days ago they planned to drown themselves in a cold lake?

Give me whatever medication you want. I don't care. I have a lengthy session with someone whose occupation I forget the moment she tells me. I fill out endless questionnaires and tests, all designed to poke into the depths of my brain. My answers confirm my belief that it is a dark, empty cave. The next couple of days, I spend time between groups filling my green notebook with scribbled notes on other patients. I use the word *scribbled*, because when I look at it now, I see uneven chicken scratch, slowly giving way to legible printing as my mind improves. I assign the patients code names. Sleeping girl. Persian princess. Neck scar guy. Slit wrist man. European dancer. Crying lady. I carry the notebook everywhere I go, hiding it under my thin, plastic hospital pillow at night. The early April sun streams through the locked windows, and I watch people outside in T-shirts and shorts, coming and going, living their normal life. I want to bang on the window and make them notice me. "I'm here!" I want to shout. In the afternoons, we pass through the double locked doors and down a long hallway.

We are a parade of mental patients, in hospital scrubs and grippy socks, on our way to absorb some vitamin D. In a small, fenced courtyard, the nurses pull flip-flops out of a bag for those of us without shoes. For 30 minutes we enjoy the warm spring air. A young nurse, maybe only 25, has a speaker, and asks us if we'd like to hear any particular songs. When she asks me, I can't think of anything. I can't remember a single artist. Instead, I walk in circles around and around the small courtyard, one solitary tree as the centre point. Back on the ward, I call Al again, asking for shoes (no laces, of course) and my own pillow from home.

When he says he's on his way back from Uncle Alfred's funeral and isn't sure he will have time to stop by the house, I feel a pit in my stomach.

"It's today?" I ask, feeling stupid for having forgotten. His uncle died last week, and I hadn't even thought about the funeral – too busy thinking about my own impending one.

"What did you tell people? They must think I'm terrible for not going." Once again, I'm crying. "I just told them you're sick. It's the truth, isn't it? Ethan was at the funeral, but Connor had an exam today. Tim let them know you are in the hospital." Tim? I don't remember telling him but, apparently, I texted him from the ER, asking him to talk to Ethan and Connor.

"The kids know I'm here? What did they say?" I feel panicked. I'm their mom. I'm supposed to take care of them. "They're just concerned. You should give them a call." I call Connor, but there's no answer.

I leave a voicemail, trying to sound ok, but I can hear my voice crack. Ethan picks up my call, tells me how glad he is I'm safe and that he left two books of poetry with Al for me. I don't want to tell him my mind can't follow a story or a poem, but I love the gesture. I call Connor back, and he says he is going to come as soon as he can.

He has year-end exams, and I feel guilty that now he has one more thing to deal with. When Al arrives with my pillow and Birkenstocks, I see he has no food and no poetry books. I'm angry. I'd given away my dinner tray, assuming he'd bring food. With a sigh, he leaves and returns 30 minutes later with McDonald's, which I devour without speaking. It's hard for people to understand how little we have here, and that everything matters. After visiting hours are over and Al has left, I realize that I wasted my time with him being angry. My parents are out of the country, as is Andrea, so I should be grateful for every visit.

Two days later, my mind feels clearer. I can't believe I wanted to die. I'm not happy, but I'm not suicidal. Dr. P. deems I am no longer at risk, so while he wants me to remain in hospital, he can't force me. But instead of being desperate to leave, I now feel safe here and agree to stay. If I can't hurt myself, I can't inflict the pain of my suicide on my family.

After that decision, my mood fluctuates wildly through the day. I've changed my mind. I want to be discharged, but nothing can be done until I meet with Dr. P. tomorrow. I calm myself enough to attend both afternoon groups, "CBT" and "Social Skills." (Of course, the calming is often assisted by a dose of Ativan.)

My sister-in-law Frances has consistently picked up the phone when I've called. We socialize, but don't really confide in each other, but now my emotions are an open book. She works from home, and takes time to listen to me cry – because every time I call, I'm crying. On Saturday, I call her convinced that Al has died in an ATV accident.

I had told Al he should go to the cottage on the weekend. Why stay back just for a short visit with me? This week can't have been easy on him either. Besides, the kids will be visiting this weekend. It's been 7 days and I feel more like myself and am looking forward to seeing them.

When I can't reach him Saturday, I become hysterical. I tell the nurses my husband is dead. I call Frances, asking her to text him, to call his brother. I hoard the ward phone, leaving Al so many messages his voicemail fills up. I call my neighbour Kim too, asking her to text him. I tell the other patients my husband may have died in an ATV accident, which gets me immediately pulled aside for a one-on-one chat with my nurse. As she is trying to help me realize that there may be other reasons he hasn't answered his phone, another nurse approaches.

"I think you will be very happy to get this phone call," she says. Al is alive – he just left his phone at the cottage when he went out. The world shrinks and stops for us in here, but not for others out there. When I hear his voice, my mood shifts from relief, to anger, to shame at my behaviour. Then my focus switches again. Hygiene is suddenly important to me. I ask Al to bring deodorant, face wash and hand cream. I now have enough personal items that I need to store them somewhere, but I have nothing except a bed and a chair. The nurses hand me a small cardboard bowl. It's a vomit bowl, and the best thing they can offer. Something is wrong with our healthcare system.

Later, I sit by the window in the hall, looking into the dark sky, lit only with parking lot lights. It's pouring rain, and even through the closed window I can smell the damp earth telling me spring is passing me by. Another patient sits beside me on the couch and points to the sky. "Look at that red light. It's moving."

I squint at it. "It's not moving, it's hovering. See, it's in the same spot."

"Oh yeah," he says. "It looks like it has a tail."

My mood has lifted a bit, but that doesn't mean my thoughts are logical.

"It's a phoenix," I state confidently. "That's why it's not moving. See? The body is there, and the tail is hanging down. Have you seen Harry Potter? Phoenixes are a sign of rebirth. They rise from the ashes." I start writing in my green notebook, describing it, and then tears start. I will never be a phoenix. I will never rise from the ashes. I'm devastated. I approach a nurse, busy typing at her computer, to show her the phoenix. At my insistence she reluctantly follows me to the window. I search the sky to show her, but it is gone.

"It was probably a plane. The airport is 20 minutes away," she says, turning and walking away. The next morning, I question the little cup of pills handed to me twice a day. This would have been a better time for the pharmacist to talk to me, now that my mind is clear. I recognize the lithium and Lamictal, but not the other two pills. When I learn it's Seroquel, the antipsychotic that made me gain 25 pounds in 1999, I refuse it, even though it is probably the reason I am feeling more logical and stable. The other pill is vitamin B6. Working in the supplement industry, I know the importance of B vitamins, but don't understand why it's being given to me.

"The liver," the nurse says dully. "Excess alcohol depletes the liver of B6." I'm stunned. "I'm not an alcoholic." "The pharmacist recommended it based on your intake notes." Kim often pops by for a quick visit after her hospital shift, and she laughs when I tell her this. "We usually double the amount of alcohol a patient tells us, because most aren't as honest as you!

If you told them 10 drinks a week, they probably wrote 20!" Ethan and Bretten will be visiting tomorrow. I hadn't wanted the kids to see me until I was feeling more myself, but I had thought I'd be home by now. I explain to Dr. P. that I'm not suicidal and feel much better. I'm desperate to be outside, on my back deck, watching the trees, maybe even getting on my bike. I listen as he talks to Al on speakerphone, and between the two of them they agree I should continue in-patient treatment. I feel like a child listening to my father and doctor make my healthcare decisions, while I sit on the sidelines.

When Ethan arrives, I'm in my room, holding a Scrabble box, hoping we can play. But before we make it to the visiting room, my roommate Love is all over him.

Talking in rapid, manic sentences, she admires his outfit, put together from his thrift store hunts.

"Maybe you could take me shopping. You could be my personal stylist. Do you like Indian food? Are you in school?"

With a gracious smile, Ethan thanks her for the compliment, looking at me and chuckling. As a psychology major, he understands what's going on. We set up the game, but I can only think of small three-letter words. We abandon keeping score, then eventually the game. Ethan pulls out his phone and asks if there's any music I'd like to hear.

I can only think of Alanis Morissette, the soundtrack of my many hospital stays in the '90s. Seeing his phone reminds me that I can access the internet. Who knows what I have missed! Appointments, classes, messages from tenants. He passes it to me and I try logging into my Gmail. Incorrect password. I try again. No luck. I move on to Outlook. Incorrect. Facebook. Incorrect. While my mood is improving, my brain functioning is obviously not, and it's frustrating. A nurse taps on the door, saying I have another visitor. In walks Bretten with a Starbucks latte in hand. I inhale the rich scent of coffee, and smile as the taste flows over my tongue.

Looking at these two young men, I begin to remember why life is good. But the next day, I break again. I need nature. I need fresh air. I need movement. I leave Frances a message. I understand that I was not in any shape to have visitors for the first few days, but it's now been been 8 days. "I'm not sure if you're aware, but I'm allowed visitors. Between 4:00 and 8:00. Oh, and if you come, please bring food – no glass containers or bottles."

I'm trying to be as specific as possible, wanting to sound calm and logical, like someone worth visiting. While questioning Al for details for to write this chapter, he was surprised that I felt this way.

"Your family never came to visit," I complained. "They would have come if I'd had a broken leg. It's like they were embarrassed about me."

He was driving and turned his head to me in surprise. "What? You told me you didn't want them to come! You specifically said, 'I don't want anyone to see me like this."

"I did?" I asked, feeling ashamed that I'd harboured resentment about this for months.

"Yes. They asked, and I told them you didn't want visitors."

What he doesn't understand is that when someone's mental state is fragile, nothing is a straight line. Our perceptions and moods shift hourly. Maybe I told him on my first day that I didn't want visitors, but he should have asked again.

After leaving that message for Frances, I pass time walking up and down the hallways – slowly, sometimes in step with another patient, sometimes alone. I once heard someone joke, "A Psych ward sounds just like the break I need right now." But for those of us whose minds are tormenting us, there is no break.

The nurse finds me to tell me I have two visitors. Kim had just been by, dropping off hot, cheesy pizza for my dinner, and Connor isn't coming until tomorrow. I'd already forgotten my voicemail to Frances pleading for visitors.

Coming through the locked doors is my niece Melissa, with her fiancé Minor. With my belly full of pizza, and the surprise of unexpected visitors, I'm smiling as they walk toward me, especially when I see food in Melissa's hand. Her mom passed on my message.

Sunday passes much the same as Saturday, until visiting hours when Connor arrives, chai latte and ginger cookie in hand. He has to slouch his six-foot-tall frame low to hug me. He's always been a curious kid, and now he asks, "Can I see your room?" I show him the three beds squeezed into a space meant for two, and our toilet and sink with its half-height, non-locking door. Frosted, unbreakable plastic.

It's Sunday and the visiting rooms are full, but we find a spot in my favourite corner, looking out at the parking lot, the afternoon sun streaming in. My roommate Love sees us and comes over, enthusiastically asking Connor what university is like. He is as amused by her chatter as Ethan was. Everyone loves to be around a bipolar person in a hypomanic state, until it climbs over the edge to mania or off the cliff to depression. Then we're not so much fun to be around.

Two more days slip by, the monotony broken into meds time, meal time, group time and visitor time. The ward is in constant flux, patients being discharged and new ones arriving. In the 10 days I've been here, half of the faces have changed. When I arrived, there were more men than women. Now it's the reverse.

At my morning appointment, Dr. P. asks, "Have you been working on your discharge plan?" He is referring to the 12-page Crisis Management Plan we complete to help transition smoothly back to stability.

"Actually, I finished it," I respond. "One of the nurses, Marianna, spent 45 minutes helping me last night. I have all the supports in place. My son even booked me an appointment with my therapist – as I couldn't do that without my phone," I add bitterly, desperate to have my phone back. "I'll check in with CMHA and see what programs fit me. I really feel a lot better. I'm ready to go home." (The CMHA, or Canadian Mental Health Association, has a number of excellent programs, as I mentioned in Chapter 10.)

Dr. P. nods slowly. "All right, let's talk with Al and see what he thinks. My suggestion is that you stay here two more days. Yes, your suicidal thoughts are gone and, yes, you feel better, but I hear you are still quite emotional. Remember, it was only a couple of days ago that you thought you saw a phoenix and that your husband was dead. And we still aren't at the full dose of Lamictal yet."

I feel betrayed that the nurses reported these things to him.

When Dr. P. calls Al, it rings to voicemail.

"He's expecting me to come home today,"

I lie. "He even adjusted his work schedule to be around this week."

"At this point, you are a voluntary patient," Dr. P. says. "You can choose to go home against my recommendation. If that's what you really want, I can start the discharge documentation. But I wish you would reconsider." I feel like I'm soaring! I can go outside today! Sleep in my own bed! Eat good food!

I rush to the ward phone and call Al. This time he answers. "I've been discharged!" I exclaim enthusiastically. "I was in the shower. I tried to call back, but they wouldn't put me through," Al says. "He wanted me to stay a few more days, but I can't. I need air. I need food." My words start choking. "You're crying. How can you be ready to come home?" "It's because I'm here that I'm crying. I need to go outside!" "Ok, ok," he sighs. "I'll get you after work." "It doesn't work that way, Al. I have to be out by noon. I'm officially discharged, and my bed will be cleared for someone else." As I say it, I feel like I'm a hassle to him. A burden. It was probably easier for him with me locked up in here, unable to breath fresh air.

"I'll rearrange some stuff. I'll be there for noon," he finally says. I call him two more times that morning to ensure he will be on time. I tell the other patients I'm going home and we break the "no touching policy," sharing hugs. Bonds form quickly in the Psych ward. At 11:30, the nurse hands me a bag with my name on it. My clothes.

With my own leggings and T-shirt on, I feel like a real person again, not a patient. My running shoes feel constrictive and stiff on my feet after 10 days in slippers. I wait by the nurses' station, my eyes glued on the cubicle between the two locked doors, looking for Al. I carry my pillow in one arm and a brown paper bag in the other, filled with my green notebook and pen, my lip balm, hand cream and face wash. Items that have meant the world to me these last few days. We stop for takeout on the way home. The chicken and fries taste like a party in my mouth. As we pack up the leftovers, Al announces he's off to work. A wave of fear washes over me. I had assumed he'd stay home with me today. I suddenly don't feel safe.

The house has so much colour, so much stimulus. In the hospital, the walls were a pale beige. No pictures on the walls or knick-knacks on shelves. Everything was plain, boring – and calming. What will I do when he leaves? There is no one telling me when to go to group, when to eat, when to sleep. The things I hated in there I now crave. Stability. Being looked after. Knowing I am safe. Al suggests I go outside, read a book and enjoy the sunshine. "I can't," I say, my eyes brimming with tears. "I think I should take you back to the hospital. You obviously aren't ready."

"No, no. I'll go outside. It's just...

I can't explain," I whisper, letting my voice fade away. I step out onto the porch and watch his car drive away. My heart races. Within seconds

I go back inside. I retreat to my bed, crying at the absurdity of being unable to simply go outside. It's just too unpredictable out there. Lying in bed, I scroll through my phone. Dozens of missed texts.

Did they wonder why I never responded? A message from the gym asking when I will be back. Emails from tenants of our building. An email that I missed an appointment. I'm overwhelmed by everything waiting on me now.

I open Facebook. The world kept posting and sharing while I was away. Did I even matter?

When Al calls, I'm distraught at all I missed. He's logical as always. Tackle only one thing at a time, then take a break. Gmail, then rest. Outlook, rest. Facebook, rest. Instagram, rest. Texts, rest. It seems like a good idea, but I keep scrolling, unable to put my phone down even though it's only increasing my agitation. I get out a step ladder and hide the phone on a high shelf, out of temptation. It's time to go outside. I open the sliding doors heading to our backyard and notice that Al must have opened the pool: the brown spring cover is gone, replaced with welcoming blue water. I take a few steps onto our wooden deck.

The boards are old, needing replacement, and I feel them soften with my weight. A crow caws loudly, startling me. I turn swiftly around, retreating inside and to the safety of my bed. That night Al helps me create a grocery list, thinking it will be a good task for me tomorrow. Something simple to get me out of the house. I've taken another week off work, feeling my anxious brain needs time to recover.

All morning, I push myself to go to the store, only a five-minute walk away. But I can't get out the door. I'm scared of the outside – the thing I wanted most. I'm bawling, frustrated that I can't shop for eight simple items. It's at that moment my friend Joan calls to check in on me. Hearing my tears, she says, without hesitation, "I'm on my way."

This is the beauty of friends who have your back. Someone who will drive 30 minutes to take you to a store one minute from your house, for eight simple items.

The next day, I have no choice but to leave my house to see my therapist. Every stay in a Psych ward feels traumatic, but it's especially so when it wasn't your choice.

I need to tell my story, get it all out there, and work through it with her guidance. We use my green notebook to jog my memory, and my Crisis Management Plan to ensure this doesn't happen again. In the weeks that follow, Al and I lay low, avoiding making any concrete plans, letting me slowly lead my own recovery. Just as I'm beginning to feel more like myself, I undergo surgery for my torn rotator cuff, the same surgery I'd had seven years ago on my other shoulder.

I'm aware of the recovery ahead, and I'm dreading it. I'm scared the stability I've found will be ripped away by losing the biggest tool in my toolbox – exercise. So, I prep for it. Knowing I won't be able to drive for four to six weeks, I register for three online groups through CMHA: Mindfulness, Self-Esteem and Bipolar Support. I arrange for my parents to stay for a few days and for friends to pick me up to get me out of the house.

Something good comes from this forced downtime. I have the summer off. My mind and my body can take the time they need to heal together.

In September, Kim encourages me to join her on a yoga and writing retreat, with the goal of writing a short memoir piece. I never imagined that those 1,000 words would become 80,000 words. And those 80,000 words would become a book.

And that book would become a way to heal myself, and to help others who experience what I've experienced. I thank the women on that retreat, who sat under a tree with me on a perfect September day, listening with empathy, compassion and understanding as for the first time I read aloud these first words:

"The sterile smell of hospital sheets hits my nose. In the corner of the room I see a young woman, whose name tag indicates she is a student. A look of fear shows in her eyes as she sees me waking up.

Hospital regulations require restrained patients to have continuous monitoring. A perfect job for a second-year nursing student. The room – in fact, the entire hospital – seems eerily quiet.

It's 1996, I'm 23 and I have no idea how I got here.

I'm grateful for the matted sheepskin lining the stiff leather restraints around my wrists and ankles. They almost make me feel as though I'm being embraced by a hug.

Years later, I'll learn that restraints may be effective for some people going through a psychotic episode. The person may naturally calm down when restrained, as opposed to becoming more agitated.

Maybe giving in to the situation is a means of finally feeling safe from yourself.

But at this point in my life, I have neither accepted my diagnosis nor feel safe yet."

And you know the rest of the story...

Six weeks out of hospital, celebrating my 50th birthday. Al and Andrea planned the party, despite being unsure how I would be doing by then, and despite me begging them to cancel it. I'm happy they didn't listen to me. This wasn't just a milestone birthday party: it was a celebration of making it: living and thriving-ish with bipolar.

Acknowledgements

My parents – I can't imagine how many nights you have lain awake worrying, yet never let me see it. I want to say I'm sorry, but I know that would be giving in to the feelings shame and guilt I work hard to let go of. Instead I will say thank you – for always helping when I have needed it, for raising me to be a positive person even amongst challenges. And for never giving up.

Al, even after all my other started and abandoned projects, you still encouraged this one. And I finished! Thank you for always helping me be the best me I can be. Knowing you hoped I'd succeed, but wouldn't judge if I didn't, allowed the words to flow, and the book to come alive.

My kids, I'm sure reading some parts of this was hard. Everything in here is things that parents try to keep from their children, so you don't carry our burden. Your responses have melted my heart. You give me hope that your generation is open to the exceptionalities in all of us, mental or physical

There is an expression "People come into our lives for a reason, a season, or a lifetime". *Tim*, you were in my life for a long and tough season. Thank you for carrying me through that.

And for each friend who has responded with empathy and curiosity, you break down my shame with your love. I appreciate you.

If not for my writing coach Anne Bokma, who encouraged my words, chapter by chapter, this story would not be as alive and flowing as it is.

I'd also like to acknowledge all the health care workers who have chosen to work in the mental health field. The psychologists, social workers, nurses, occupational therapists, doctors and psychiatrists who dedicate their days to those of us who may sometimes resist their help. But you see our potential to be well. I wouldn't be where I am without that support throughout my life.

Can You Help Me Out?

Can you help me spread the word?

The best way to help indie authors get our book into reader's hands is to leave a review.

The more 5 stars and positive reviews, the higher up on the algorithm it goes.

Purchased on Amazon? – Go to 'Your Account', click 'Your Orders", find 'A Sparkling Tornado', click 'Leave a Review'

Purchased on Kobo or Kindle? Review directly from your device.

Gifted or Borrowed? Review on www.goodreads.com Enter 'A Sparkling Tornado' in the search bar, click 5 star (hopefully!), click 'review'

Thank you so much for reading and enjoying my book!

About the Author

Sandra Steiner has risen above the challenges of multiple mental health hospitalizations to become a successful fitness professional, motivational speaker, mother, and advocate living with bipolar.

Sandra considers herself to be "thriving-ish" -never quite out of the woods, but always walking, or pedaling her bike on a sunny path beside the trees.

Curious what she is up to now? Stay connected!

www.sandrasteiner.com